D0984786

# Patriotism, Morality, and Peace

# Studies in Social and Political Philosophy

*General Editor: James P. Sterba, University of Notre Dame*

# Patriotism, Morality, and Peace

## Stephen Nathanson

Rowman & Littlefield Publishers, Inc.

ROWMAN & LITTLEFIELD PUBLISHERS, INC.

Published in the United States of America
by Rowman & Littlefield Publishers, Inc.
4720 Boston Way, Lanham, Maryland 20706

**Copyright © 1993 by Rowman & Littlefield Publishers, Inc.**

British Cataloging in Publication Information Available

**Library of Congress Cataloging-in-Publication Data**

Nathanson, Stephen, 1943-
Patriotism, morality, and peace / Stephen Nathanson.
p.    cm. — (Studies in social & political philosophy)
Includes bibliographical references and index.
1. Patriotism—Moral and ethical aspects. I. Title. II. Series.
JC329.N325   1993    323.6'5'01—dc20       92-32412       CIP

ISBN  0-8476-7779-0  (cloth : alk. paper)
ISBN  0-8476-7800-8  (paper : alk. paper)

Printed in the United States of America

The paper used in this publication meets the minimum requirements of
American National Standard for Information Sciences—Permanence of
Paper for Printed Library Materials, ANSI Z39.48–1984.

For Linda,

"Of thee I sing, . . . "

# Contents

Part IV—Challenges to Moderate Patriotism

# Acknowledgments

I would like to thank the many people who have provided stimulation, encouragement, and helpful criticism during the years that I have been thinking and writing about patriotism.

A talk by Lawrence Blum in the fall of 1985 helped me to set my concerns about patriotism in a philosophical context. I have also benefited from Larry's published works and from conversations.

Nelson Lande has provided helpful comments on a number of papers that preceded the book and has been a valued partner in marathon lunchtime conversations on moral and political questions.

A number of my Northeastern colleagues have listened and responded to yet another paper of mine on patriotism over the last five years. I thank Bill DeAngelis, Walter Fogg, Pete Gilmore, Bart Gruzalski, Michael Lipton, Michael Meyer, Gordon Pruett, Gene Saletan, and Susan Setta for their interest in what I had to say. In addition, Deborah Welsh's continuing interest in my work has been an important source of encouragement.

Norman Care and Andrew Oldenquist provided helpful comments when I presented papers at philosophical meetings. I have also benefited from correspondence with Marcia Baron and from her published work. I have a more general debt to Bernard Gert, whose thinking about the nature of morality has deeply influenced my own.

Audiences at American Philosophical Association meetings, the conference of Concerned Philosophers for Peace, the Peace Studies Association, Northeastern University, and St. Andrew's College provided good responses and much encouragement.

In the pages that follow, I criticize the works of several thinkers from whose writings I have learned a great deal. I owe a great debt to work by Alasdair MacIntyre, Andrew Oldenquist, and Michael Walzer. Along with the Russian writer Leo Tolstoy, their writings have been especially valuable to my efforts to think about these issues. My criticisms of their views should not obscure my indebtedness to them.

John Post and Nelson Lande read an earlier version of the entire manuscript. I thank them for their comments and suggestions.

This book would have taken considerably longer to write had it not been for a Faculty Research Appointment that I received from the College of Arts and Sciences at Northeastern University. This relieved me from teaching duties for the Spring quarter 1991 and enabled me to capitalize on motivation provided by the Persian Gulf War. I am deeply grateful for the opportunity this leave provided.

My thinking about many issues and my commitment to peaceful ideals owe much to the influence of Everett Gendler. More recently, my friends in the Newton Peace Vigil have been an important source of inspiration.

Finally, my wife, Linda, and my children, Michael and Sarah, have provided the usual everything. I thank them especially for their love and patience during the most intense periods of writing. With great love, I dedicate this book to Linda.

✳　　✳　　✳

Portions of this book are based on articles that originally appeared in the following publications: "In Defense of 'Moderate Patriotism,'" *Ethics*, 99 (1989), 535–52; "On Deciding Whether a Nation Deserves Our Loyalty," *Public Affairs Quarterly*, 4 (1990), 287–98; and "Patriotism and the Pursuit of Peace," in K. Klein and J. Kunkel, eds., *In the Interests of Peace* (Wakefield, N.H.: Longwood Academic, 1990), 315–23.

# Introduction

This book is the result of my efforts to come to terms with patriotism. While the book consists of philosophical arguments and analyses, the reflections that have produced it are not merely abstract or academic. They arose from my own personal wrestlings with the ideal of patriotism and from my desire to get beyond gut reactions to an understanding of the nature and value of patriotic attitudes.

There is no reason, of course, why the problems that disturb or perplex one person should be of interest to others. Many people are apparently quite undisturbed by patriotism. They either embrace or reject it automatically. Nonetheless, there are deep divisions in American culture about patriotism. While patriotism is often lauded as an unquestionable value, the status of patriotism is a problem for many thoughtful people. It is particularly troublesome for people who care about the common good but are alienated by the all too frequent use of patriotism and patriotic symbols to stifle debate, tarnish the images of rival candidates, or arouse popular support for aggressive military policies. Because the things that have troubled me about patriotism reflect tensions and confusions about the place of patriotism in American political and cultural life, my hope is that this book will contribute to a public working out of problems about the nature and value of patriotism.

My primary goal in the book is to describe a form of patriotism that is worthy of support by morally conscientious people. I call it "moderate patriotism." In defending this form of patriotism, I try to show that it has no connection with such attitudes as hostility to other countries and enthusiasm for war. My defense of patriotism does not imply that everyone ought to be patriotic. There may be countries that are unworthy of patriotic devotion or people with special reasons that make patriotism difficult or unattractive. Nonetheless, showing that patriotism is a possible virtue is a significant result, since there are powerful reasons for thinking that it is no virtue at all.

My own first serious reflections about patriotism led me to think of it as a dangerous and destructive attitude, something to be shunned and viewed with suspicion. The reasons for this do not derive from childhood indoctrination in anti-Americanism. I grew up with conventional political attitudes, happily pledging allegiance to the flag in school, marching in holiday parades, and learning about the glories of American history. I was taught to cherish America as a land of "liberty and justice for all."

These attitudes were shaken by the evils exposed by the civil rights movement of the 1950s and 1960s. Nonetheless, like many other people, I saw the federal government as the most effective instrument for implementing national ideals of justice and equality. The negative feelings that were aroused by the injustices of racial segregation were directed mainly at state and local officials who stood in the way of progress toward equal rights for black Americans.

Like many others, however, my sense of the nation's value was deeply shaken by the Vietnam war. Here again, cynicism and suspicion were certainly not my first reactions. I remember watching Lyndon Johnson on the TV screen in August, 1964, describing the "unprovoked" attacks by North Vietnam on American ships and declaring the necessity of retaliatory bombing. I remember a meeting the following spring at which a film showed Senator Wayne Morse criticizing the Gulf of Tonkin resolution that authorized the president to bomb North Vietnam. But I was not instantly convinced that "we" were in the wrong. By the fall of 1965, however, when repeated administration denials of North Vietnamese interest in negotiating were shown to be false, my belief in the government's credibility disappeared.

In the years that followed, I felt deeply that the actions of the American government were wrong and that we were fighting an immoral war. And in this time, while many began to doubt and criticize, the president—first Johnson, then Nixon—and other officials appealed to the patriotism of Americans in urging support for the war effort. Time after time, officials claimed that patriots would support the war and that people who questioned or opposed the war were unpatriotic. The American flag, whether worn on lapels or displayed on decals in cars, was universally understood to be a symbol of support for the war. Patriotism and support for the war became synonymous. As an opponent of the war, it seemed clear that I was no patriot.

Moreover, to the extent that patriotic feelings helped to sustain support for the war, it seemed clear that patriotism was not a good thing. For patriotism to be good, it would have to be true that blind support for an immoral policy was good. That was something I could not believe, and so, I began to feel that patriotism was an evil. Just as patriotism seemed to want no part of me, so I wanted no part of it. That remained my attitude for a good many years.

My thinking about patriotism began to change in the early 1980s, again as a result of debates about national policy. Like many other citizens, I was concerned about the threat of nuclear war. Because I believed that this threat was created in large part by dangerous policies of the United States, I once again found myself as a critic of our government. And, once again, I saw people who shared my views labeled as unpatriotic. Why? Because they did not support aggressive and dangerous military policies.

Initially, I felt inclined to acknowledge that I was not a patriot, and I sensed in people I knew a lack of inclination to protest when they were labeled "unpatriotic." They might resent the charge as an irrelevant attempt to discredit their views, but they would not deny it. Most typically, they hoped that they could just stick to "the issues" and that the subject of patriotism wouldn't come up.

More and more, I began to see this kind of response as a political liability. If, in the popular mind, a non-patriot is someone who lacks loyalty to or concern for the nation, then it is no wonder that non-patriots are not listened to in public debates. For, people want some assurance that those who advocate or oppose national policies do care about the nation. People who disavow patriotism seem to lack this quality. They undermine their own credibility and thus rule themselves out of the debate. So, I began to see the great political cost that people like myself paid for their alienation from patriotism.

A second thing struck me and made me question my previous attitudes about patriotism. I became aware of an odd paradox. The people I knew who did not consider themselves to be patriots were in fact *exemplary citizens*! They worried about our country's well-being. They wanted our country to have sensible and decent policies. They took seriously the rights and duties associated with the democratic process—such as voting, trying to be well-informed, trying to influence public opinion, lobbying for better policies, etc. Judged by their behavior, these "non-patriots" were model citizens, doing all the things that any citizen education program would want people to do. These "non-patriots" did not fit the image of the "disloyal citizen." Maybe, unbeknownst to themselves, they *were* patriots! Maybe *I* was a patriot, though I didn't know it.

But what is a patriot? And why do so many people see these exemplary citizens as non-patriots? How do we square the apparent requirement that patriots give unquestioning support to the nation's military policies with the democratic ideal that citizens should make independent judgments, debate about issues, and be free to criticize government policies?

I found myself at a loss to answer these questions and felt the need to try to think through just what patriotism is and whether it is compatible with moral principles and ideals that I took to be fundamental.

In the years that I have been thinking about this subject, there have been other occasions for perplexity. There were, to name a few, the popular reaction to Oliver North during the Iran-Contra hearings and the use of the American flag as a partisan symbol in the 1988 presidential election. Most important was the war in the Persian Gulf, which resurrected strong patriotic feelings in many people, rekindled charges that opponents of the war were unpatriotic, and left many anti-war citizens with feelings of alienation and confusion.

Patriotism remains a powerful force, capable of both uniting and dividing people in profound ways. It is a force that requires more systematic thought and discussion than it has received. This book is my attempt to help to fill that gap.

There are many ways to try to understand patriotism. One might want to know its history or understand the psychological and sociological bases of patriotism. My approach is dictated by two things. First, as a citizen and a human being, I care most about certain basic ethical questions about patriotism. I want to know whether patriotism is good or bad. I want to know whether I and others should or should not be patriots. I am less concerned about explaining patriotism in a detached way than I am in coming to terms with patriotism as an involved human being.

Second, my approach is dictated by my education and my work as an academic philosopher of a generally analytic orientation. Approaching questions about patriotism, my inclination is to try to render concepts and arguments explicit so that they can be handled more effectively. If we want to know whether patriotism is good, we need to have a definition of what patriotism is. In addition, since patriotism has both supporters and detractors, we need to ask how they defend their claims that patriotism is either worthy or unworthy of acceptance. We need to look for and at arguments in a careful way. We need to take the burning personal issues that provoke our thinking and subject them to the cooler activities of analysis and deliberation. That is what I attempt to do in the pages that follow. For all of its apparent simplicity and its associaton with visceral emotions, patriotism is a complicated concept and its evaluation involves us in a host of complex and sometimes theoretical issues.

I have divided my discussion of patriotism into four overall parts. In Part I, I describe and evaluate the most compelling arguments for rejecting patriotism. I use some essays by the great Russian writer Leo Tolstoy as sources of anti-patriotic ideas, and I consider Tolstoy's claims that patriotism is immoral and is necessarily linked to enthusiasm for war. I argue that in spite of the power of Tolstoy's criticisms of patriotism, they can be answered if we distinguish between moderate and extreme forms of patriotism. I defend "moderate patriotism" as a form of patriotic loyalty that does not have the chauvinistic and belligerent qualities that anti-patriotic critics rightly reject. Nor does moderate patriotism conflict with valid principles of morality or worthwhile moral ideals. An important part of this section is a description of the nature of morality. If we want to know whether patriotism is compatible with morality, we need some understanding of the nature of morality, just as we need to understand what patriotism is.

In Part II, I defend moderate patriotism against a number of criticisms. Some critics suggest that a moderated patriotism of the form I defend is too weak to be a real form of patriotism. It lacks the passionate devotion associated with patriotism and requires an ability to distance oneself from the values of one's own society. Some thinkers believe that such a critical attitude is either impossible to achieve or is incompatible with genuine loyalty. I consider these criticisms and defend the genuineness and coherence of the moderate patriotic ideal. This requires a discussion of such topics as the nature of special duties, ethical relativism, and the nature of loyalty.

In Part III, I take up the issue of how to determine if a country is worthy of our loyalty. Then, I consider how moderate patriots should respond to the involvement of their country in unjust wars. Should they be willing to fight in such wars? Does patriotism require them to withhold criticism during a war? I argue that patriotism is compatible both with opposition to war and with a refusal to fight for one's country in an immoral war.

Finally, in Part IV, I consider the meaning of moderate patriotism in a world of vast disparities between nations in the amount of resources they possess. If concern for one's own country leads to neglect of others in greater need, then patriotism may seem inappropriate. I also consider the criticism that patriotism is undesirable because it is a form of nationalism. I try to answer this by distinguishing between various forms of nationalism. Some forms of nationalism are, I argue, both morally and politically dangerous, but others are legitimate. Finally, I consider the relationship between moderate patriotism and the popular patriotism that is dominated by flags, parades, and military values. I argue that moderate patriotism is true to the basic conception of patriotism, which is love of one's country, even if it clashes with many typical forms of patriotic expression.

As this brief overview indicates, the road to a reasoned evaluation of patriotism is less direct and more complicated than one might expect. Nonetheless, I have tried to keep the discussion from being unduly complicated. My aim is to use philosophical methods to produce a broader understanding and not to restrict the discussion to professional academic philosophers. To this end, I have tried not to presuppose any prior understanding of specific philosophical theories, writings, or specialized terminology.

In arriving at the views expressed in this book, I feel that I have resolved many of my own previous confusions about patriotism. While I would not claim to have solved all the problems, I believe that I have removed the key obstacles that stand in the way of a reasoned assessment of patriotism. The pages that follow are the test of whether that belief is true. My deepest hope is that by clarifying these difficult issues, this book can make some contribution to strengthening a humane, positive, non-militaristic patriotism and to weakening the elements of patriotism that have contributed to intolerance, hatred, and war.

*Part I*

# Anti-Patriotism:
# Pro and Con

# 1

# The Case Against Patriotism

When we think of patriotism, we are likely to think about a strong passion that unites people in support of their nation. We think about national symbols that inspire patriotic pride. We think about our country itself and what it stands for. Most people think of patriotism as a trait that is valuable and worth encouraging. Indeed, patriotism is something that most citizens of a country expect of one another. They expect other citizens to care about and support the country and assume that patriotism is a virtue.

It is no accident that patriotism is generally viewed in a positive light. All societies need and value social cohesion and cooperation. On occasion, they call on citizens to make significant sacrifices for the common good. No society can endure and flourish without some degree of commitment to its overall good. So it is no surprise that the people and institutions of all societies promote patriotism and group loyalty as worthy ideals. Nor is it surprising that societies do not look kindly on people who scorn patriotism, for those who scorn patriotism appear to reject the good of the society as a worthwhile goal. Opposition to patriotism is bound to be unpopular.

Nonetheless, patriotism has not been lacking in critics. Despite the standard pieties that patriotism usually evokes, one of the most familiar comments about patriotism is Samuel Johnson's remark that "patriotism is the last refuge of a scoundrel." Other less well known comments are similarly cynical in spirit. Mark Twain described patriotism as "the spirit of the dog and the wolf." J. B. Zimmerman wrote that "the love of one's country . . . is in many cases no more than the love of an ass for its stall." And Thorstein Veblen expressed his scorn for patriotism by noting that "its highest and final appeal is for the death, damage, discomfort, and destruction of the party of the second part."[1]

Just as patriotism has inspired passionate feelings in its advocates, so has it inspired equally passionate feelings in its detractors. The most powerful criticisms of patriotism that I have discovered come from the great Russian writer and thinker, Leo Tolstoy. In two extraordinary essays, "On Patriotism" and "Patriotism, Or Peace?", Tolstoy presents both a strong denunciation of patriotism and an analysis of why it is an evil. Although Tolstoy wrote almost a century ago, he expressed views and arguments that remain both relevant and worthy of our attention. They are an excellent starting point for serious reflection about patriotism.

The following passage is typical of Tolstoy's thought and feeling about patriotism. He writes:

> The sentiment [of patriotism], in its simplest definition, is merely the preference of one's own country or nation above the country or nation of any one else; a sentiment perfectly expressed in the German patriotic song, "Deutschland, Deutschland über Alles," in which one need only substitute for the first two words, "Russland," "Frankreich," "Italien," or the name of any other country, to obtain a formula of the elevated sentiment of patriotism for that country.
>
> . . . [T]his sentiment is by no means elevated but on the contrary, very stupid and immoral. Stupid, because if every country were to consider itself superior to others, it is evident that all but one would be in error; and immoral because it leads all who possess it to aim at benefiting their own country or nation at the expense of every other—an inclination exactly at variance with the fundamental moral law, which all admit, "Do not unto others as you would not wish them to do unto you."
>
> . . . [H]ow can patriotism be a virtue . . . when it requires of men an ideal exactly opposite to that of our religion and morality—an admission, not of the equality and fraternity of all men, but of the dominance of one country or nation over all others?[2]

While Tolstoy's language is highly charged, it would be a mistake to dismiss what he says as mere rhetoric, for his remarks contain a definition of patriotism, an analysis of its implications, and arguments to discredit it.

Tolstoy's definition of patriotism is "the preference of one's own country or nation above the country or nation of any one else." In support of this definition, he cites the title of the German anthem

"Deutschland über Alles" (Germany over all), and claims that this exemplifies the typical attitude of patriots of all lands.

The patriotic preference that Tolstoy describes and criticizes has two parts. The first part is the belief that one's nation is better than others. The second is the desire that one's own nation enjoy greater benefits than other nations. Tolstoy rejects both of these.

## AGAINST NATIONAL SUPERIORITY

Tolstoy argues that the belief in national superiority is "stupid" because only one nation could be superior and yet all nations believe in their own superiority. All but one must be wrong, and, though he does not put it this way, the odds of any patriot's nation turning out to be *the* superior nation are exceedingly slim. Not everyone can be best, and if everyone claims to be best, then virtually everyone is wrong. Moreover, since none have actually compared their country with all others, none are in a position to have a justified belief about their relative merits. They simply assume that their own country is best.

We can strengthen Tolstoy's argument by noting that the idea of being the best country may not even make sense. Countries possess many different qualities: size, climate, political power, economic productivity, natural beauty, cultural richness, justice of institutions, and so on. Even if one grants that there are objective ways to evaluate these qualities, it is hard to believe that any single nation would score highest on every scale.

Nonetheless, the belief in the superiority of one's own group is a common one. Jews are not the only ones to have thought of themselves as "chosen people." American leaders frequently tell us that we are "the greatest nation on earth," and many of us take it to be an obvious truth that we are "Number 1." Until World War II, Germans had a strong sense of national superiority and were attracted to the racial version of this view expressed by the Nazis. The French are notorious for their sense of linguistic and cultural superiority. The ancient Greeks contrasted themselves with non-Greeks by calling them "barbarians," a word whose negative connotations have persisted. The name "China" means "central country," with the connotation that the rest of the world radiates out from it, just as "Japan" means "the place where the sun rises." A nineteenth-century Japanese writer proudly asserted that "our sacred country is where the sun rises and the spirit of matter starts . . . the center of the world and the foundation of creation."[3]

These are just a few examples of ethnocentric attitudes and ideas. Belief in the superiority and importance of one's own nation may be stupid, as Tolstoy says, but it is nonetheless widely held. People who suggest that their own nation is not as great as is claimed are likely to be met with hostility. Their remarks will be taken as signs of betrayal. Political leaders flatter the public vanity and are rewarded for doing so. No political candidate would get very far by telling people that our country is not the greatest and that, indeed, there are things that we could learn from other nations.

It is not hard to see why the belief in one's own country's superiority persists. Unless their experience as citizens is extremely negative, people tend to feel affection for and a kinship with their own country because of its familiarity. In developing as persons, we absorb the language, the customs, and the values of our society. When we come to judge our society, we are likely to judge it by its own criteria, and it probably will measure up to at least some of its own centrally important standards better than other countries will. Other countries presumably have somewhat different standards which they satisfy better than we do. So, people of every nation are likely to think of their own way of doing things as more reasonable, more natural, and better than that of others. And, even if we fail to live up to our own values, the fact that those values represent our aspirations will differentiate us from others and make us appear superior to ourselves.

In making these points, I am not disagreeing with Tolstoy. I am trying to explain how the belief in national superiority can persist, in spite of the fact that it is absurd. Tolstoy is correct in claiming that if we reflect on the belief in national superiority, we will see that the chances of its being true are somewhere between slim and non-existent. If this belief is an essential part of patriotism, then Tolstoy is correct to criticize patriotism.

## THE CONFLICT OF PATRIOTISM AND MORALITY

The belief in the actual superiority of one's own country is but one part of the patriotic preference for one's own country. The other part is the desire that one's country flourish and be superior. Tolstoy says that patriots "aim at benefiting their own country or nation at the expense of every other." Elsewhere, he describes patriotism as "the exclusive desire for the well-being of one's own people."[4]

There are several possible attitudes encompassed by Tolstoy's description. What is central and common to all is a special concern about the well-being of one's own nation. No one would qualify as a patriot without this special concern. But Tolstoy attributes more to the patriot than just this concern. He claims that the concern for one's own country is "exclusive," that patriots have no positive concern for other countries. In addition, he claims that patriots want their own country to benefit "at the expense of" other countries. This last statement identifies the most aggressive form of patriotism, since exclusive concern by itself is compatible with indifference to others and does not require dominance over them.

From a conceptual point of view, we can distinguish three possible types of patriotic concern. First, there is *special* concern for one's country, a higher degree of concern for one's country than for others. Second, there is *exclusive* concern. This couples concern for one's own country with indifference or hostility to others. Finally, there is *aggressive* concern, a form that requires not only benefits to one's own country but dominance over others. The desire for national well-being is common to all three, while the desire for national superiority is only required by aggressive concern.

While the first of these might appear to be less objectionable than the others, Tolstoy's argument is designed to discredit them all. He rejects them as being incompatible with fundamental moral principles and ideals. Patriotism, he says, is "exactly at variance with the fundamental moral law," the Golden Rule, and represents "an ideal exactly opposite to that of our religion and morality—an admission, not of the equality and fraternity of all men, but of the dominance of one country or nation over all others" (75). Elsewhere, he stresses that patriotism is incompatible not just with the highest moral ideals but also with "the very lowest demands of morality in a Christian society" (108).

Tolstoy's moral criticism of patriotism is simple but powerful. Even in its non-extreme form, patriotism requires special duties toward our own fellow citizens. It implies that we ought to treat them better than we treat other people. Our basic moral principles, however, are universal in form and presuppose the fundamental moral equality of human beings.

The Golden Rule does not say "do unto your fellow countrymen as you would have them do unto you." It says "do unto *others*," and the lack of a qualifying term shows that *all* others are meant. Likewise, the Ten Commandments do not tell us to refrain from killing or stealing from our fellow citizens. They say "Thou shalt not kill" and "Thou shalt not steal." Here, too, the lack of a qualifying term indicates that our duty is to refrain from killing or stealing from *any* human being. The fact that a particular person is not a citizen of our own country does not mean that we are free to do anything whatever to that person, as the more extreme forms of patriotism suggest.

Tolstoy's appeal is to Christian ethics and biblical sources of morality, but the point he is making is affirmed in other traditions and by major figures in philosophical ethics. Jeremy Bentham's utilitarian principle requires that we act so as to maximize the amount of happiness among all beings that are affected by our actions. Each person's happiness or unhappiness is to count as much as any other person's.[5] Immanuel Kant tells us to treat all persons as "ends in themselves"— objects of unique, intrinsic value—and not as "means only."[6] Neither view limits our duties to people of our own country.

Patriotism, however, sets up a moral hierarchy. In its extreme forms, it encourages the abuse and degradation of people of other countries as a means toward achieving the dominance of our own country. It focuses on promoting the national good, no matter what the effect on persons in other countries might be. Even in its milder forms, it calls for special forms of attention to members of our own nation. In effect, patriotism rejects the moral egalitarianism and universalism that play so central a role in moral thought. Patriotism, Tolstoy argues, is incompatible with the fundamental nature of morality and hence must be condemned by any person who aspires to live a moral life.

This conclusion is further strengthened by Tolstoy's comparison between patriotism and egoism. Virtually no one believes that morality permits individuals to pursue dominance over all others, to use any means necessary to achieve their ends, or to be totally indifferent to the well-being of others. Patriotism, however, is nothing other than national egoism, and it sanctions actions and attitudes that are condemned at the individual level. As Tolstoy points out,

> the public opinion which punishes every violent act of the private individual, praises, exalts as the virtue of patriotism, every appropriation of other people's property made with a view of increasing the power of one's own country. (106)

Here again, the inconsistency between genuine morality and the group egoism that we call patriotism is evident. If we were true to the universalist values that we often profess, then, Tolstoy writes,

> just as now a young man is ashamed to show his rude egoism by eating everything and leaving nothing for others, by pushing the weak out of the way that he may pass himself, by forcibly taking that which an-

other needs: so he may then be equally ashamed of desiring increased power for his own country; and . . . just as it is now considered stupid, foolish, to praise oneself, it shall then be seen to be equally foolish to praise one's own nation, as it is now done in . . . national histories, pictures, monuments, text-books, articles, verses, sermons, and silly national hymns. (110)

What is not permitted at the level of individual egoism should not be permitted at the level of group egoism. Egoism in any form violates our fundamental moral principles and ideals.

## SHAMS AND DELUSIONS

Just as a small amount of reflection reveals how preposterous is the belief in national superiority, so the incompatibility between patriotism and morality is equally striking. How, then, is it that we generally fail to see this?

One answer is that patriotism and group loyalty are natural feelings that are deeply embedded in human nature. Tolstoy rejects this view and accounts for the existence and strength of patriotism by arguing that it is produced by the public relations efforts of the government and those who benefit from it. What is called patriotism, he argues, is

only a certain disposition of mind, constantly produced and sustained in the minds of the people . . . by the existing government, by schools, religion, and a subsidized press. . . . (74)

Patriotism exists, he says,

because the governments and ruling classes, aware that not their power only, but their very existence, depends upon it, persistently excite and maintain it among the people, both by cunning and violence. (77)

Anticipating today's critics of media politics, who denounce rule by sound bites and photo opportunities, Tolstoy discusses in detail the creation of military and diplomatic spectacles, the manipulation of news and education, and other means by which patriotic sentiments are created, shaped, and exploited.[7]

I noted earlier that all societies value patriotism because they need a certain degree of loyalty and cohesion in order to function. Tolstoy believes, however, that group loyalty does not in fact enhance the well-being of the group as a whole. Rather, it is a means for creating and protecting the status of ruling powers. Patriotism is in the interest of rulers but not of the community itself.

> Patriotism in its simplest, clearest, and most indubitable signification is nothing else but a means of obtaining for the rulers their ambitions and covetous desires, and for the ruled the abdication of human dignity, reason, and conscience, and a slavish enthrallment to those in power. (79)

What Tolstoy presents is a cynical hypothesis about the origin and function of patriotism. Its function is to maintain the power of those who rule, and it originates in their efforts to deceive the public about the nature of their government. The creation and sustaining of patriotism is part of a gigantic deceit. Patriotism itself is a sham and a delusion.

Tolstoy is not the first person to have expressed such beliefs. Similar ideas are found in Marx and Engels, but they are also expressed in Plato's *Republic* by the character Thrasymachus. In each case, the explanation for patriotic ideals is a deflationary one. What is thought to be lofty is shown to be base. What is thought to be a shared commitment for the good of all is revealed as a manipulated attachment for the good of a few.

What are we to make of these disquieting claims? I will limit myself to two comments here.[8] The first is that this cynical hypothesis possesses undeniable plausibility. Ruling groups do need to ensure support for their policies, and patriotic emotions often serve to provide that support. The second is that if patriotism is created in the way Tolstoy describes and serves the function that he ascribes to it, then it would be irrational to continue to feel this sentiment. If one accepts Tolstoy's account of patriotism, it would make no more sense to continue to be patriotic than it would to feel great loyalty to "friends" who only want one's money or other extrinsic benefits of friendship. It makes no sense for us to be devoted to a person or group that seeks only to manipulate and exploit us. If patriotism is such a phenomenon, then Tolstoy is correct that we ought to free ourselves of it.

## THE ROOT OF WAR

All of Tolstoy's arguments culminate in his most powerful criticism of patriotism, his claim that war is the "inevitable consequence of patriotism" (104). "The root of war," he writes, is "the exclusive desire for the well-being of one's own people; it is patriotism. Therefore, to destroy war, destroy patriotism" (106–107).

Even if we believe that patriotism has some value, the basis for supporting patriotism would be seriously undermined if it could be shown that patriotism makes war inevitable. Ideals need to be evaluated in part by looking to their effects in the world. While love of one's country might appear to be a noble sentiment, it should certainly be rejected if it in fact leads inevitably to armed conflict and widespread human suffering. How, Tolstoy asks,

> can this patriotism, whence come human sufferings incalculable, sufferings both physical and moral, be necessary, and be a virtue? This question . . . must be answered. It is needful, either to show that patriotism is so beneficent that it redeems all those terrible sufferings which it causes to mankind; or else, to acknowledge that patriotism is an evil, which . . . should be struggled against with all one's might. . . . (109)

We already know Tolstoy's answer to this question and can therefore understand his radical proposal, the eradication of patriotism. How plausible, however, is his argument that patriotism is an evil because it inevitably leads to war?

On the face of it, Tolstoy's argument possesses a great deal of force. It begins with the plausible assumption that war is a grave and serious evil. This is a central belief of Tolstoy's. He was an absolute pacifist, who rejected both warfare and individual killing as intrinsically immoral.[9] Even if we reject his pacifism, however, and believe that some wars may be morally justified, virtually everyone would acknowledge that war is at best a necessary evil and that even justified wars cause terrible destruction and suffering. The moral constraints that forbid killing, injuring, and destroying and that are the minimal requirements of civilized life are all lifted in wartime. Indeed, the very acts of violence whose restraint defines civilized life are the same acts whose performance defines warfare. Those who fight in wars are permitted to kill, injure, and destroy because these are done in the name of their country and in the context of war. Tolstoy is not exaggerating when he speaks of the "incalculable" suffering, "both physical and moral," that results from war. For these reasons, I agree with him that the avoidance of war is a goal that any moral person must support.

The next question is whether and how patriotism leads to war. Tolstoy's essays suggest three different ways. In each case, patriotism fosters the development of a trait or attitude that makes wars much more likely to occur.

The first way that patriotism leads to war is through its connection with aggressive attitudes. If, as Tolstoy claims, patriots "aim at benefiting their own country or nation at the expense of every other," then the goal of patriotism is inherently aggressive. Of course, not every benefit to a nation requires that other nations be less well off, but some goals do require this. Dominance, greatness, and superiority are all relational goods. In order to be enjoyed, a country must possess greater amounts of power and wealth than other countries. So, the country that pursues greatness must necessarily seek to weaken others so that it can dominate and control them. In order to be "number 1" or "über alles," it must act aggressively toward others, either threatening or initiating war as a way of getting its own way.

The second way that patriotism leads to war involves the connection between patriotism and ruthlessness. Recall Tolstoy's statement that patriotism is the "exclusive desire for the well-being of one's own people." This desire need not lead directly to the goal of harming others. It is compatible with indifference as well as hostility to others. Even if patriots are indifferent rather than hostile, however, their attitude is conducive to warfare. This is because when conflicts exist between their own and another country, they will not care either about recognizing the legitimate needs of the other country or placing moral limits on the means that are used to get their own way. Exclusive concern with one's own people leads to the idea that morality stops at the border, that the rules and principles of morality apply only to one's dealing with one's fellow citizens and not to dealings with people of other nations.

This kind of ruthless indifference is often expressed and defended in terms of the amorality of the international realm. It is called "realism" or "realpolitik," and it is an acceptance of the law of the jungle in international affairs. It assumes that nations will seek their own good and use whatever means they have at their disposal to achieve it. It implies that "might is right" and that war, which certainly does determine who has the might, likewise determines who has the right. It is clearly an attitude that is conducive to war.

Finally, the third way that patriotism leads to war is by encouraging passive, uncritical acceptance of the decisions of rulers to go to war. Even though people know of the horrors that war causes, both to themselves and others, their patriotism makes them believe that they must accept war and support their own side. Citizens do not have to be aggressive or ruthless in order for patriotism to lead to war. It is enough if most people are passive and will support a war once it starts. Tolstoy gives a bitterly sarcastic description of the process by which this occurs.

> We all regard ourselves as freed, educated, humane men, or even as Christians, and yet we are all in such a position that were [Kaiser] Wilhelm tomorrow to take offense against [Czar] Alexander, or Mr. N. to write a lively article on the Eastern Question, or Prince So-and-so to plunder some Bulgarians or Servians, or some queen or empress to be put out by something or other, all we educated humane Christians must go and kill people of whom we have no knowledge and toward whom we are as amicably disposed as to the rest of the world. (88)

What this passage makes clear is that hostility is not even necessary as a basis for war. All that is necessary is that people be willing to accept and act on the judgment of others that a particular crisis is sufficient to justify a war. All that is necessary is the uncritical passivity that is implied by the slogan "my country, right or wrong."

Tolstoy's remarks also suggest that the willingness to go to war is completely unrelated to the gravity of the cause or the rightness of embarking on war. The issue may be trivial, but when it becomes a matter of national honor, people will support a war. They will kill other ordinary people like themselves, even if they had no prior hostility toward them. They will put their own lives and the lives of people they love at risk no matter how slight the cause. They will support the war because "theirs is not to reason why." Their only role is to stand behind their own country.[10]

Patriotism, then, yields an explosive mix of attitudes—aggressiveness, ruthlessness, and passive acceptance of government decisions. Undoubtedly, there are other causes of war, but Tolstoy's insights about the contribution of patriotic attitudes toward war make a powerful case for his conclusion: "to destroy war, destroy patriotism."

How would the eradication of patriotism help to prevent war? Presumably, Tolstoy believes that this would occur because each of the components of the patriotic attitude would be replaced by a more pacific attitude. The aggressiveness of patriotism would be replaced by a commitment to equality and a desire that no one be dominated by others. The hostility and indifference toward people of other nations that produces ruthlessness would be replaced by a concern for these other people. This concern would lead us to honor moral constraints in our dealings with others, even when our interests conflict. The passive acceptance of war that patriotism encourages would be replaced by a refusal to support aggressive and unjustified wars and by a disposition to oppose government decisions to engage in such wars.

For Tolstoy, then, there is only one way to prevent war, and that is to root out patriotism and replace it with a universal commitment to the well-being of all human beings. If we do not do that, he wrote (in 1895), then we face a grim, destructive future.

Seas of blood have been shed over [patriotism]; and will yet be shed for it, unless people free themselves of this obsolete relic of antiquity. (108)
Patriotism promises men nothing but a terrible future, but the brotherhood of nations represents an ideal which is becoming ever more intelligible and more desirable to humanity. (87)

In places, Tolstoy expresses optimism that patriotism can be rooted out and that a universalist ethic will gain the upper hand. Almost a century after his writing, it seems fair to say that his optimistic prediction has not been confirmed by subsequent events. Subsequent history has, however, added force to his claims about the connections between patriotism and warfare and has made his moral criticism of patriotism even more forceful.

## NOTES

1. These quotes are from Morton Grodzins, *The Loyal and the Disloyal* (Chicago: University of Chicago Press, 1956), 18–19.

2. "On Patriotism," in *Tolstoy's Writings on Civil Disobedience and Non-Violence* (New York: New American Library, 1968), 74f.

3. Quoted in Harold Isaacs, *Idols of the Tribe* (New York: Harper and Row, 1975), 73. For his source, Isaacs cites Hiroshi Wagatsuma, "Problems of East and West in Japanese Culture," ms., December 1972. Also relevant to the idea of greatness is Isaacs, chapter 7.

4. "Patriotism, or Peace?," op. cit., 106. Subsequent page references are in the text.

5. *Introduction to the Principles of Morals and Legislation* (1789).

6. *Grounding for the Metaphysic of Morals*, James Ellington, trans. (Indianapolis: Hackett Publishing, 1981), 36.

7. For a disturbing, sophisticated version of this view, see Murray Edelman, *Constructing the Political Spectacle* (Chicago: University of Chicago Press, 1988).

8. For further discussion of political cynicism, see my *Should We Consent to be Governed?* (Belmont, Calif.: Wadsworth, 1992), 12–15, 41–65.

9. For his pacifism, see, e.g., his "Letter to Ernest Howard Crosby," op. cit., 181–90.

10. For two other descriptions of the process by which automatic support for war is generated, see Edmund Wilson, *Patriotic Gore* (Boston: Northeastern University Press, 1984), xxxvi; and Randolph Bourne, "The State," in Carl Resek, ed., *War and the Intellectuals* (New York: Harper & Row, 1964), 66–67.

# 2

# Problems for Anti-Patriots

Tolstoy makes the case against patriotism with great power and acuteness. Standing back from the patriotic ardor that we are encouraged to feel and rejecting the tendency to see patriotism as the natural love of people for their country, he perceptively analyzes patriotism and gives a very negative account of its origins, functions, moral status, and effects.

I find Tolstoy's account very plausible and agree with much that he says. Nonetheless, in spite of their great power, there are serious difficulties with his anti-patriotic arguments and conclusions.

## THE POLITICS OF ANTI-PATRIOTISM

Much of the impetus for Tolstoy's critique of patriotism comes from his belief that the "us vs. them" mentality that it creates is conducive to violence and warfare. His attempt to undermine patriotism arises from his desire to promote an end to violence and to create a peaceful world.

Richard Barnet expresses a similar desire for global values in an essay written in the late 1960s. Speaking of anti-war critics who had lost a sense of loyalty to the United States, Barnet points out that these people did not simply shift their loyalty to some other nation.

> Those who question the legitimacy of the American nation are not looking for a better nation-state or the conventional model of world government. They are groping for a system of countervalues applicable

across the planet . . . [and a] world community that transcends accidents of birth and race.

This quest is bound to be resisted, Barnet thinks, by those who are responsible for carrying out foreign policy. The "national security bureaucracy," he writes,

> is threatened by the myth of human brotherhood, the curious suggestion that the world need not be divided up into rival teams. To any national security bureaucracy, enemies are much more important than friends . . . for without them the very *raison d'être* of the state would be undermined.[1]

Like Tolstoy, Barnet links progress toward peace with the idea of transcending the artificial barriers of national sovereignty and loyalty to national groups. Likewise, his opposition to war leads him to oppose patriotism. While this is an understandable reaction to the horrors of war and to the use of patriotism to gain support for war, there are many reasons for doubting that one can oppose war effectively by opposing patriotism and national loyalty.

First, as utopian a goal as the end of war might be, the end of patriotism and group loyalties seems even more utopian. After all, war is at least widely recognized as an evil, while group loyalties like patriotism are almost universally thought to be good. Harold Isaacs concludes his extensive, cross-cultural study of group loyalties by stressing their pervasiveness and enduring qualities. In his words,

> Here to stay, then, are the idols of our tribes, . . . granite-like in their power to survive, mobile and vital in their power to reproduce themselves, to be reborn, to evolve. . . . Despite occasional impulses and even efforts in a number of cultures to see if it could be otherwise, this remains the essential order of human existence.[2]

The prospects for destroying these forms of human attachment are not very good. Even if Tolstoy, Barnet, and others are correct in thinking that we must escape from parochialism to universalism in order to end war, it does not follow that we can in fact achieve this. Given the evident staying power of group loyalties, it might be worth exploring other alternatives first.

This conclusion gains support from the fact that the short-term effects of opposing patriotism are bound to be negative. In the short term, opponents of war and militaristic policies make their task even more difficult by publicly opposing patriotic values. This is evident from the fact that opponents of war are often charged with being unpatriotic and that when the charge is taken seriously, their proposals go unheeded.

When critics of belligerent policies are charged with being unpatriotic or disloyal, they can make one of two replies. Either they can deny that they are unpatriotic and claim, in the words of one recent slogan, that "peace is patriotic." Or, they can admit that they are not patriots and denounce patriotism as an evil. If they admit to being unpatriotic but nonetheless wish to advance ideas and proposals as part of the public debate on foreign policy issues, then they must argue that their lack of patriotism does not matter. On this view, charges about lack of patriotism are an irrelevant smear that has nothing to do with the issues.

This second response, however, has its liabilities. By disavowing patriotic sentiments, advocates of peace-oriented policies alienate themselves from the very citizens they hope to address and persuade. They reinforce the associations that already exist between militarism and love of country and between peace and lack of loyalty. By rejecting the patriotic label and attacking patriotic values, they discredit the peace-oriented views they seek to promote.

Moreover, they are not clearly correct that the presence or absence of patriotic sentiment is irrelevant to public debate. Many people believe that if one is not a patriot, then one is lacking in loyalty to the nation. While one may dismiss this view as irrelevant, this response misses an important point about the place of loyalty and trust in debates about national policy.

The charge of disloyalty—while it is often (perhaps even typically) used unfairly—is not in fact irrelevant to make or irrational to take seriously. It occurs in the context of disagreements about what policies a nation should adopt. The policies are important because they affect the nation's security and well-being. Moreover, there is usually a great deal of uncertainty, both about the nature of the problems facing the country and about the likely results of different policies. In such debates, it is rational to want some assurance that parties to the debate at least share common goals and concerns. While shared concerns about the nation are no guarantee that a person will recommend good policies, at least they assure people that no traps are being set and that we seek the same ends.

Imagine going to a physician for advice and not being sure that she cares about promoting your health. If the physician seems indifferent or sadistic, you would not be likely to take her advice, no matter what medical qualifications she possesses. We want an assurance of a common commitment to personal well-being as a precondition for trusting what a physician says. Likewise, when faced with difficult personal choices, we seek advice from people who love and care for us, not from people who dislike us or have an interest in our failing. This is not irrational.

Similarly, it is not irrational in disputes about public policy to be influenced by our sense of a person's loyalty to worthwhile ends. If people publicly deny that they are patriots, this suggests that their degree of concern for the nation is not sufficient to make them worthy sources of advice. As Michael Walzer has written, "An enemy is not recognizable as a social critic; he lacks standing. We expect and simultaneously discount criticism from our enemies."[3]

People who want to promote peace-oriented policies need to claim the role of *loyal* opposition if they are to avoid being cast as enemies. They need to present their ideas as *friendly* advice, and this requires that they avoid calling into question their concern for the well-being of the nation. If they portray themselves as anti-patriots, they undermine the standing they need if their views are to be taken seriously.

One practical argument, then, against Tolstoy is that professing a lack of patriotism makes it harder to be an effective advocate of peace-oriented policies. Even if he is right that patriotism is an important cause of war, it remains true that lack of patriotism makes it harder to advocate peace in a politically effective way. As a political prescription, his view has serious problems.

## ALTERNATIVES TO PATRIOTISM

There is a second practical problem with Tolstoy's view. Implicit in many of his arguments is the idea that loyalty to one's country is a barrier to wider loyalties. Tolstoy seems to assume that it is patriotism alone that stands in the way of commitment to a universalistic moral attitude. Because one is a patriot, one is not committed to "the equality and fraternity of all men." He seems to think: If only we could get rid of patriotism, then people would treat all human beings with proper regard.

Tolstoy and other universalists often seem to assume that there is a powerful, natural tie between each person and all other human beings. Patriotism imposes an artificial barrier to the expression of this natural tie, limiting human sympathy to the national group and keeping it from expanding to its natural, universal scope. This assumption is extremely unrealistic.

Whether through nature or by social acculturation, human beings have many different objects of concern, and most of them are considerably narrower than either the world community or the nation. If patriotism were to disappear, the result might well be a narrowing, rather than a broadening, of the scope of people's sympathies and moral concerns. Patriotism might be replaced by overzealous commitments to the interests of the self, the family, the local community, or to racial, ethnic, or religious groups.

In recent years, a wide variety of books and articles have dealt with the fact that the pursuit of narrow aims is the cause of many social ills. Competition, self-interest, greed, and lack of social concern are widely cited as causes of social disarray. These forces in turn have been unleashed, it is argued, because of a diminished level of loyalty and a sense of alienation from public institutions. Andrew Oldenquist, a strong defender of loyalty and patriotism, claims that a lack of loyalty among citizens leads to "indifference, automatic negative votes on tax and bond levies, cynical exploitation of the social services system, vandalism, and crime."[4]

In their much-cited book, *Habits of the Heart*, Robert Bellah and his co-authors describe the commitment to individualism in American culture as undermining the concern for the public good that is necessary for maintaining a just society.[5] They describe the problems of sustaining what they call "civic virtue" in a society that is so dedicated to allowing individuals to exploit all opportunities to benefit themselves. Even if people are constrained in the pursuit of self-interest by a minimal set of rules and procedures, this may not be enough to create the climate needed for democratic compromise and the distribution of a fair share of civic responsibilities.[6]

In effect, what Oldenquist, Bellah, and others are calling for is more patriotism. Their call has some plausibility. Social peace and social justice are threatened by the narrow range of people's concerns and the lack of commitment to the common good. Genuine patriotism, in this setting, may provide an important corrective by broadening the range of people's concerns. Without patriotism, what we may see is not the humanitarian universalism that Tolstoy advocated but rather the narrow pursuit of well-being by individuals for themselves, their families, or their social group. Patriotism is less narrow and particularistic than its most likely alternatives.

This is especially so in countries like the United States where there is no ethnic, racial, or religious basis for defining the nation. Where nations are homogeneous and national identity rests on religious or ethnic ties, then patriotism may be especially conducive to narrow loyalties. When, however, a nation is racially, religiously, and ethnically pluralistic, then national loyalty is a force for overcoming otherwise divisive distinctions among people. As Hans Kohn notes, "nationalism provides the foremost . . . emotional incentive for the integration of various traditions, religions, and classes into a single entity. . . ."[7]

Tolstoy might be correct in opposing patriotism if national spirit were the only barrier to universal morality, but there are many other divisions among people. Patriotism may in fact broaden people's sympathies, bringing them closer to a universalist morality. Undermining patriotism may lead to individual and group self-seeking rather than increasing the scope of people's concerns. For this reason, one should be wary of undermining this uniting force. Even if the unity that patriotism creates is dangerous, the demise of patriotism could strengthen forms of disunity that are not very appealing.

## COULD PATRIOTISM BE GOOD?

In looking at the arguments that I have given so far, anti-patriots might well feel that I have damaged Tolstoy's policy prescription ("destroy patriotism") but that I have not undermined his claim that patriotism is an evil. Even if patriotism is ineradicable, that does not show it to be good. After all, a virulent disease might be ineradicable, but it would remain an evil nonetheless. Likewise, if it turns out that eradicating patriotism would have the effect of strengthening self-interest and narrow group loyalties, this would not detract from the genuine evil effects of patriotism itself. Perhaps the evils of patriotism are inseparable from some good effects that it produces, but that does not show patriotism to be good. A physician may not be able to remove a tumor without also removing a vital organ, but the tumor remains undesirable, even if it cannot safely be extracted.

Finally, the argument that publicly disavowing patriotism weakens advocates of peace-oriented policies politically is less a defense of patriotism itself than an argument for hypocrisy and the expression of fake patriotic sentiments. It is an argument for appearing to be patriotic rather than for being patriotic. So far, then, one could argue that there has been no genuine reply to Tolstoy's central contention that patriotism is an evil.

While these objections do not fully undermine the force of the previous arguments, they do show that the arguments fall short of a full refutation of the anti-patriotic position. For this reason, I would like to turn to the central issue and show that Tolstoy fails to establish that patriotism must be an evil.

We can see that something is wrong with Tolstoy's overall argument if we look away from patriotism and consider religion, something to which he himself was strongly committed. Tolstoy was deeply committed to upholding the teachings of Christianity as he understood them. He must, therefore, have thought that religious commitment was capable of being a valuable trait.

Nonetheless, without much difficulty, we can construct arguments against religious commitment that exactly parallel Tolstoy's arguments against patriotism. If we look at the history of religions, we see that supporters of particular religions have tended to think of their own religion as being far superior to other religions and have wanted to promote the dominance of their particular religious faith. Frequently, when conflicts have developed between themselves and persons of other religions, they have felt free to treat others in violent and abusive ways.

Harold Isaacs notes that when different religions "have confronted one another, they have not ordinarily done so in any mutually tolerant spirit" and goes on to claim that the "accumulated evidence suggests that the more strongly religious beliefs and affiliations are held, the greater the hostility toward other religious beliefs and those who hold them."[8] The same kind of "us vs. them" mentality that Tolstoy finds among patriots has been common among religionists, frequently with the same bloody results that patriotic attitudes lead to.

Because religious people distinguish between their own true religion and the false religions of others and because they see people of other faiths as rejecters of what is true and most important, they are led to accept and act on strong distinctions between those who are in and those who are outside of the fold. Isaacs, commenting on these distinctions, writes:

> Hence, then, the great separations of the chosen from the unchosen, the saved from the damned, the believers from the infidels, the pure from the impure, the children of the true gods from the victims of the false. Hence, then, the need, the duty, indeed the divine command to slay the Amalekites, to stone the sinner, to put heretics to the torch, nonbelievers to the sword. From these passions, . . . great streams of blood have flowed through the courses of much human history.[9]

In support of this last claim, Isaacs refers to the conquests of Islam, the Crusades, the Inquisition, and other instances of religiously based conquest and violence.

It hardly needs saying that cynics have seen in religion the same kind of sham and delusion that Tolstoy saw in patriotism. Marx and Engels' reference to religion as the "opiate of the people" is but one of the most famous of such remarks. Tolstoy himself was a critic of established religious institutions and might well have agreed with many of these points. How then could he avoid the conclusion that to destroy war, we must destroy religion? If there are arguments that link aggression, exclusive concern, acceptance of war, and belligerence with religion, we might wonder why Tolstoy does not reject religion as well as patriotism.

## THREE POSSIBLE REPLIES

There are three ways that Tolstoy could respond to the view that the argument for eradicating religion is as strong as his own argument for eradicating patriotism. First, Tolstoy could accept it, acknowledging that he was mistaken in failing to see that his commitment to religion was inconsistent with the principles that led him to reject patriotism. This is not the path that Tolstoy himself took, in spite of the fact that he rejected and criticized many features of established religion.

A second response would be to claim that his own religious creed was the only genuine religion and that the so-called "religions" that have given rise to conquest, bloodshed, and enmity are fake religions. They are not religions at all, he might argue, because any genuine religion must include the universal, pacific values that he finds in the teachings of Jesus. To adopt this view would be to deny that it was actually religion that produced the evils of war and hostility. Other forces, masquerading as religions and falsely accepted as religions, are responsible for these evils.

The problem with this response is that it requires a radical redefinition of the term "religion." For now, in order to be a religion, a body of thought and practice must coincide with Tolstoy's pacifist universalism. If it fails to do so, it is not a religion at all. According to this definition, something is a religion only if it conforms to Tolstoy's criterion for being the correct religion. There can be no false religions, only genuine ones and pretenders. This definition, however, is linguistically arbitrary. It denies the label "religion" to virtually all of the major religious traditions of the world. In addition, it does nothing to avoid the evil consequences of dissension between "religions." For, even if we accept Tolstoy's definition, the same battles would be fought. Now, however, they would be battles between adherents of genuine religion and those who make fraudulent claims to the status of religions. Finally, while it might seem presumptuous to claim that "only my religion is true," it seems even more arrogant to claim that "only my religion is a religion." In short, this second response does not provide Tolstoy with a plausible reply to the argument for eradicating all religions.

Tolstoy's third option is to grant that many religious traditions have had features that have encouraged aggression, hostility, and acceptance of war. Nonetheless, he could argue, it would be a mistake to reject all religion. Why? Because *not every form* of religion has the evil qualities that these arguments have highlighted. So, for example, Tolstoy might distinguish between different forms of religion, saying that some of them are true while others are false, some are fanatical while others are reasonable, some are cruel while others are humane, some are moral while others are immoral. More generally, he might claim that religion may take many forms and that, unfortunately, many of the forms that religion has taken throughout history have stimulated hatred and violence. From this, he might conclude not that we must eradicate religion as a whole, but only that we must work to promote *other forms* of religious commitment that do not have these effects. Presumably, Tolstoy believed that his own form of religious commitment did not have the same defects as the extreme forms of commitment that the anti-religious argument focuses on.

Of the three replies available to Tolstoy, the last one seems most plausible. Religions do differ, both in their beliefs and practices and in their attitudes toward other religions. It is a mistake to condemn all religion because of the evils that grow out of some of its forms. This reply would allow Tolstoy to condemn bad forms of religion, while still supporting what he takes to be its good forms.[10] It succeeds, therefore, in allowing him to maintain both his general moral principles and his belief in the value of his religious beliefs and attitudes.

But now a new problem arises for Tolstoy. The very same type of argument that allows him to defend religion can be used to defend patriotism. A defender of patriotism could acknowledge that extreme, fanatical, and immoral forms of patriotism have generated hostility and war, while denying that every form of patriotic commitment must have this effect. Tolstoy thinks that the qualities he attacks in patriotism are essential to its nature. Suppose, however, that there is a form of patriotism that does not have the qualities Tolstoy rightly condemns. That form of patriotism would not be vulnerable to Tolstoy's criticisms.

In particular, if we can describe a form of patriotism that does not involve absurd notions of national superiority, that does not sanction hostility, indifference, or ruthlessness toward people of other countries, and that is not conducive to war, then we will have a strong defense of patriotism and a powerful reply to Tolstoy's argument that patriotism must be eradicated if the horrors of war are to be prevented.

## MORAL UNIVERSALISM AND SPECIAL TIES

Tolstoy could defend his view in the following way. He could concede that there are different forms of religion, some of which are worthy of commitment and others of which are not. However, he could deny that this helps the patriot's cause because patriotism is essentially flawed in a way that religion is not.

Religion may indeed lead to many of the same evils as patriotism, but in its essence it is a commitment to certain truths that are universally available to people. The way of life that Tolstoy found in Christianity is available to all people and makes no distinctions among people. Those who call themselves Christians may forget its universalism and may fall into a special preference for their fellow religionists. When they do so, however, they are departing from Christian ideals that call for regarding all people as equally worthy.

In contrast, Tolstoy might say, patriotism is essentially particularist. Patriots are necessarily committed to showing greater concern for their fellow citizens than they do for others. Patriotism is therefore necessarily in conflict with the fundamental principles of morality, for morality is essentially universalist. Patriotism is necessarily immoral because particularism—the belief that one ought to show special concern for some group—is inconsistent with moral universalism, the belief that all human beings ought to be treated with similar care and consideration.

This reply restates one of Tolstoy's original arguments—that patriotism is unacceptable because it is immoral, violating both the Golden Rule and the ideal of morality equality. By emphasizing the special tie between citizens and their country, patriotism encourages special preferences that are inconsistent with morality.

This is a powerful argument, but it has implications that are quite radical and that are unacceptable to virtually all people. The argument requires us to believe that all forms of special concern conflict with morality. While the point of the argument is to condemn the special tie that people have to their countries, the argument works by condemning all special ties. Therefore, if we accept this argument, we are forced not just to reject the ties that link us to our country but also the ties that link us to our families, our friends, and to any other groups to which we feel especially connected.

This implication is quite extraordinary. It requires us to ignore all emotional and historical connections between ourselves and others and simply to focus on the common humanity of all people as the only morally relevant connection. Such a view conflicts with our ordinary sense of things in two ways. First, on an emotional level, it requires us to act against some of our deepest feelings of love, attachment, and loyalty to particular people and to groups with which we identify strongly. Even if we accept the universalist view as the correct moral perspective, we might find it very difficult, if not impossible, to ignore these emotional connections.

Equally important, however, most of us think that morality actually requires us to be especially attentive to the needs of people we love and have special attachments to. Parents, we think, have special duties to their children that go beyond their duties to all human beings. The same is true of spouses and friends. Likewise, doctors have special duties to their patients and teachers to their students. The list could go on indefinitely. All of us are embedded in webs of special connections to other people. Necessarily, however, these webs of relationships do not include all human beings. Nonetheless, if these special connections imply moral duties, as virtually all of us think, then it would actually be immoral for us to ignore these duties and embrace a purely universalist morality. Special ties and special duties are exclusionary, but they are, we think, morally legitimate.

To accept this conclusion, however, is to reject the extreme universalism that serves as the basis of one of Tolstoy's main arguments against patriotism. If some special ties (such as those that bind family members together) are legitimate, then the special tie that exists between citizens and their countries may be legitimate as well. Patriotism may be morally legitimate even though it falls short of a universal moral concern.

Once we see that the extreme universalism Tolstoy appeals to is not acceptable, it becomes possible for us to see how a form of patriotism might be morally legitimate. This is not to deny Tolstoy's correct perception of the evils of patriotism, but it does raise the possibility that just as other forms of special connection might be good, so patriotism might also be a possible good.

What we must do then is to see whether it is possible to describe a form of patriotism that does not generate the evils that Tolstoy claims are inherent in patriotism. We have just seen that the mere fact of special, non-universal preferences and duties is not enough to discredit patriotism morally. If it were, we would have to reject many other forms of close personal connections and relationships. That all ties to family and friends are immoral, however, is not a plausible or attractive moral claim.

If Tolstoy's extreme version of moral universalism is an essential part of his anti-patriotic argument and if this view is false, then Tolstoy's claim that patriotism is inherently and necessarily immoral is severely weakened. A morally permissible form of patriotism may be possible.

## NOTES

1. "The Twilight of the Nation-State," in R. P. Wolff, ed., *The Rule of Law* (New York: Simon and Schuster, 1971), 238–39.

2. *Idols of the Tribe* (New York: Harper & Row, 1975), 205.

3. *Interpretation and Social Criticism* (Cambridge, Mass.: Harvard University Press, 1987), 59.

4. "Loyalties," *Journal of Philosophy* LXXIX (1982), 189.

5. Harper and Row, 1986, *passim.*

6. For similar concerns about the lack of "civic consciousness," see Morris Janowitz, *The Reconstruction of Patriotism* (Chicago: University of Chicago Press, 1983).

7. "Nationalism," in Philip Wiener, ed., *Dictionary of the History of Ideas* (New York: Charles Scribner's Sons, 1974), Vol. III, 324.

8. *Idols of the Tribe*, 151.

9. Ibid., 153.

10. In fact, Tolstoy takes just this approach in his discussions of religion. See his "What Is Religion and of What Does Its Essence Consist?" in *A Confession and Other Religious Writings* (London: Penguin Books, 1987).

# 3

# Sketch of a Reasonable Form of Patriotism

In this chapter, I want to sketch a form of patriotism that is not subject to the criticisms of Tolstoy and other anti-patriots. I do not deny that some forms of patriotism are open to their criticisms, but I do deny that every form of patriotism is vulnerable to their charges.

As a preliminary, let us recall the features that Tolstoy identified with patriotism and the reasons why these features are dangerous and immoral. The features Tolstoy emphasizes are:

1. A belief in the superiority of one's country
2. A desire for dominance over other countries
3. An exclusive concern for one's own country
4. No constraints on the pursuit of one's country's goals
5. Automatic support of one's country's military policies.

These qualities are dangerous because the belief in superiority, coupled with the desire for dominance, leads to *aggressive* policies. Exclusive concern for one's own country involves either hostility or indifference to others, and this in turn leads to *ruthless* pursuit of one's own goals because no constraints are recognized on what one may do on behalf of the nation. Finally, automatic support of policies, in the spirit of "my country, right or wrong," leads citizens to *passive* acceptance of immoral decisions by the country's leaders.

My view is that while these are all recognizable traits of a familiar kind of patriotism, they are not essential features of patriotism itself. One kind of evidence for this view is linguistic. Our repertoire of words for describing forms of national attachment includes not only the word "patriotism" but also words like "chauvinism," "jingoism," and "xenophobia." The attitudes named by the latter terms are clearly related to patriotism in important ways. The existence of these distinct terms, however, calls our attention to certain excesses that patriotism is liable to and differentiates these excesses from patriotism itself.

While patriots must love their country and think well of it, chauvinists have an excessive love for their country and an inflated conception of its worth. While patriots must want their country to flourish and must be concerned about its defense, jingoists are overly eager to engage in conflicts and wars with others. While patriots feel a special connection with their fellow citizens, xenophobes have an unnecessary hostility to people who are citizens of other lands.

What is most significant about these terms is that their presence in ordinary language reveals a general awareness that patriotism may take different forms and that some of its forms are extreme and excessive. These terms suggest a general awareness that extreme forms of patriotism are bad and that patriotism must be moderated in certain ways if it is to be a valuable trait.

## MODERATE VS. EXTREME PATRIOTISM

We can see what a moderated form of patriotism would look like by returning to the undesirable features listed above and replacing each of them with a related but more reasonable alternative.

### Superiority

Patriots need not believe in the superiority of their country. All that is required is that they have a special affection for their country. The belief in national superiority is, as Tolstoy said, a stupid belief. Reasonable patriots will know that their country is not best, but they will love it nonetheless. They will not pretend to love it because it is "objectively" best but will acknowledge that they love it because it is their own country. It is their home. It is familiar to them and contains the values and ideals they have been brought up with. Their sense of self is tied up with its language, culture, history, and natural features.

Faced with the question "why does one love one's country?" a character in Bertolt Brecht's play *The Caucasian Chalk Circle* gives the following explanation:

Because the bread tastes better there, the air smells better, voices sound stronger, the sky is higher, the ground is easier to walk on. Isn't that so?[1]

While these lines explain love for one's country in a quasi-objective fashion, the idiosyncratic, personal nature of the qualities that are described calls attention to their subjectivity. It calls attention to the fact that for people in other countries, their bread will taste better, their air will smell better, etc. It highlights the relational ties between people and their countries and so undercuts any presumption to genuine superiority.

In describing a moderated patriotism, then, we can substitute the quality of special affection or love of one's country for the chauvinist's absurd conviction that one's own country is objectively superior to all others.

### Dominance

Patriots need not desire that their country dominate over others. All that they need to desire is that their own country prosper and flourish, that its citizens live well, and that their ideals are realized.

In some conflict situations, it may be that one's own country can only flourish if it dominates over others. In a war, for example, the victory of one country requires the defeat of another. This "zero-sum" situation, however, is not representative. There are many forms of flourishing that do not require dominance. A country can be secure, for example, if it has sufficient strength to resist aggression. It need not have the power to conquer all others. Likewise, a country can meet the economic needs of its citizens and provide them a decent standard of living without having the highest per capita gross national product. Finally, a country need not possess the greatest number of artists and thinkers, so long as it possesses enough creative people to sustain a culture that enriches its citizens.

Patriots will want their countries to possess the things that are needed to sustain a viable way of life. Achieving this, however, does not require that their country be better than other countries. Dominance is not a goal to which patriots must be committed.

### Exclusive concern

Patriots must care about their country and their fellow citizens. They need not, however, be hostile or indifferent to other countries and peoples. Caring for one person or group is perfectly compatible with having concern about others. Caring may have its limits, but it is not exclusive, and greater degrees of care for some people may coexist with limited but genuine concern for others.

The idea that patriotism requires exclusive concern for one's own country is undermined by many facts. No one thinks, for example, that it was unpatriotic of Americans to donate money for victims of famine in Ethiopia. Even people who believe that "charity begins at home" can see that the extreme suffering of people beyond our borders requires some kind of humane response.

Likewise, however cynical one's view of foreign policy ideals may be, it remains true that the defense of other peoples' well-being is often put forward as a rationale for foreign policy decisions. John Kennedy proclaimed that "the world cannot exist half slave and half free." Lyndon Johnson claimed to be protecting the rights of the Vietnamese to self-determination. Jimmy Carter promoted human rights as an important component of foreign policy. George Bush spoke of a "new world order."

These professions may be genuine or may be ploys for generating support for other less lofty goals. In either case, they express concern for people who are not citizens of our own country. Even if we interpret them cynically, it remains true that those who professed these goals assumed that American citizens would share them. They did not think there was any inconsistency between a commitment to our country and a commitment to these goals.

Patriotism, then, requires a strong concern for one's own country, but it does not require exclusive concern. It does not rule out concern for people of other countries.

### Ruthless pursuit of national goals

Ruthlessness, as I have noted, arises out of a lack of concern for others. If we are hostile or indifferent to others and care only about ourselves, then we will think it legitimate to do anything whatsoever in pursuit of our goals. We may trample on the rights and interests of others because they do not matter to us. Their well-being does not enter into our calculations.

This may be the attitude of the xenophobe, but as we have seen, patriots need not have an exclusive concern for their own country, and if their concern is not exclusive, then they will be concerned about the effects of their actions and policies on others. One way that this concern is reflected is in the recognition of constraints on what may be done in pursuit of the national interest.

These constraints take a number of forms. Among the primary constraints is the disavowal of aggressive war as an instrument of policy. One may not kill people simply because they are in one's way. Likewise, one may not simply plunder the resources of others, even if one has a legitimate need for those resources. These and other limits on the means by which we may pursue our interests grow out of a recognition that we share a common humanity with people of other countries and that they, too, are ends in themselves, not simply means to the satisfaction of our needs and desires. We may not think that these moral ideals and constraints are sufficiently recognized or acted on, but there is nothing in our conception of patriotism that rules them out. Patriots may well want their nation to pursue its good within the limits of moral rules and principles.

## Automatic acceptance

If patriots have special affection and concern for their own country, then they will want to support actions and policies that promote its well-being and its national ideals. They need not, however, be committed to the automatic acceptance of any policy. Criticism of one's own country's policies and actions are entirely compatible with a patriotic attitude. Indeed, genuine patriotism requires that one criticize government policies in some situations. Such criticism may arise because one believes that actions by the government are likely to harm the country rather than benefit it. If, as a patriot, one is concerned about the well-being of one's country and believes that the government has adopted a policy that will harm the nation, then one's patriotic commitment will show itself in efforts to criticize and alter the policies. It would be an odd patriot who would acknowledge that the government's policies were harmful to the country and yet would think that it was wrong to criticize them. Supporting one's country is not the same as supporting all the policies that public officials adopt or pursue.

One may also criticize government policies because they are insufficiently attentive to the rights of people in other countries. If we grant that patriotism need not involve exclusive concern for the well-being of one's own nation and that there are moral constraints on what a nation may do in pursuit of its goals, then a patriot may well criticize a national policy because it violates these moral constraints. Wanting our country to do what is right, we may criticize its policies because they violate moral principles and ideals that we believe it should follow. Patriotism does not require passive acceptance of the particular policy choices and decisions that public officials make. "My country, right or wrong" is not a principle that patriots need subscribe to.

## FORMS OF PATRIOTIC CONCERN

We can now see that patriotism need not have the features that Tolstoy attributes to it and thus that it need not be open to his criticisms. Moderate patriotism involves the following features:

1. Special affection for one's country
2. A desire that one's country prosper and flourish
3. Special but not exclusive concern for one's own country
4. Support of morally constrained pursuit of national goals
5. Conditional support of one's country's policies.

People who possess these traits would be patriots without being chauvinists, jingoists, or xenophobes. They would be specially attached to their country without believing that it is best, without wanting it to dominate over others, and without feeling hostile toward others. However strong their sense of attachment to their own country, their patriotism would be moderated by their recognition of the humanity of people in other countries.

I do not want to deny that chauvinism, jingoism, and xenophobia are forms of patriotism. My view is that because of their extremity, they are bad forms of patriotism. Nonetheless, they embody genuine forms of attachment to one's country. Both the moderate and extreme forms of patriotism are members of a more general class of patriotic attitudes. Having described both of these special forms, I can now give a general description of the general category of patriotism.

There are in fact two senses of the word "patriotism." In its primary sense, "patriotism" names a set of attitudes. In a second sense, it is the name for an ideal or principle. This second sense, which stresses the "ism" in "patriotism," is the general principle that patriotic attitudes are valuable and that we should take steps to encourage and promote patriotic attitudes in people.

This second sense of "patriotism" presupposes that we understand patriotism in its primary, attitudinal sense. The primary sense can be defined by listing the complex of attitudes that all patriots must possess. These are:

1. Special affection for one's own country
2. A sense of personal identification with the country

3. Special concern for the well-being of the country
4. Willingness to sacrifice to promote the country's good.

Any person with these four features is a patriot. Other attitudes such as exclusive or non-exclusive concern, belief or disbelief in national superiority, etc., are traits that patriots may or may not possess. These four attitudes, however, are essential.

Without special affection, a person would lack the love of country that is most frequently cited as the heart of patriotism. Beyond that, patriots feel a sense of identification with their country, a sense of "my-ness" that gives rise to feelings of pride when the country acts well or shame when it acts poorly. One can only feel these attitudes about one's own country.[2] Normally, special affection and personal identification give rise to a special concern about the nation's well-being, and together, all of these traits generate a willingness to act on the country's behalf, even if this requires some sacrifice by a person. If such willingness to act and sacrifice is lacking, that would call into question whether the affection and concern that a person expresses are genuine. A person who merely professed these attitudes but was unwilling to act on them would be a hypocrite, not a patriot.

We can use this definition, then, as a criterion for the genuineness of patriotism, while continuing to remember that it is not a criterion for the goodness of patriotism, since both extreme and moderate patriotism possess these traits.

The definition is also helpful in differentiating patriots from an extreme type of universalist. Such universalists are committed to the equal worth of all human beings and to equal activity on behalf of all people. Universalists might feel special affection for their own country and a special identification with it simply because it is the place where they have grown up. Nonetheless, they would not feel any special concern for its well-being since they regard national boundaries and other differentiations among people as arbitrary. Hence, they would be committed to acting on behalf of all people and would not be primarily concerned with people of their own nation. Universalists would only act on behalf of their own country if it had, so to speak, the best case, i.e., the greatest need or the most pressing rights, or if it were the only country that they were in a position to assist.

## IS MODERATE PATRIOTISM DEFENSIBLE?

My main goal in defining patriotism and distinguishing its different forms has been to describe a form of patriotism that is not subject to the criticisms of Tolstoy and others who see patriotism as an impediment to peace and human cooperation. Does the moderate patriotism I have sketched achieve this?

Recall Tolstoy's main criticisms. Patriotism he said, is stupid, immoral, a sham, and the cause of war.

Moderate patriotism, however, is not stupid because it is not committed to the false belief in the superiority of one's own nation. Nor is it immoral, since it recognizes that people in other countries have rights and that there are moral constraints on what any country may do to promote its own good.

Whether moderate patriotism is a sham or not depends in part on whether those who espouse it are sincere in what they say. Tolstoy believed that patriotism was simply an instrument of propaganda to generate support for unworthy government policies and maintain the power of public officials. There is no doubt that patriotism is frequently used in these ways. Nonetheless, moderate patriotism is much less useful for these purposes than extreme patriotism. Since moderate patriotism permits and even encourages a critical attitude to government policies, it is not useful for bolstering either unjustified policies or the power of political officials. Like any other ideal (love, charity, religious devotion, etc.), patriotism may be invoked for ulterior motives or manipulated for evil purposes. The moderate patriotic conception, however, contains some built-in safeguards against these abuses that other forms of patriotism lack.

Finally, for all these reasons, moderate patriotism is not warlike or belligerent. It does not include the qualities of extreme patriotism that are conducive to war. Having excised the belief in superiority, the desire for dominance, exclusiveness of concern, and non-recognition of moral constraints on national actions, moderate patriotism permits the pursuit of legitimate national goals by morally legitimate means. Because it does not encourage belligerence, hostility, or aggression, however, it is compatible with a commitment to international cooperation and the nonviolent solution of conflicts between nations.

For all these reasons, we can accept the validity of Tolstoy's arguments as they apply to extreme patriotism while rejecting them as a refutation of moderate patriotism. While there are good reasons to reject extreme forms of patriotism, these reasons do not show that we should reject every form of patriotism.

## NOTES

1. Translated by Eric Bentley (New York: Grove Press, 1966), 21.

2. Cf. Andrew Oldenquist, "Loyalties," *Journal of Philosophy* LXXIX (1982), 173–93.

# *4*

# Patriotism Within the Limits of Morality

Tolstoy attacks patriotism for being incompatible with morality. I have argued that the form of patriotism he attacks is not the only form and that the features of patriotism he finds incompatible with morality are not essential to it. My argument so far has focused on the nature of patriotism. Since the central issue is the relationship between patriotism and morality, we need to consider the nature of morality as well. In this chapter, I will focus on some important features of morality in order to clarify the ways that moral standards constrain the actions we are allowed to perform on our country's behalf.

If a form of patriotism is to be a morally acceptable ideal, it must combine two features: a positive commitment to act on one's country's behalf in ways that one would not normally act for other countries, and a negative commitment to avoid acting in ways that fail to respect the common humanity we share with people of other countries. Both of these features are essential. Without the positive, special commitment to one's country, we do not have patriotism. Without the negative commitment to avoid ill treatment of people in other countries, we have an extreme, belligerent, immoral form of patriotism.

In chapter 3, I contrasted two forms of patriotism. Extreme patriotism involves the following features:

- A belief in the superiority of one's country
- A desire for dominance over other countries
- An exclusive concern for one's own country
- No constraints on the pursuit of one's country's goals
- Automatic support of one's country's military policies.

Moderate patriotism, the form that I am defending, is characterized by the following related but significantly different set of features:

- Special affection for one's country
- A desire that one's country prosper and flourish
- Special but not exclusive concern for one's own country
- Support of morally constrained pursuit of national goals
- Conditional support of one's country's policies.

Both of these forms of patriotism are specific versions of the more general category of patriotic attitudes. Patriotism in general is characterized by:

- Special affection for one's own country
- A sense of personal identification with the country
- Special concern for the well-being of the country
- Willingness to sacrifice to promote the country's good.

In defending moderate patriotism, I am trying to show that it includes both the special concern for one's country that makes it a form of patriotism and the respect for others that makes it a morally acceptable attitude.

It is part of the universalist aspect of morality that while special preferences are permissible, there is no genuine moral hierarchy among people. All people possess hopes and aspirations. All people possess vulnerabilities to death, injury, pain, and disappointment. In general, all people have, at least initially, an equal claim on the pursuit of a happy life. One famous expression of this belief occurs in the American Declaration of Independence, which states that all people have "inalienable rights" to "life, liberty, and the pursuit of happiness." The possession of these rights is not limited to members of any particular national group, race, or religion. These are universal rights, and the recognition of these rights in others is one way that we show a minimal respect for them as human beings.

Extreme patriotism fails to show this respect. It encourages a sense of overcommitment to one's own national group, while failing to support attitudes of respect and concern for those beyond one's borders. Moderate patriotism, however, is not attached to delusions of grandeur and superiority. It recognizes that we have special ties to some people but does not inflate the special connection we have into illusions about the moral superiority of our own group.

Moderate patriotism, then, is morally superior to extreme patriotism because it is consistent with a recognition of human equality and the universality of basic rights that belong to people simply by virtue of their humanity.

## CONSTRAINTS ON PURSUING
## THE NATIONAL INTEREST

Extreme and moderate patriots both want their country to prosper and flourish. Because that is all that extreme patriots care about, however, they are committed to the view that any actions that advance the interests of their own country are right. Contribution to national well-being is the only factor they take to be relevant when they evaluate actions.

This is why Tolstoy describes patriotism as a form of group egoism. While individual egoists care only about themselves and will do whatever promotes their well-being, group egoists approve of whatever contributes to the well-being of their group. Extreme patriotism is one form of group egoism, as are extreme forms of racism, "religionism," "familyism," or "friendism."

What is the matter with these forms of overcommitment to oneself or one's group? In order to answer this question, we need to consider how morality impinges on the pursuit of *individual* goals and purposes. Then we can extrapolate to the relationship between morality and the pursuit of benefits for *groups* that we belong to. We can begin by recalling Tolstoy's description of a crudely egoistic young man who shows his indifference to others

> by eating everything and leaving nothing for others, by pushing the weak out of the way that he may pass himself, by forcibly taking that which another needs. . . . (110)

The problem with the egoist is not that he cares about himself. Nor is it that he cares more about himself than he does about most people. This kind of self-concern is quite natural and even healthy, since each of us bears a primary responsibility to manage our own lives. The problem with the egoist is that he has an exclusive concern for himself. He cares for himself alone. The egoist honors the first part of the Jewish sage Hillel's maxim "If I am not for myself, who will be?" But he neglects the second part, "If I am for myself alone, what am I?"

Caring only for himself, the extreme egoist recognizes no value in other people or the satisfaction of their needs. Because he has no respect for them or their rights, he feels free to do whatever is necessary to get what he wants. He eats without leaving for others, gets to his destination by pushing the weak out of his way, and simply takes from others what he wants from them. In short, he pursues his own good without recognizing any constraints on his actions.

If we want to transform Tolstoy's egoist into a moral person, we do not need to destroy his self-concern or make him a perfect altruist. Instead, we can leave his self-concern intact and add to it some degree of concern for others and a recognition of their rights, needs, and interests. Likewise, we need not forbid him from pursuing his own good. Rather, we need only limit the ways in which he pursues them. He may eat, but he may not take others' food. He may go where he wants, but he may not push aside the weak. He may strive for what he wants, but he may not forcibly take what belongs to others.

So, if we want to change the extreme egoist into a moral person, we will change his attitude from one of exclusive concern with himself to one of special but non-exclusive concern. Likewise, we will allow him to pursue his own good but only within the limits of a set of constraints on his actions.

These two features are central to morality: some degree of regard for all people and an acceptance of constraints on what we do in pursuit of our goals. Adding these features to the egoist would render him immune to moral criticism without requiring him to forfeit a special concern for his own well-being.

## THE STRUCTURE OF MORALITY

This description of what is required to transform an egoist into a moral person provides an insight into the nature of morality, and I would like to describe what I take to be the structure of morality. Given the many controversies about the nature of morality, it may be presumptuous to attempt a brief description. Nonetheless, we need some sense of what morality is and how it operates in order to understand how morality impinges on our actions and, ultimately, how it relates to patriotism.

Someone might object that any attempt to describe morality must fail because there is no single entity called "morality." If what exists is a plurality of diverse moral visions, codes, ideals, theories, and principles, then morality—as a *singular* thing—cannot be described.

While I do not deny that there is both moral diversity and moral controversy, I also believe that there is widespread agreement about certain basic features of morality, and it is these features that I will try to describe.[1]

We can think about the structure of morality in one of two ways. The first way sees morality as specifying some goal that we are all to achieve. The goal might be our own happiness, the happiness of some group, universal well-being, the production of knowledge or strength of character, the production of love and affection, or other things. If this were the structure of morality, then there would be a mandatory goal that everyone would be morally required to strive for.

I do not think that this is how morality works. There is no one goal that is mandatory for all of us. Rather, as my remarks about egoism suggest, morality permits us to have our own goals. My goal may be my own happiness or the greatest amount of wealth for people I love or the achievement of fame or high office. Or, like most of us, I may have no single goal at all. Rather, I may have many different goals and desires, some more central than others but all things that I hope to achieve. To a great extent, morality leaves open what I choose to strive for. It does not have a goal-oriented structure.

According to a second model, morality places constraints on our actions. It places certain actions "out of bounds." It tells us that while we may pursue our own goals, there are certain things we must not do to achieve them. Morality, according to this second view, imposes what have been called "side constraints" on our actions.[2] From this perspective, moral rules are analogous to the rules of a game. The rules of a game do not tell us what strategy to use in order to win. In fact, they do not even require that we try to win. Allowing a child to win a game of checkers, for example, does not violate the rules.

What the rules do is to define the ways in which we are permitted to play. An important part of this is negative, for the rules forbid certain means of trying to win. In checkers, for example, a person may not make two moves consecutively. After each move that I make, my opponent must have a chance to move one of his pieces. So, one way that I am not allowed to seek victory is by moving twice in a row. Other rules are not written down but are presupposed. For example, it would violate the rules to use threats and intimidation to keep an opponent from taking a piece that I do not want to lose, even though this is not written in the official rules of checkers.

So, in a competitive game, we are allowed to strive for victory, and we are not required by the rules to be altruistic. Nonetheless, our quest for victory (if that is what we seek) is limited by the rules. It is worth noting that rules do not derive only from competitive aspect of games. Even in non-competitive games, like solitaire or ring-around-a-rosie, there are things one is not permitted to do.

Similarly, while morality leaves it up to us to choose our own goals, it imposes constraints on our pursuit of these goals. What are these constraints? The main constraints prohibit inflicting certain kinds of harms on people. They forbid us from killing or injuring other people, as well as inflicting pain and unhappiness on them. To take some common examples, I may pursue my goal of driving to New York, but in doing this, I must avoid running into other cars and pedestrians. I may compete for a job, but I may not do so by killing or disabling other applicants. I may pursue pleasure for myself but not by means of inflicting pain on others.

It is important to add here that the rules forbidding killing, injuring, causing pain, etc., are presumptive rules. That is, while generally forbidding these actions, they allow that there are special occasions on which they are permitted. In the case of killing, for example, morality generally forbids killing other people but permits doing so in exceptional cases. It permits a person to kill in self-defense or in defense of others, provided that there are no available alternative means for preventing severe injury or death to oneself.

Common sense morality, then, consists of a core set of rules that generally forbid certain kinds of actions.[3] From this perspective, morality has a negative function. It does not prescribe goals, but it does proscribe actions done in pursuit of goals. Within the limits set by these constraints, a person may do what he or she wants to do.

## SPECIAL DUTIES

There is a second part of morality, and that is the realm of special duties. People may acquire positive obligations by virtue of making promises, signing contracts, or having a certain social role or status. When this occurs, they have a special duty either to work for a certain goal or to promote the well-being of other people.[4]

Family obligations are a good instance of such special duties. If one becomes a parent, one takes on a host of rather demanding duties toward one's children. These duties need not be regarded as onerous. People who love and care about their children have strong, natural motivations to act on their behalf. In saying that one has a duty to do these things, I am not suggesting that parents must be directly motivated by a sense that there are certain rules they must follow.[5] The motivation to act for one's children flows from deep emotional ties, and acting for them may often be quite pleasurable. Nonetheless, such actions are still duties. A parent who did not seek to promote the well-being of his children or who was distracted from parental demands by other pursuits would be failing to carry out the duties of parenthood. Parents who dislike their children do not have an excuse to neglect them.

Parenthood is not the only social role that generates special duties. Being a lawyer, teacher, plumber, nurse, elected official, or waiter carries special duties and requires forms of behavior that one would not otherwise engage in. The same is true of being a member of a club or a team. There are many special roles and many sets of role-related duties. Moreover, one person can occupy many such roles, so that these duties are an important part of our moral life.[6]

While there are many such duties, I will continue to focus on the family, since it is a familiar institution that has an important place in virtually everyone's life. Even people who do not marry have, for the most part, grown up in families. Moreover, it is widely thought that family commitments ought to be among our most central ones and that ties to family members will be taken seriously by all involved. We expect, for example, that parents will be strongly committed to the well-being of their children and will care deeply about them. We expect parents to devote considerable time and energy to the raising of children and the promotion of their interests.[7]

Often, we think of our families as extensions of ourselves. Within the family, we do not seek our own well-being directly but are happy to pursue that of our spouse or children. It is probably more appropriate to say that the distinction between self and other is not significant rather than saying that others become extensions of ourselves. What is crucial is that other people's well-being can come to have a higher priority than our own and that our own well-being comes in part to be defined by the extent to which others flourish. If my children suffer, then *my* life is diminished, not simply theirs.[8] So the well-being of our closest family members is a goal that duty requires us to pursue and that some of our strongest feelings may motivate us to pursue as well.

Nonetheless, as important as these goals are and as central as families are to our lives, the kinds of moral constraints I have discussed apply to us in our roles as committed spouses or parents. One is not permitted to pursue the well-being of one's children or spouse by any and all means. There are many things that we are morally forbidden to do while pursuing our family's well-being. I may not, for example, injure or kill another child because that child may win a scholarship that my child needs in order to attend college. I may not beat another child to provide pleasure for my own child. I may not threaten another family in order to force them out of a house I would like for my own family. If these examples seem bizarre, it is because we take it for granted that these actions would be wrong. That is precisely my point, however. As deeply committed as we may be to the well-being of our spouses or children, there are actions that are "out of bounds" and that we may not do, even if we are motivated by love or familial duty.

The situation with respect to our families exactly parallels that which applied to the egoist. People have a right to pursue their own self-interest, but only within the limits that morality imposes. Likewise, people have a right and even a duty to pursue the well-being of their families, but there are moral constraints on what they may do in the course of this pursuit. Carrying out the special duties that morality imposes on us must be done in a way that is consistent with the constraints that morality also imposes.

## PATRIOTISM AND MORALITY

With this model of the structure of morality in mind and with the examples of how it applies to self-interest and to the carrying out of family duties, we can now understand the relationship between patriotism and morality.

Patriots seek the well-being of their country and believe that they have a special duty to it. The patriot's desire for her country to prosper and flourish is a particular goal, and, as we have seen, morality is very permissive about our choice of goals. It permits us to pursue our own interests, other people's interests, and a variety of specific goods that we find appealing or believe to be valuable. Because morality does not forbid us from having a special desire that certain people, groups, or institutions flourish, there is nothing about morality that forbids one from seeking the good of his or her country.

Likewise, if being a citizen carries with it special duties to the country, morality permits us to act on these duties and may even require us to do so. If there are duties that one has by virtue of being a member of a family, team, club, or profession, then there can be duties that grow out of our status as citizens. National well-being is not a goal that morality forbids, and it thus permits the special preference of patriots for their country and the special efforts they are motivated to make on its behalf.

Nonetheless, just as the pursuit of the well-being of our selves, our families, and other groups must be carried out within the constraints imposed by morality, so must the pursuit of our country's interests be carried out within these same constraints. While many means of promoting our national well-being are open to us, some means violate moral side constraints and are therefore morally forbidden. Just as individuals may not engage in wanton killing and injuring in the course of pursuing their personal goals or the well-being of their families, so they may not engage in wanton killing and injuring of others in pursuit of the good of their country. Actions done on behalf of one's country are no more exempt from the constraints of morality than actions done on behalf of oneself, one's family, one's team, or one's religious group.

As we have already seen, the recognition of constraints on how we may pursue our goals is one important characteristic that differentiates moderate patriotism from extreme patriotism. It is this recognition that makes moderate patriotism compatible with both the form and the substance of universal morality.

Likewise, we can see that moderate patriotism would not lead to war in the way that extreme patriotism does. From a moral point of view, war is always a disaster, since the conduct of war involves the widespread performance of actions that are our paradigms of what we must avoid doing. The infliction of death, injury, and pain on people are essential to the conduct of war. Yet, these are precisely the actions that morality most stringently forbids. These are actions that may only be performed when we are most seriously threatened. They may not be performed simply because they are useful means to achieving our goals. Because moderate patriots recognize these constraints, they will seek to avoid the violence and destruction of war. If circumstances appear to make war justified, moderate patriots will subject both the decision to go to war and conduct in the course of a war to serious moral scrutiny.

Just as one may only injure or kill individuals to defend oneself or others from the most serious threats, so one may only perform these actions for one's country if its vital interests and rights are severely threatened. In other circumstances, moderate patriots will not support a country's entry into war. There is, then, no grounds for accusing moderate patriots of belligerence or indifference toward the suffering that war inevitably causes.

## MY COUNTRY, RIGHT OR WRONG?

Once we understand the structure of morality, we can see why the
slogan "my country, right or wrong" is fundamentally misguided and
why it can only be taken as an expression of fanaticism.

As we have seen, morality has a certain structure. It imposes constraints on what we may do to anyone, as well as special duties to
promote the well-being of particular persons or groups. The special
duties, however, are always limited by the constraints that morality
imposes. "My country, right or wrong" asserts that a person should do
whatever is necessary for his own country, whether or not it violates
moral constraints on how one may treat others.

It is hard to see how such a position can be defended. It is hard to
see what properties countries have that would make the constraints of
morality inapplicable to actions done on their behalf. In fact, there
are good reasons for denying that countries are beyond the reach of
morality in this way.

First, as we have seen, the constraints of morality apply to the
pursuit of all other goals and to the carrying out of our special duties
toward other individuals and groups. If these moral constraints apply
to our promoting the interests of ourselves, of people we care about,
and of other groups to which we belong, it is very odd to think that
they do not similarly constrain the actions we may perform in promoting the interests of our country. There is no reason to think that
while all other concerns are constrained by morality, the pursuit of
national interest is alone free of such moral limits.

Second, if one looks to history, one can see that many immoral
deeds have been done in the name of national interest, and one can
certainly make retrospective judgments of these acts. If we can condemn past actions because they led to large-scale death and destruction, then it is hard to see why it would be wrong to condemn present
or future actions that one can see will have similar consequences. If
a citizen believes that her country is considering policies that are
immoral, she may evaluate and oppose those proposed actions in the
same way that she could condemn them after the fact.

In this context, it is important to recall Tolstoy's remarks about the
misuse of patriotic ideals and patriotic sentiment to gain support for
unworthy policies. No matter how enamored one might be with one's
own country and its historical record, it is evident that such abuses do
occur. Knowing that this is a possibility, we can all at least conceive
of situations in which we would disapprove of our country's actions,
and, knowing the imperfections of human institutions, we can at least

imagine our own country embarking on evil policies. Given these possibilities, the ideal of unconditional support appears to have little in its favor.

There is a third basis for rejecting "my country, right or wrong." As I noted above, it is characteristic of patriots that they have a sense of special identification with their country. This identification leads patriotic people to feel pride in their country's achievements. Patriots feel proud when their country promotes good causes, when it champions respect for human rights or joins with others to fight illness and hunger. They take pride when their country lives up to valuable ideals.

The corollary to this is that when a country fails to live up to high ideals or standards of moral decency, then its citizens may both disapprove of its actions and feel shame. Mere disapproval is evoked by the failings of other countries, but when it is our own country whose actions are immoral, then we feel shame that *we* have behaved badly. Because patriots want their country to behave in ways that merit pride rather than shame, they will urge that their country live up to high moral standards and avoid pursuing its interests by immoral means.[9]

In saying this, I do not deny that some patriots take pride in their country's strength and power and do not care whether it violates moral ideals. My point is that this attitude is not a necessary part of the patriotic attitude. Once we see that patriotism and national pride can lead to a desire that the country live up to high moral standards, then we can see that love of country might lead to especially strong denunciations of aggressive, immoral national policies. The denunciations are especially strong because of the special connections between citizens and the actions and policies of their own government.[10]

So, while many think that patriotism requires citizens to abstain from criticizing their country, it may in fact give special urgency to the need to be critical. Citizens have special reasons for wanting their country to behave well. Their own integrity is at stake in the behavior of their country. We can see this in a statement Thoreau made in discussing slavery and the Mexican war. "How," he asked, "does it become a man to behave toward this American government to-day? I answer that he cannot without disgrace be associated with it."[11] Thoreau himself may not have been a patriot, but his comment brings out one of the special motives—the desire to avoid personal disgrace—that patriots have for holding their country to high moral standards.

Part of the problem with extreme patriotism is that it makes the support of one's country and its policies unconditional. Moderate patriots, on the other hand, see that taking morality seriously requires that our commitment to our country be conditional in two ways. First, the actions or policies of a government must be worthy of support or, at least, must not be serious violations of morality. When nations behave immorally, patriots need not support them.

Second, we must recognize the possibility that a nation itself might be unworthy of support. It might be so dedicated to immoral goals or ideals or so unconstrained in its pursuit of its interests that no moral person could support that nation. The fact that a country is *my* country does not mean that it is worthy of patriotic devotion.

This last point brings out an important limitation in my view. My defense of patriotism does not imply that anyone ought to be a patriot. That only follows if we assume that one's country is worthy of patriotic loyalty. What I have shown is that patriotism is a morally permissible ideal, that it does not in itself violate any fundamental moral values. But just as a defense of friendship would not show that any specific individual is a worthy object of friendship, so a defense of patriotism does not show that any particular country is a worthy object of patriotic loyalty.

"My country, right or wrong" is unacceptable both because it overlooks the possibility of nations that do not deserve our support and because it fails to take seriously the importance of withholding support from immoral policies. These are the reasons that moderate patriots reject this slogan and the ideal it expresses.

## LOOKING AHEAD

The moderate patriotic perspective arises from an attempt to balance the claims of universal morality with the claims of one's own country. It is a middle position, located between the extremes of unconstrained, fanatical loyalty to one's country and a purely universalist moral perspective that refuses to see any relevance in the emotional, personal, and historical ties between people and the political communities they inhabit.

While I hope that my sketch has shown moderate patriotism to possess some significant virtues, it is the fate of middle positions to be subject to criticism and attack from both sides. Moderate patriotism will satisfy neither extreme universalists nor extreme patriots. Extreme universalists will criticize it because it grants too much special status to one's own country, while extreme patriots will attack it for not granting enough.

What seems like a straightforward, commonsensical position provokes strong criticisms, and these criticisms need to be addressed before we can be sure that the moderate patriotic perspective is reasonable and worthy of our embrace. Fortunately, the criticisms raised against this view are themselves of considerable interest, so trying to understand and reply to them is not without its pleasures. More important, by considering them, we can deepen our understanding of ourselves as moral beings who are at the same time separate individuals, members of numerous groups, and members of the human species.

## NOTES

1. Much of what I will say is heavily indebted to the views of Bernard Gert. These were first set out in *The Moral Rules: A New Rational Justification for Morality* (New York: Harper & Row, 1973) and have been further developed in *Morality: A New Justification of the Moral Rules* (New York: Oxford University Press, 1988).

2. The term is Robert Nozick's. See his *Anarchy, State, and Utopia* (New York: Basic Books, 1973), 28–30.

3. For Gert's full set of rules, see *Morality*, 157.

4. Cf. Gert, who includes "do your duty" as one of his ten basic moral rules.

5. Lawrence Blum makes a similar point about friendship, arguing against Kant's view that morally worthwhile actions must be motivated by a desire to do one's duty. See Blum, *Friendship, Altruism, and Morality* (Boston: Routledge and Kegan Paul, 1980).

6. For an insightful description of the ways in which roles generate duties, expectations, and rules of behavior, see Erving Goffman, *The Presentation of Self in Everyday Life* (Garden City, N.Y.: Doubleday Anchor, 1959).

7. For a rich description of the complexities of raising children, see Sara Ruddick, *Maternal Thinking* (Boston: Beacon Press, 1989).

8. For a helpful discussion of the relationship between self-interest and the interests of others, see Joel Feinberg, *Harm to Others* (New York: Oxford University Press, 1984).

9. Pride and shame are also mentioned in connection with patriotism by Andrew Oldenquist in "Loyalties," *Journal of Philosophy* 79 (1982), 175.

10. The idea that loyalty requires criticism can be found in the idea of friendship as well. Robert Bellah notes that the Aristotelian conception of friendship involves a "shared commitment to the good" and a duty to help one's friends "to be better people." He goes on to say, "The 'unconditional acceptance' that was supposed to go with true love and friendship did not mean the abandonment of moral standards, even in the most intimate relationship." See Bellah et al., *Habits of the Heart* (New York: Harper and Row, 1986), 115.

11. Quoted from "Civil Disobedience," in *Walden and Other Writings* (New York: Modern Library, 1937), 638.

*Part II*

# Is Moderate Patriotism Patriotic Enough?

.

# 5

# The Basis of Loyalty

For me, moderate patriotism is both a plausible ideal and the solution
to a problem. It enables us to make patriotism consistent with universal morality. This is a problem because the demands of morality are
universal in form, while the requirements of patriotism are directed
toward the members of a particular society.

Moderate patriotism appears to be a straightforward, commonsensical view. It recognizes the value of loyalty and special concern for
one's country without losing sight of the common humanity we share
with members of other societies. It takes seriously the common knowledge that governments are often evil and that even good governments
can initiate evil policies. Finally, it recognizes that ideals can be either reasonable or fanatical and that extreme patriotism is a form of
fanaticism.

In spite of its virtues, moderate patriotism will not please everyone. That it will appear weak and tepid to extreme patriots is to be
expected. Reasonable people can never compete with fanatics in degree of devotion to a cause. But, of course, no one ought to compete
with fanatics in this way, for this is the path to excessive and unreasonable commitment. If some people are more patriotic than I am,
that does not mean that I am unpatriotic. Nor does it establish them
as better patriots. Patriotism, like everything else, has its limits, and
moderate patriots try to define those limits and honor them.

For all its apparent reasonableness, moderate patriotism has been
attacked directly by some philosophers and has implications that appear to conflict with a number of widely accepted views. The objections to moderate patriotism are of several types. Some purport to

show that moderate patriotism is not a genuine form of patriotism. Some claim that it is impossible to combine patriotic concern for a particular country with the impartial perspective of a universal morality. Finally, others argue that moderate patriotism requires a kind of moral judgment that is, for one reason or another, impossible to achieve. My aim in this and the next few chapters is to strengthen the claim that moderate patriotism is genuine and to show that whatever obstacles appear to block the way to moderate patriotism are illusory.

## TWO CRITICS

The most direct philosophical attacks on moderate patriotism can be found in essays by Alasdair MacIntyre and Andrew Oldenquist. Both MacIntyre and Oldenquist raise strong challenges to moderate patriotism and thereby provide valuable sources of the doubts and arguments that moderate patriots must address.

The title of MacIntyre's essay—"Is Patriotism a Virtue?"[1]—shows that he takes seriously the need to defend patriotism and sees that patriotism and morality may conflict. Like Tolstoy, MacIntyre begins his discussion by describing the tensions between two "standpoints," the standpoint of ethical universalism and the standpoint of patriotism. He then describes a proposal for reducing these tensions. "It might be argued," he writes,

> that the two standpoints need not be in conflict. For patriotism and all other such particular loyalties can be restricted in scope so that their exercise is always within the confines imposed by morality. Patriotism need be regarded as nothing more than a perfectly proper devotion to one's own nation which must never be allowed to violate the constraints set by the impersonal moral standpoint. (6)

The proposal that MacIntyre describes for resolving the tension between universalism and patriotism is exactly the view that I have called moderate patriotism: a special devotion to one's own country that is constrained by "impersonal" moral standards and that, therefore, does not motivate actions that violate these standards.

While I have argued that this view resolves the tensions between patriotism and universal morality, MacIntyre rejects it as a false solution and raises the question whether it is genuinely patriotic. This constrained form of patriotism is, he says,

> the kind of patriotism professed by certain liberal moralists who are often indignant when it is suggested by their critics that they are not

patriotic. To those critics however patriotism thus limited in scope appears to be emasculated. . . . (6)

MacIntyre's subsequent remarks show that he shares the critics' view and has little sympathy with the "liberal moralists" who believe that their patriotism has been unfairly challenged.

Earlier, I defined patriotism as a special affection for, identification with, and concern for one's own nation and a willingness to act on its behalf. Since moderate patriotism satisfies all of these conditions, we might wonder what it lacks and why critics would view it as an inauthentic and "emasculated" form of loyalty.

MacIntyre tries to answer this question by distinguishing true patriotism from another attitude that resembles patriotism but is, he thinks, essentially different. Some people, he says, support their nation but do so only because it promotes or conforms to high and worthy ideals. So, for example, some Americans may view the United States as worthy of allegiance because it is committed to freedom, democracy, or capitalism. In such cases, MacIntyre says, "it is the ideal and not the nation which is the primary object" of loyalty (4). Such people are not genuine patriots because their primary attachment is not to the country itself but to the ideals the country happens to support.

MacIntyre claims that real patriots are attached to their country because it is *theirs*, not because it supports high ideals or has other valuable features. It is the sense of personal attachment to that particular country that underlies their loyalty. Patriots do value their country's worthy qualities, but they value them in a way that is different from the way they value the worthy qualities of other countries. Genuine patriots are directly attached to their country and not indirectly linked to it by virtue of its commitment to proper ideals. Patriotism is not based on reasons in the sense that we decide to be loyal to a country because it has valuable features. Rather, we are patriotic because the country is our country.

Patriotism, MacIntyre notes, is one of a number of "loyalty-exhibiting virtues" that include marital fidelity, love of one's family, and such things as school or team loyalty. Each of these forms of loyalty involves a special "regard founded upon a particular historical relationship of association between the person exhibiting the regard and the relevant person, institution or group" (4). Because of its historical roots, there is a contingency and a particularity that is essential to these loyalties and that is not captured by universal evaluative criteria.

For MacIntyre, patriotism is grounded on contingent facts about our personal connection to our country. Moderate patriotism, however, is criterion-based. It emphasizes the necessity of judging one's country to see if it is worthy of loyalty. Moderate patriotism, he claims, overlooks the personal connectedness that is central to patriotism. It may look like the real thing, but for MacIntyre, it lacks an essential feature of genuine patriotism, a rootedness in contingent personal connections between people and their country.

Andrew Oldenquist develops a similar argument in his essay "Loyalties."[2] Like MacIntyre, Oldenquist sets out to defend loyalty against the claims of universal morality. He argues that genuine loyalties are morally important and wants to defend them even if they conflict with impersonal morality. In one part of his essay, he draws a distinction between two kinds of patriotism, which he calls "loyalty patriotism" and "impartial patriotism." He tries to show that while loyalty patriotism is genuine, impartial patriotism is not.

A loyalty patriot, Oldenquist says, is someone whose "judgment [about] what he should do is partly determined by the fact that the good of *his* country is at stake" (184). In contrast, an impartial patriot is someone for whom "the thought '*P* is my country' is not conceded to count for anything." The impartial patriot

> says that he supports his country just because it has [some set of valuable] features . . . and therefore he is committed to the position that if his country and its adversary exchanged features . . . he should support the adversary. If it is true that he supports his country solely because he thinks it is in the right, it follows that the fact that one of the countries is his own does not enter at all into his decision. Such "patriots" believe themselves to be objective, like ideal observers, and simply lucky that their own country is right. . . . (183)[3]

Oldenquist comments that impartial patriotism is not a genuine form of loyalty because it contains no "uneliminable singular terms," no terms that refer to the relationship between specific individuals and a specific country. That is, the fact that it is *his or her own country* does not count for the impartial patriot. All that counts is that it is a country with certain good features. Because impartial patriotism lacks the essential element of personal connectedness, it is not a real form of patriotism.

Again, it is easy to see that the impartial patriot is like the moderate patriot. Both take seriously the idea that a nation and its policies must meet some criteria of value in order to merit our loyalty. So, if Oldenquist is correct that impartial patriotism is not genuine, then this would be true of moderate patriotism as well.

After rejecting impartial patriotism, Oldenquist goes on to suggest that most people who think of themselves as impartial patriots are self-deceived. They actually do feel personally connected to their country because it is theirs. Nonetheless, because they want to believe that their commitments conform to universal moral standards, they assure themselves that their devotion to their own country is based on the fact that it has such valuable features.

Oldenquist's conclusion, then, is that impartial patriots are either not genuinely patriotic or they are self-deceived. People cannot both be genuine patriots and support their country solely because it has valuable features. Like MacIntyre, Oldenquist believes that a specific, contingent bond is what links patriots to their country.

## AMERICAN PATRIOTISM

While Oldenquist deals with the contrast between "loyalty patriotism" and "impartial patriotism" as a purely logical distinction, MacIntyre believes that both forms occur in history. Modern states, he claims, have tried to combine an older form of contingent, personal loyalty with a loyalty based on universal values. During the French Revolution, for example, the revolutionaries saw themselves as champions of humanity at large and not just of France. They proclaimed the Rights of Man, not just the rights of French citizens. Similarly, the American Declaration of Independence postulates natural, inalienable rights that derive from God and that belong to all people, rather than affirming rights for Americans that derive from their membership in the American political community. Later, in absorbing immigrants from many nations, American society stressed the value of universal standards that applied to and could unite all these diverse peoples, contrasting this with the customary moralities of the immigrants' original ethnic homelands. Thus, MacIntyre tells us,

> the cause of America, understood as the object of patriotic regard, and the cause of [universal] morality . . . came to be identified. (19)

MacIntyre believes that the attempt to identify these two distinct causes gives rise to a set of values that is fundamentally incoherent. Why? Because it attempts to combine a highly particular commitment to a specific political community with a highly general commitment to universal human principles. This hybrid conception, he thinks, makes no sense. Patriotic loyalty must derive directly from a sense of personal connection to a country, not indirectly from universal ideals that the country possesses.

An interesting fact about MacIntyre's historical analysis is that it suggests that something like the moderate patriotic view is an essential component of traditional American political values. This idea is made explicit by Anthony Hartle. Hartle begins by citing a description of American patriotism as "loyalty to national institutions and symbols *because and in so far as they represent values that are the primary objects of allegiance*" [emphasis added]. He goes on to praise American patriotism for the very reason that it makes loyalty conditional on the qualities of the nation. In his view, this

> characteristic [of American patriotism] saves us from the dogmatic form of nationalism that can be a severe threat to peace. . . . American nationalism [is] based upon . . . fundamental moral values . . . [and] is linked to the idea that "the American way" is a shining light that should lead to a morally superior existence.[4]

Unlike MacIntyre, Hartle sees it as a strength of American nationalism that it is criterion-based. MacIntyre, however, views this as a fundamental weakness. He believes that adherence to universal standards can never produce genuine commitment to a particular group.

While both MacIntyre and Hartle identify this type of patriotism with American political culture, it is not obvious that the United States is essentially different from other cultures in this regard. As we saw earlier, there is a widespread tendency for people in different cultures to view themselves as superior to others. They tend to see their own group as exemplifying the highest values and view others who lack these values as inferior. Hence, in addition to whatever loyalty their members feel by virtue of personal connectedness, that loyalty is buttressed by a confidence that their own society measures up to high standards of worth. Even racial theories of membership, like that held by the Nazis, supplement their claim that primordial blood ties define the nation with assertions about the superiority of their race. They make assertions of value as well as assertions of connectedness.

What Hartle and MacIntyre see as a peculiar feature of the United States or some other modern societies may not be limited to them. Likewise, MacIntyre and Oldenquist may be wrong to think that it is only "liberal moralists" and universalists who wish to combine a personally based and a criterion-based form of loyalty.

## ON COMBINING PERSONAL AND
## PRINCIPLED PATRIOTISM

Both Oldenquist and MacIntyre take genuine loyalty to be based simply on the fact of personal connectedness, and they reject principled, criterion-based loyalty as lacking the essential qualities of genuine loyalty. Patriotism, they claim, always rests on the fact that the country is my country or your country. This "my-ness" is essential. One can only be patriotic toward one's own country. As MacIntyre says, "Only Frenchmen can be patriotic about France, while anyone can make the cause of *civilisation* their own" (4). He and Oldenquist believe that moderate patriotism does not recognize this personal connection.

While both MacIntyre and Oldenquist assume that this personal connection is missing from and incompatible with moderate patriotism, their assumption is false. No one would deny that patriotism involves "uneliminable singular terms" and that one can only be patriotic toward one's own country. At one level, this is merely a trivial semantic point. The only kind of devotion or loyalty that we call "patriotism" is loyalty toward one's *own* country. If a person admires or assists another country, that may be a case of loyalty to another country, but it won't count as *patriotic* loyalty. This is no different from the definitional truth that I can only bestow "fatherly affection" on my own children or feel "brotherly love" only toward my siblings. Any other use of these terms would be metaphorical.

It is true, then, that one can only be patriotic to one's own country, but this semantic point does nothing to show that criterion-based patriotism is not patriotism.

No doubt MacIntyre and Oldenquist do not mean to make a purely semantic point. More likely, the point they are making is *psychological* rather than semantic. What they have in mind is that the genuine patriot is devoted to her country *because* it is her own. In the same way, one bestows affection on one's children because they are one's own or on one's siblings because they are one's own brothers and sisters. In the case of the genuine patriot, they want to say, loyalty is *based on* a sense of personal connectedness, while in the case of the moderate patriot, it is based on conformity with universal value criteria.

This criticism, however, is misguided for two reasons. First, as I have noted, an essential component of patriotism is a sense of personal identification with a nation. While moderate patriots want their country to live up to universal moral standards, they do have a particular connection to their own country. It is typically the country in which they have grown up and acquired a sense of themselves. The language and culture are most familiar to them, and they are more likely to feel "at home" in their own country than in others. While the deeds of other countries may inspire either admiration or disdain, the deeds of one's own country, and *only* one's own country, may produce pride and shame. The latter emotions require a sense of identification and membership. As Randolph Bourne notes,

> We may be intensely proud of and congenial to our particular network of civilization, or we may detest most of its qualities and rage at its defects. This does not alter the fact that we are inextricably bound up in it. The Country, as an inescapable group into which we are born, and which makes us its particular kind of a citizen with the world, seems to be a fundamental fact of our consciousness, an irreducible minimum of social feeling.[5]

These facts about the psychology of identification are as true of moderate patriots as they are of extreme patriots. In this way, the loyalty of moderate patriots is based on emotional, historical, and personal ties between them and their own country. It is because of these ties that moderate patriots feel specially connected with their country, caring for it and wishing it well in a way that is different from their feelings for other countries.

Moderate patriots believe, however, that we must test our commitments against a set of universal moral values. While our sense of loyalty may arises from an emotional, non-rational sense of attachment, the actions motivated by this loyalty are subject to evaluation. The fact that patriotic devotion must measure up to moral criteria does not mean that it originates out of a judgment that the country and its policies deserve one's support. Patriotic feeling does not come about through a rational process of comparing all countries to see which is most deserving of loyalty. Rather, a person grows up and acquires loyalties that he can later evaluate to see whether they are appropriate or not.

The story for "naturalized" citizens who are patriotic about their "adopted" country is obviously different but will contain a slow process of acculturation and the gradual development of a sense of identification. Such patriots, like their native counterparts, will acquire the sense of "my-ness" that patriots must possess. Likewise, evaluation of their new country will be no more impossible for them than was evaluation of the country they left behind.

In meeting the objections of MacIntyre and Oldenquist, I have commented on the origins of patriotic attachment. It is important to see, however, that moderate patriotism is not itself a theory about how people become patriotic. Rather, it expresses norms for assessing our personal connections from a moral point of view. MacIntyre himself agrees with the spirit of this critical attitude when he disavows "mindless patriotism." Likewise, Oldenquist acknowledges both that an object of loyalty "must have features that make it worth having" and that "it could deteriorate to the extent that shame ultimately kills [a person's] loyalty" (178). In making these points, they both acknowledge the necessity of evaluating objects of loyalty, without suggesting that patriotism develops out of a prior evaluative process. This is precisely the view I have supported. Moderate patriotism is not committed to a picture of the origins of patriotism that requires evaluation to precede commitment.

In short, the particularity that is essential to patriotism is as much a part of moderate patriotism as it is of any patriotism. MacIntyre and Oldenquist are simply mistaken in thinking that there is an inconsistency between particular attachments and commitment to moral standards. It is simply a fact that human beings both feel personally connected to particular individuals or groups and want their objects of loyalty to be *worthy* of devotion. While the delusion of grandeur that may infect national pride is a dangerous phenomenon, it can be seen as an outgrowth of a deep and admirable need to believe in the goodness of the groups to which we are attached. There is no reason to believe that a commitment to general standards of value is incompatible with the personal attachment that patriots have to their country.

## ARE MODERATE PATRIOTS FICKLE?

Oldenquist, in spite of his remark that it may be appropriate for loyalty to deteriorate in some cases, seems to suggest that moderate (or "impersonal") patriots will be fickle in a way that loyalty patriots will not. Recall his remark that an impartial patriot

> supports his country just because it has [some set of valuable] features . . . and therefore he is committed to the position that if his country and its adversary exchanged features . . . he should support the adversary. (183)

Even if moderate patriotism does not develop from a process of evaluation, moderate patriots are committed to evaluating their country by universal standards. If a country ceases to possess valuable features and an adversary acquires those features, then (Oldenquist suggests) a moderate patriot would be committed to switching his loyalties. Such a switch, he argues, is inconsistent with genuine patriotism and would show that the moderate patriot never was loyal in the proper way.

In this version of the argument that moderate patriotism is not genuine, Oldenquist assumes that the commitment of moderate patriots to universal standards forces them into choosing the best country as the object of their loyalty. They will do this even if it means betraying their own country. This conclusion does not follow, however. While there may be cases in which a "divorce" from one's own country is the right thing to do, it is surely not the first step. If a country that possesses morally valuable features begins to depart from them, moderate patriots may exhibit their commitment both to moral standards and to the country itself by trying to work for a return to high standards. They will not simply abandon their country. Contrary to what Oldenquist says, abandonment is not the only possible response to deterioration, even though (as he himself concedes) it might at some point become appropriate.

Moderate patriotism does not commit citizens to the role of a fickle judge, shifting loyalties from one country to another as one or another is more successful in conforming to moral and other ideals. If another country is admirable, one may admire it and even lend support to its efforts. To do so, however, is not to be patriotic toward that country since, as we have seen, one cannot be patriotic toward a country that is not one's own. Likewise, one's own country's failings may call for activity and effort to change it for the better.

We can see a similar pattern in the relations between parents and children. Parents who are committed to high moral standards will apply these standards to the behavior of their children. That does not mean, however, that they will be constantly surveying other children to see if they are more deserving of parental attention. Nor does it mean that if they are disappointed in their own children's actions they will simply abandon them for "better" children. Instead, out of concern for the child, they will do what they can to help the child live in a more morally appropriate way. In short, whether we are considering our attachments to children or to countries, Oldenquist's understanding of how people committed to universal moral standards will behave when faced with failure to meet these standards is misleading. Moderate patriots need not react in the way Oldenquist describes. They can maintain their commitments both to their particular country and to their general values.

## SUMMING UP

In this chapter, I have considered two critics' charges that moderate patriotism lacks an essential feature of genuine patriotism, namely the sense of personal connectedness that patriotic people have to their country. I have tried to show that these criticisms are misguided. There is no incompatibility between personal commitments that are based on emotional and historical ties and principled commitments to uphold universal standards of morality. Our personal attachments need not derive from moral criteria in order to be compatible with them.

## NOTES

1. The Lindley Lecture (Lawrence: University of Kansas Press, 1984). Subsequent references are in the text.

2. *Journal of Philosophy* LXXIX (1982), 173–93.

3. For the claim that this type of impersonal, criterion-based patriotism is central to American patriotic attitudes, see Anthony Hartle, *Moral Issues in Military Decision Making* (Lawrence: University of Kansas Press, 1989), 93–94.

4. *Moral Issues in Military Decision Making* (Lawrence: University of Kansas Press, 1989), 93–94.

5. "The State," *War and the Intellectuals*, 68.

# 6

# Are Patriotism and Universal Morality Compatible?

In chapter 4, I described two important components of the structure of morality. One component consists of constraints on what we may do in seeking to achieve our goals. While morality does not require us to adopt any particular goals, it does limit the ways in which we may pursue the goals we seek. In particular, central moral rules forbid us from inflicting serious harms on others as a normal means of achieving our goals.

A second feature of morality is that it includes positive duties to persons with whom we share special ties. We acquire these special duties in many ways: by making promises, signing contracts, or by occupying certain social roles, like being a parent, spouse, friend, or teacher. In these circumstances, we have special duties either to strive for a certain goal or to promote the well-being of particular people.

The relationship between patriotism and universal morality can be thought of in relation to these two aspects of morality. First, we can think of patriots as people who have the goal of promoting their country's well-being. Like other goals, this goal is morally permissible and may be pursued, as long at its pursuit is limited by the appropriate moral constraints on harming others. Second, we can think of patriots as people with a special social role, citizenship in a country. This role generates special duties to one's country in the same way that parenthood generates special duties to one's children.

Critics of moderate patriotism think that this picture of universal morality makes matters too simple. They deny that patriotism and universal morality are compatible. For them, the essence of universal morality is its stress on *impartiality*. In addition, they believe that the kind of impartiality required by universal morality forbids the kind of *partiality* required by special duties, whether they be duties to one's family or to one's country. If this is so, then patriotism and universal morality cannot be compatible with one another. Moderate patriotism's critics argue that its attempt to combine partiality and impartiality is doomed to failure.

## EXTREME UNIVERSALISM

In order to answer this criticism, I need to clarify the universalist position and see what gives rise to the belief that it conflicts with moderate patriotism. Taking my cue from Tolstoy, I understand extreme universalism as the view that morality requires us to give equal consideration to every human being who is affected by our actions. I have already cited evidence for the view that morality is universalist in this sense. Paradigms of morality such as the Ten Commandments and the Golden Rule are expressed in an unqualified way, telling us how to treat people generally rather than specifying particular groups or individuals who are to receive special attention. Another traditional maxim instructs us to "love our neighbors" as much as we love ourselves. This suggests that special attention to oneself is illegitimate, that a moral person will never put her own needs over the needs of others.

This impersonal aspect of morality is not only found in religious conceptions of morality. Utilitarianism, the most influential secular moral theory, is similarly impartial. Jeremy Bentham, John Stuart Mill, and other utilitarians instruct us always to act so as to produce the overall best consequences. In determining what is best, we are not to value the pleasures and pains of any person or group more than the pleasures and pains of others. Mill states this point explicitly, noting that

> the happiness which forms the utilitarian standard of what is right in conduct, is not the agent's own happiness, but that of all concerned. As between his own happiness and that of others, utilitarianism requires him to be as strictly impartial as a disinterested and benevolent spectator.[1]

On the face of it, this would forbid me, for example, to buy ice cream for myself if I can buy it for someone who would enjoy it more. Likewise, in choosing between ice cream for my child and for some other child, the fact that one child is *mine* is not regarded as directly relevant. It would be relevant only if it affected the amounts of pleasure and pain produced by my action.

If this is an absurd conclusion, utilitarians may seek ways of avoiding it. Mill himself later qualifies these remarks, but the function of this impartial ideal is central to utilitarian thinking.[2]

Many philosophers have thought that an impartial attitude is essential to the nature of a moral judgment. On their view, a judgment cannot be a moral judgment at all if it is not made from an impartial perspective. As James Rachels notes,

> Almost every important theory of morality includes the idea of impartiality. The basic idea is that each individual's interests are equally important: from within the moral point of view, there are no "privileged" persons; everyone's life has the same value.[3]

There are several reasons why this emphasis on an impartial perspective is found among so many different moral views.

First, in many cases, although we might want to act so as to benefit ourselves or someone we care about, we would not approve if others acted in the same way. For example, I might prefer not to pay taxes and to use the money for a vacation for my family. Apart from the problem of legal punishment, we generally want to say that such an action would be wrong. While the prospect of using tax money for personal benefits is attractive to us all, we would judge such an action to be wrong if done by others. Morality requires that we judge our own actions from an impersonal perspective, putting aside our own interests and seeing that it is inappropriate to treat ourselves differently from others. If I judge it to be right for me to keep tax money for myself and my family but am unwilling for others to act in the same way, then I have failed to make a genuine moral judgment because I have failed to judge from an impartial perspective.

Second, if we think about the role that morality plays, we can see that it can only play this role if it is impersonal. One of the central functions of morality is to provide a guide for us when our interests conflict with those of other people. If morality simply involves invoking our interests, it could play no role in settling conflicts. In order to be useful in conflicts, it must involve taking a point of view that is the point of view of neither party. Like the law, morality must be an impartial perspective, for if it is merely partial, it cannot resolve differences.[4]

These universalist ideas appear to raise problems for moderate patriotism. According to critics of moderate patriotism, any form of patriotism—whether moderate or extreme—must operate from a "partialist" perspective, not from the impartial, universal point of view of morality. All forms of patriotism involve a special preference for one's own country and special duties to it. Because patriotism is not impartial, it appears to be inconsistent with universal morality. Whoever adopts one must renounce the other.

This criticism of moderate patriotism could be advanced both by extreme universalists and by extreme patriots. They both agree that patriotism is incompatible with universal morality, but they disagree about whether this discredits universal morality or discredits patriotism. As we have seen, MacIntyre and Oldenquist take particular loyalties to be central and thus reject universal morality. Tolstoy takes the opposite approach, rejecting patriotism for failing to square with the egalitarian impartiality that he thought universal morality requires.

## A PARTIAL DEFENSE OF PARTIALISM

Critics of impartial morality are at least partly right. There is something wrong with the kind of moral universalism that prohibits family relations and the special ties and duties that go with them. Given the familiarity of many universal ideals, we may simply fail to see how radical they are. Alternatively, we may dismiss them as noble visions that are just too difficult for ordinary human beings to attain. I want to argue that extreme universalism is not a worthy ideal and that special ties need to be respected by any reasonable morality.

As critics of impartial morality have argued, it appears to rule out many features of ordinary life that are central to our understanding of how we should live. Extreme universalism is radically impartial and radically egalitarian. Following its standards would prohibit us from giving any preference to ourselves over others, to our families over non-family members, to friends over strangers, or to fellow citizens over citizens of other nations. Treating all perfectly equally and in the manner of an impartial judge or spectator would make love, friendship, and family ties impossible. It would also undermine many less intimate but nonetheless important relationships—physicians to their patients, teachers to their students, mayors to their towns, etc.

In attempting to expand the range of the caring, attentive attitudes that characterize our close relationships at their best, radical universalists threaten to destroy these relationships. To talk about the "family of humankind" sounds like a noble ideal, but it is literally impossible to treat everyone as family. To do so would require treating everyone with special attention, but "treating everyone with special attention" is no more possible than creating square circles. By necessity, *special* attention can only go to some restricted group of people. For this reason, it requires that others be at least partially neglected.

Finally, partialists are correct that morality not only permits us to favor those whom we love but indeed requires us to devote special attention to our spouses, children, parents, friends, and others to whom we have special ties. By entering these relations, we incur obligations we would not otherwise have. Since commonsense morality recognizes and encourages these special ties and special duties, it is incompatible with extreme versions of universalism. The ideal of perfect impartiality to which extreme universalists appeal is not an attractive ideal.

Having acknowledged the truth of these "partialist" ideas, it is important to see that they must be accepted with care. Many thinkers, looking for the psychological basis of morality, have found it in human sympathy and the special, caring relationships that human beings have to one another. But just as universalists may leave no room for special relationships, so partialists run into difficulty when they try to support any form of universal moral duties. If moral duties can only arise out of emotional connections and social ties, then how can we account for duties to people who are strangers to us? How can we uphold moral rules that require decent treatment of people whom we do not know, do not care for, have no sympathy for, and with whom we stand in no special relationships? If we accept Andrew Oldenquist's provocative claim that "all morality is tribal morality," then how can we account for duties to those who do not belong to our tribe?[5]

By stressing the importance of partiality and special ties, anti-universalists appear to legitimate the kinds of behavior that characterize extreme patriots. Once one looks at life through partialist lenses, then the kind of exclusive concern for which Tolstoy criticized patriotism begins to look morally possible. If we forego universal morality, how do we rein in the ardor of patriots? How do we get them to take seriously the moral constraints on what they may do to promote their country's well-being?

These questions bring us back to the claim that we must choose between universal morality and special ties, that we must choose between our own group and humanity as a whole, and that no compromise is possible. In order to assess this criticism, we need to look more closely at the moral status of special preferences and duties. Are these really incompatible? Or can a universal morality leave room for personal ties and special duties?

## UNIVERSAL MORALITY AND SPECIAL DUTIES

The idea that universal morality is incompatible with duties based on affection or special relations rests on several confusions. Once these are sorted out, we can see that special duties are compatible with at least some versions of universal morality.

Part of the difficulty arises because there are different senses in which morality can be universal. In one sense, morality is universal if it requires absolutely equal treatment of everyone. In this sense, universal morality does rule out special duties to particular individuals or groups.

We can speak of morality as being universal in another sense, however. In this second sense, morality is universal if there are moral standards that apply to everyone's behavior. Often when we talk about universal morality, this is what we have in mind, a set of principles that applies to everyone. These standards are also impersonal in the sense that they do not depend on anyone's personal commitment to them. If, for example, a professional killer feels no compunctions about murdering as a way of making a living and has no commitment to the moral rule that forbids killing (except in special cases), that does not mean that the rule against killing does not apply to him. It does apply to him even though he does not personally feel committed to it, and when he kills, he acts immorally by virtue of his violating this rule.[6]

If the rule were a personal rule, then it might be right for the killer to murder anyone he does not feel personally attached to and wrong for him to kill only in cases where he feels a personal attachment to the victim. Morality does not operate this way, however. Whether a rule limits a person's behavior or protects someone from mistreatment does not depend on whether the people involved know or care about one another. For these reasons, moral rules can be described as impersonal and universal.

Once we distinguish these senses of "impersonal" and "universal," then it is easy to see that special preferences and duties may be permitted within a universal moral code. I have already referred to the Ten Commandments as an example of a universal code. Its rules tell us simply not to kill or steal. They do not tell us only to refrain from killing or stealing from our friends and fellow citizens. Nonetheless, the Ten Commandments contains the rule "Honor your father and mother," and this rule clearly specifies particular people as recipients of special treatment. In spite of this, the rule itself is a universal rule since it applies to everyone. It imposes on all people a special duty to honor those particular people to whom they are related in a specific way. It requires me to honor my parents and you to honor yours.

This rule illustrates a simple but important point. It shows that a moral code can be universal in form and still permit special attention to particular people. A universal moral code need not require that we treat everyone in the very same way. It can contain principles that recognize personal connections as relevant to determining what is morally right or wrong for us to do. Once we see this, it is easy to see that there is no incompatibility betweeen a universal moral code and special preferences for or duties toward specific people. A universal code can permit (or require) parents to devote special efforts to their children, children to devote special attention to their parents, teachers to devote special attention to their students, etc.

Likewise, there is no reason why a universal, impersonal code cannot recognize special duties that citizens have to their country. "Honor your country" is a possible candidate for such a code. It could apply to everyone, even though not everyone has the same country. Just as "honor your parents" requires each of us to honor different people, depending on which parents are ours, so likewise, "honor your country" requires us to honor different countries, depending on which is ours.

## UNIVERSALIZING SPECIAL DUTIES

Andrew Oldenquist denies that we can combine the impartiality of universal morality with the partiality that special duties require. We have seen, however, that the familiar rule "Honor your mother and father" does precisely that. Why does Oldenquist think this is not possible?

Oldenquist's argument for the incompatibility of special duties and universal morality is based on his belief that universal morality permits actions only if they can be "universalized." Many philosophers, following Kant, have thought that the mark of a genuine moral judgment is our willingness to "universalize" it. According to this view, we can test whether our behavior is morally correct by seeing whether we would be willing to generalize the kind of behavior we are engaging in.

In criticizing impersonal morality, Oldenquist argues that special duties cannot be universalized. When a special duty exists, he says, we believe we ought to act toward one person in a way that we need not act toward others. If I have a duty to protect my own child, Oldenquist argues, a universalized form of that duty requires me to protect all children who are like mine in relevant ways. For example, if my child is in danger and I have a duty to rescue it, then I would also have a duty to rescue any similar child. If this is so, however, then I don't have any special duty to my own child. Indeed, that is the point of Oldenquist's criticism, to show that universal morality rules out special duties.

This argument simply repeats the confusion that I have been trying to dispel. Since the confusion is easy to fall into, however, it is important to take it seriously. In seeing how the argument goes wrong, we can clarify the way that special duties fit into a universal moral scheme.

Suppose I believe both that I ought to take special care of my child and that all moral duties are universalizable. Is my duty to care for my child universalizable in the way that morality requires? I think it is, but this may be obscured by confusions about what it means to universalize a judgment. Oldenquist seems to understand it as the requirement that someone who acts in a certain way must be willing to act in the same way whenever she is confronted with similar circumstances. In fact, however, there are several different ways to universalize a belief like "I ought to take care of my child." Oldenquist goes wrong because he focuses on unattractive forms of universalized judgments while overlooking more plausible ways of meeting the universalizability requirement.

All of the following are universalized forms of the judgment that "I ought to take care of my child."

A. I ought to take care of all children.
B. I ought to take care of all children similar to mine.
C. Everyone ought to take care of all children.
D. Everyone ought to take care of my children.
E. Everyone ought to take care of their own children.

Consider A, "I ought to take care of all children." This requires me to generalize my treatment of my child to all children and to treat them all in the same way. It is this form that gives rise to the extreme universalist position that we have already considered and that genuinely does rule out special duties. It rules them out because it is impossible to treat all specially. To treat someone in a special way is, by definition, to treat her in a way that is different from the way one treats others.

"I ought to take care of all children" is an absurd requirement for other reasons too. To "take care of" a child in the way that parents ought to requires large amounts of time, energy, and attention. The work of "protection, nurturance, and training" that goes into raising children is very demanding.[7] Human beings do not have the time, energy, or emotional resources to bestow such efforts on more than a few people.

If A were the only way to universalize the duty "I ought to take care of my children," then special duties and universal morality would be incompatible. Since this universalized duty imposes absurd and impossible demands, this would discredit impersonal morality in the way that Oldenquist suggests. We need not accept this conclusion, however, if there are other more plausible forms of universalizing.

Consider B, "I ought to take care of all children similar to mine." This form is ambiguous, depending on how we interpret the phrase "similar to mine." Oldenquist understands this to mean "possessing similar features," and he has in mind features like curly hair, being six years old, or suffering from a fever. For this reason, he thinks this form requires me to care for all curly-haired, feverish six-year-olds and forbids me from considering the fact that a particular child is my child. While this interpretation of B is less demanding than A, it is similarly absurd. There are too many such children, and the specialness of my tie to my own child is lost in this formulation.

Suppose, however, that the feature we have in mind is "being my child." Then, there is no problem about universalizing in this way. According to this interpretation, the universalized form of "I ought to take care of my child" is "I ought to take care of all children who are mine." This form is quite reasonable and describes a genuine parental duty. Even if a parent is especially fond of one of his children, he still has a parental duty to care for them all. Further, all parents have this duty. So, there is no reason to reject this universalized idea. Nor is there any incompatibility between this special duty to *all* of one's children and an impersonal moral code that imposes this duty on all parents.

Oldenquist overlooks this interpretation because he assumes that "being my child" is not a general feature like "having curly hair." This is a mistake, however. "Being my child" is a general feature that can be possessed by more than one person. (In my case, it is possessed by two.) And, I have parental duties toward all the children who are my children. Their being my children is an important biological and social fact about them, and because they and I occupy the roles of parent and children, we are bound together in a network of historical, emotional, and moral ties. These kinds of relational features of people are quite important, and it is arbitrary to omit them when we think about what it means to take care of "all similar" children.

Understood in this way, then, B expresses a reasonable form of a universalized special duty and shows the compatibility of specialness and universality.

## WHAT IF EVERYBODY DID THAT?

Immanuel Kant expresses the most famous version of a universalizability test in his "categorical imperative."[8] He tells us that we must be willing to have everyone act according to the rule that we are adopting. This suggests some other ways of universalizing the belief that "I ought to take care of my own child."

Consider C, "Everyone ought to take care of all children." This generalizes in two directions, dealing both with the bearers of duties and the recipients of special treatment. It improves on A ("I ought to take care of all children"), since it brings out that there is nothing special about me that imposes a unique duty for me to care for all children. Rather, according to C, everyone has this duty.

In spite of this improvement, C remains absurd. It is impossible to follow for the same reason that A is. If by "take care of" we mean the intensive kind of caring that good parenting requires, then it is impossible for anyone to bestow this treatment on all children. Such care is beyond our capacities to provide. This fact allows us to reject C.

Consider D, "Everyone ought to take care of my children." This is absurd, too, but for a different reason. There is nothing logically impossible about everyone being specially concerned with just a few children. In practical terms, too many people trying to care for the same children would get in each other's way, producing a "too many cooks spoil the broth" situation. Most important, however, is that everyone's following this rule would lead to the neglect of many other children and their needs. It is morally inappropriate to bestow too much attention on some children while others are neglected. No matter how much individual parents might love their own children, they can easily see that a grievous wrong would be done if their own children were the only ones whose needs were attended to. We can reject D for being both impractical and immoral.

Finally, consider E: "Everyone ought to take care of their own children." This is clearly a genuine, universalized form of the original "I ought to take care of my children." Moreover, it implies that I have a special duty to my children and recognizes this duty as one that applies to all parents. It is also the most reasonable rule, for it takes account of two important facts. First, parental caring can only be devoted to small numbers of children because of the effort it requires. Second, all children need parental care, so a requirement that everyone take care of just some children, while all others are neglected, is morally unacceptable. A rule that requires parents to care for their own children distributes both efforts and benefits in an appropriate way.

Here, then, is a rule that applies universally both to all parents and to all children and that assigns a special duty in a way that recognizes the equal human worth and importance of all children. Contrary to Oldenquist's assertion, then, there is a reasonable, universalized form of the special duty of parents to children. A universal morality can accommodate the special duties that parents have to their own children.

## THE RELEVANCE TO PATRIOTISM

This result is extremely important for understanding patriotism because patriotic duties have the same form as parental duties. Everything that we saw about parental duties applies to patriotic duties as well.

Suppose we formulate the patriot's duty as "I ought to support my country." We will not want to universalize this as A, "I ought to support all countries," for the same reasons that we rejected "I ought to take care of all children." The kind of support that people owe their country is a special kind of concern that cannot be universally bestowed. To attempt to bestow it on all countries would be to reject patriotism and embrace extreme universalism.

Consider B, "I ought to support all countries similar to mine." As in the parental case, this will be acceptable if in interpreting "similar to mine," we allow that the similarity must be the feature of "being my country." It will be unacceptable if we understand similarity in terms of general political, geographic, or other features of countries.

Consider C, "Everyone ought to support all countries." This is impossible because it overlooks possible conflicts between countries and undermines the genuine, special kind of support that patriotism requires.

We get an interesting result by considering D: "Everyone ought to support my country." This form might be attractive to chauvinists who believe in the superiority of their own country. While even the most doting of parents do not genuinely believe in the superiority of their own children over all others or expect everyone to cater to their own children's needs, patriots do not always have this degree of detachment. Believing in the superiority of their own country, they might actually think that people of all nations have a duty to support it.

The arguments against D are similar to those against its parental analogue. Like children, all countries have needs, and if everyone devoted themselves to the needs of just one country, then the legitimate needs of many people would be neglected. No reasonable person would expect this of others. Generally, we recognize that just as our parental duties require that we care for our own children and other parents care for theirs, so likewise our duties as citizens require us to support our country while at the same time requiring other people to support theirs.

This brings us to E, "Everyone ought to support his or her own country." Since countries need support and since the people of all countries have a common human worth, it is desirable that people of all countries do what they can to support their country's flourishing. For this reason, when we view patriotism from a moral point of view, we can see that morality allows for special duties to one's own country, while recognizing at the same time that other people have similar duties to their countries.

## SUMMING UP

In this chapter, I have tried to explain the ways in which morality is both impartial and partial. I agree with some "partialist" critics that there are forms of universal morality that are not acceptable, but that does not mean that we can scrap all elements of universality. Indeed, as I have tried to show, a universal morality can make room for the special concerns that all of us feel for particular individuals and groups.

The argument about whether parental and patriotic duties can be universalized may at first appear to be only of technical interest. Nonetheless, exploring it enables us to understand better how special duties and universal morality fit together. It also provides some insight into the rationale for the special duties we have. We can better understand why special duties are restricted in the range of people they benefit and how they are universal in the sense that they apply to all. We can also see how a morality that is both impartial and universal can recognize legitimate forms of partiality towards people with whom we share special ties.

## NOTES

1. "Utilitarianism," in Mary Warnock, ed., *Utilitarianism and Other Writings* (Cleveland: Meridian Books, 1968), 268.

2. Ibid., 270.

3. *The Elements of Moral Philosophy* (New York: Random House, 1986), 9.

4. This point is made by Kurt Baier in *The Moral Point of View* (Ithaca: Cornell University Press, 1958), 190.

5. "Loyalties," 178.

6. The idea that morality is impersonal in this sense is disputed by Gilbert Harman in *The Nature of Morality* (New York: Oxford University Press, 1977), ch. 9. For criticisms of Harman's view, see my *The Ideal of Rationality* (Atlantic Highlands, N.J.: Humanities Press International, 1985), ch. 8.

7. For these terms and a helpful description of the complexity of parental tasks, see Sara Ruddick, *Maternal Thinking* (Boston: Beacon Press, 1989), chs. 3–5.

8. See his *Grounding for the Metaphysic of Morals*, translated by James Ellington (Indianapolis: Hackett, 1981), 30.

# 7

# The Necessity of
# Choosing Sides

A critic might concede that moderate patriotism is all right in theory
but charge that it nonetheless fails in practice. This is the force of an
objection raised by Alasdair MacIntyre. MacIntyre, after noting that
some critics deny that moderate patriotism is a genuine form of loyalty, describes the basis of their complaint. "To those critics," he says,

> patriotism thus limited in scope appears to be emasculated . . . because
> in some of the most important situations of actual social life either the
> patriotic standpoint comes into serious conflict with the standpoint of
> a genuinely impersonal morality or it amounts to no more than a set of
> practically empty slogans.[1]

MacIntyre's subsequent remarks make clear that he supports this criticism. He describes two forms of conflict and argues that in each case,
moderate patriots would be forced to choose between their patriotism
and their universalism. Because such a choice cannot be avoided in
practice, the view itself amounts to no more than "practically empty
slogans." When the chips are down, moderate patriots will find themselves unable to practice what they preach.[2]

## THE PROBLEM OF CONFLICT

The first type of conflict MacIntyre describes arises when two countries must compete for scarce resources. In extreme cases, the survival of each nation might be at stake. One can survive, but not both.
When such conflicts occur, MacIntyre says,

the standpoint of impersonal morality requires an allocation of goods such that each individual person counts for one and no more than one, while the patriotic standpoint requires that I strive to further the interests of my community and you strive to further those of yours.[3]

He goes on to say that when the survival of one's country or other "large interests" are at stake, "patriotism entails a willingness to go to war on one's community's behalf."

What would moderate patriots do in such a case? MacIntyre suggests that they would be caught in an impossible bind. If they honor universal morality and the constraints it imposes, they will count equally the legitimate interests of the competing community and will avoid inflicting death and injury on its members. In adhering to these universalist ideals, however, moderate patriots will be unable to carry out their special duties to their own country. They will not give its interests priority over those of the other nation because they cannot count their own country more than the other. And, they will not commit themselves to acts of war against the other community in the way that patriots must be willing to do. In short, when conflicts arise, their commitment to universal morality will prevent them from supporting their country's efforts to survive and flourish.

Extreme patriots, on the other hand, will make an unequivocal choice for their own country. They will give greater weight to their own country's well-being and will both risk their own lives and take the lives of others in its defense. Extreme patriotism turns out, according to this argument, to be the only genuine form of patriotic loyalty. Moderate patriots must either embrace it or fail to be patriots at all. If MacIntyre is correct, moderate patriotism evaporates in the heat of tragic, real-world conflicts over scarce resources.

This troubling argument derives its force from three features of the example MacIntyre describes: first, the apparent unavoidability of conflict; second, the high stakes, the nation's need for these resources if it is to survive or escape severe impairment; and third, the brutality of the means necessary for the country to survive. It must opt for war and hence cannot avoid inflicting serious harms on members of the competing nation. The combination of these factors appears to undermine the claim that moderate patriotism resolves the tensions between universalism and group loyalty.

## HOW SHOULD CONFLICTS BE DEALT WITH?

While there is a certain power to MacIntyre's argument, I think that it can be dispelled if we consider it carefully.

First, it is important to see that MacIntyre misdescribes the moderate position. He equates it with extreme universalism, claiming that moderate patriots cannot count the interests of their own country more heavily than the interests of the competing country. This is simply false. As we have seen, moderate patriots do have a special commitment to their own country's well-being and recognize the legitimacy of special duties to it. They begin, then, with a presumption in favor of their own country's needs and interests.

Nonetheless, as MacIntyre suggests, they do take seriously the interests of the competing country, and they would wish to avoid inflicting serious harm on its citizens. Thus, they will be averse to warfare. This contrasts with extreme patriots, who consider only the interests of their own country as having value and would unhesitatingly pursue them by any means. Since their morality requires loyalty only to their own community, they would not count the destruction of the other community and its members as serious losses.

How would moderate patriots actually act in this conflict situation? They would certainly not opt automatically for war, even if their prospects for victory were assured. Because they take seriously the value of persons in the opposing community, they would examine the conflict to see if there are any ways of accommodating the needs of both communities. They would evaluate the legitimacy of the claims made by both sides, and if the moral weight of the opposing side's claims is greater, they might well urge a sacrifice by their own community. Because they count the well-being of both sides, they would strive to discover or devise a just accommodation.

MacIntyre seems to think that such an examination of the conflict is inconsistent with genuine patriotism. The standpoint of morality is, he writes,

> that of an impersonal arbiter, adjudicating in ways that give equal weight to each individual person's needs, desires, beliefs about the good and the like, while the patriot is once again required to be a partisan. (7)

The assumption here is that partisans cannot carry out the kind of assessment of competing claims that moderate patriots would call for.

Why is this? Perhaps the argument is that one cannot be a detached, impartial judge in a dispute to which one is a party. While patriots can adjudicate disputes between other countries, judging between their own country and another is totally different. For patriots, their commitment to their own country rules out impartial judgment and requires them to prejudge all issues in favor of their own country. To

judge impartially or to fail to support one's country's claims is incompatible with being a patriot.

There is an ambiguity in this argument. The argument could either
be that the partisan perspective of patriots makes them literally incapable of adjudicating disputes to which their country is a party. Or it
could be that while they are capable of taking a neutral perspective,
patriots are duty-bound to refrain from doing so. Neither of these views
is correct.

Consider the first. It is no doubt harder to be impartial in judging
one's own interests or the interests of people one cares about. That is
why it is good practice to seek disinterested third parties when ver-
dicts on such matters are necessary. Nonetheless, the ability to stand
back from one's own position is a skill that everyone has to some
degree and that can be improved with practice. With effort, one can
succeed in taking a variety of perspectives on an issue. How does the
conflict look to one's adversary? How does it look to people who are
not involved? These are questions that one can address either by using one's own imagination or by seeking out the information from
these other people. "Putting ourselves in other people's shoes" is widely
regarded as an appropriate way of thinking about our own and other
people's needs and interests.

These imaginative exercises may be difficult, but they are not impossible. Nor does commitment to one side preclude us from engaging in them. To take a different example, my commitment to my
children does not render me incapable of trying to look at a conflict
they are involved in with some degree of detachment. I am able to do
this in spite of my deep commitment to their well-being.

This brings us to the second possibility, that while we are capable
of this kind of detachment, our duty as parents or patriots requires us
to avoid it. To be detached in this way is to betray our connection to
those with whom we share special attachments. There is a grain of
truth in this argument. When we have special ties to people or groups,
a detached attitude cannot be our typical stance toward them.

Nonetheless, this argument also fails to prove its point. It assumes
that detachment and attachment are mutually exclusive. This is incor-
rect. Emotional attachment does not prevent us from trying to understand issues in a somewhat objective way or from deliberating about
them in a manner that suspends personal interests and involvements.
There is nothing to keep us from trying to take a more objective stance
toward some fact about people we care about or toward situations they
are involved in. In fact, being committed to their well-being often
requires us to do just that. As parents, we do our children no favors

by automatically backing up their plans and desires or automatically taking their side in a dispute. A concern for their well-being may lead us to seek a more objective understanding of their situation so that we can better help them to deal with it. Personal commitment may call for taking an objective view rather than ruling it out.

The same is true with respect to our country. If it is involved in a conflict that may lead to war, then citizens are faced with very serious decisions. Even from the perspective of the country's own interests alone, it is important to understand the full impact of our decisions and to see whether our goals might be achieved in other ways. To refuse to consider the merits of the other country's case or to avoid taking up their perspective may lead us into wars that needlessly consume the country's resources and the lives of its citizens. Contrary to the claim that duty requires us to take a purely partisan perspective, a concern for our own nation should lead us to seek a broader understanding of the conflict we are involved in. Only in this way can we tell whether war is necessary or worthwhile.

Suppose that we have misunderstood either our own interests or those of the other country. Suppose that we have overlooked compromise solutions that might have arisen from negotiation and discussion. Suppose that our goals can be achieved without military conflict. All of these are distinct possibilities, but they would never be discovered by MacIntyre's patriot, who appears caught in the stereotyped role of armed defender of the nation.

Admittedly, MacIntyre's example is only briefly described, and he may be assuming that all these deliberations have occurred. If so, however, he is overlooking a part of the process in which rational, objective thinking has an important role to play and can be carried out consistently with a commitment to one's country. In addition, by overlooking these prior stages of deliberation, he implicitly adopts a militarized conception of patriotic action. There is no mention of the possibility that patriotism might motivate us to avoid conflict and to seek a peaceful resolution. All we are told is that patriots view things in a partisan manner and are willing to go to war to support their country.

MacIntyre's description assumes the most extreme kind of conflict situation. It cannot be, however, that every conflict is like this, and the process of determining whether the situation is as bleak as MacIntyre says will often involve the very sort of reasoning that he thinks is inappropriate to genuine patriots. To grant the need for such reasoning is to grant the legitimacy of a kind of questioning about national policy that seems incompatible with the mind set of

MacIntyre's patriot. Since these forms of questioning are necessary and valuable, their compatibility with moderate patriotism provides an additional argument in its favor and against extreme patriotism.

## WHAT IF WAR IS UNAVOIDABLE?

Suppose that no just accommodation is possible. What if the choice is between the death of one community or the other? What if each side has an equally legitimate claim to the resources needed for national survival? What would moderate patriots do? Would their commitment to universal morality mean that they be would be indifferent to which community survives? Would it lead them to urge collective suicide by their own community? Would they be willing to fight for their community, though it had no greater moral claim than the opposition?

In this extreme and tragic situation, I assume that moderate patriots would struggle on behalf of their country. In doing so, they would not in any way be abandoning their commitment to universal morality. Morality permits actions done in self-defense, even in cases where the threat comes from innocent persons.[4] In addition, since universal morality recognizes the importance of special duties, it would not require moderate patriots to abandon or betray their own community. Morality does not require people to be indifferent to which community survives, since their deepest emotional ties are to one group. This would be like expecting a person to be indifferent to whether it is his own family that is killed in an auto accident or some family of strangers.

Nor would morality require group suicide in such a case. That degree of sacrifice and altruism goes beyond what we think is required by morality. So, if indifference and altruism are unreasonable to require in this setting, then a regretful entry into the struggle for survival would be morally permissible. Nothing in the nature of moderate patriotism would force its adherents to reject this option. The fact that they would undertake the defense of their own community with deep regret points to the moral superiority of their position. In contrast, extreme patriots, as MacIntyre describes their view, need not care in the least about the well-being of members of the opposing community. The decision to fight for survival would be made with ease and need not involve any search for alternatives.

In response to MacIntyre's argument, then, we can note two things. First, in the heat of struggle, moderate patriots are not forced to renounce their country or sacrifice its existence. They can defend it as well as extreme patriots. Second, in dealing with serious conflict, extreme patriots betray a callous disregard for the legitimate rights and interests of those in the competing group. The moderate position leads to the appropriate responses: a search for compromise and conciliation, as well as a deep sense of regret when conflict is unavoidable. Nothing in this case serves to discredit the moderate patriotic view.

## IDEALS AND WAYS OF LIFE

MacIntyre describes a second type of conflict in which, he thinks, moderate patriots will be revealed as people whose principles make them unable to offer the right kind of support to their community. This is a conflict in which the community's way of life, rather than its physical survival, is at stake.

MacIntyre illustrates this problem by describing a conflict between empires (e.g., the Roman and the British) and what he calls "barbarian border peoples." He writes:

> A variety of such peoples—Scottish Gaels, Iroquois Indians, Bedouin— have regarded raiding the territory of their traditional enemies . . . as an essential constituent of the good life; whereas the settled urban or agricultural communities which provided the target for their depredations have regarded the subjugation of such peoples and their reeducation into peaceful pursuits as one of their central responsibilities.[5]

The conflict here is between two distinct and incompatible ways of life. The border people have a way of life in which raids against outsiders have a central role and value. As MacIntyre describes it, they would be unable to live what they take to be a good life if they were to do away with this activity.

The empires, however, see themselves as having a civilizing mission that requires them to tame the border peoples and to instill new values in them. This civilizing mission is central to the empires' conception of their role in the world. They cannot forsake it without forsaking what they take to be the proper form of life for their community.

While MacIntyre does not use the term, we could describe this as an ideological conflict, a conflict between communities with radically different central values. Neither community can act on its own ideals without interfering with the other. While their physical well-being is not at stake, their ability to live according to their values is. The battle, we might say, is for the soul of each society. The successful good life of one precludes a successful good life for the other.

Once again, MacIntyre argues, the existence of conflict raises insoluble problems for moderate patriots. Patriotism cannot be combined with universalism, he argues, because universalists must try to adjudicate the dispute in the manner of an impersonal judge. To do this, however, is to fail to support the central values of their own community when it is under threat. But, MacIntyre's argument suggests, people who fail to support their community's central values and its way of life are not patriots at all.

The only way to be a patriot is simply to stand behind one's community when its way of life is threatened. Patriots cannot adopt the impartial perspective of a judge. If their commitment is serious, they must be partisans from the start. The decisions they reach must flow directly from their commitment to their community and not from a neutral, critical evaluation of the two competing ways of life.

## DEFENDING A WAY OF LIFE

This argument is similar to the first one, but the conflict is over the preservation of a society's way of life rather than its physical survival. The argument is valuable in pointing out that physical needs and interests are not the only elements of a community that may require defense. Again, however, it misconceives the nature of moderate patriotism and falsely assumes that moderate patriots will be indifferent to the special values of their community. My reply to the previous argument should make it clear that this is false. Moderate patriots may engage in impartial reasoning about their country's situation, but they are not impartial or uncommitted to its well-being.

Nonetheless, MacIntyre is correct in suggesting that moderate patriots will not automatically defend their community's way of life. This is not an objection to moderate patriotism, however, for a community's way of life may involve immoral practices. Indeed, his example seems to provide an example of just such a case. As he describes it, the raids carried out by these border peoples are not conducted in defense of their well-being. They are not under threat from the outside forces. Rather, their traditions have evolved in such a way that the skills and strengths required in these raids has come to be especially valued. The raids are carried on in order to give community members the opportunity to live up to their ideals.

While one can understand how these ideals might have developed in times during which the community's survival was threatened by invaders, it does not follow that one should approve the continuation of these activities when the community is no longer threatened. When wars are necessary, then military valor is a virtue, but when such activities are no longer necessary, they simply cease to be virtues. No one would regard raids within the community as virtuous displays of military prowess, and it is hard to see why they would be virtues when directed against innocent outsiders.

What MacIntyre appears to assume is that if a practice is an "essential constituent" of a community's conception of the good life, then all members of the community must support it. For him, the central practices of a community's way of life are exempt from moral evaluation and criticism. Why should this be, however? Why should community practices, values, and ways of life be immune from criticism?

Certainly, it is a loss to people if they are deprived of the chance to live according to the values they believe to be valid and important. Nonetheless, these values may be mistaken. If we place them beyond criticism, we are saying that *any* practice must be regarded as legitimate if it is central to a community's conception of the good life.

While it is important to appreciate diverse forms of life and to understand the desire of patriots to support their community's values, MacIntyre's argument carries these ideas too far. If we exempt from moral criticism any practices that are central to a way of life, then we would be unable to condemn the actions of religious zealots who devote their lives to wiping out "heathens." We would be unable to condemn slavery because the niceties of Southern plantation life required it. We would be unable to condemn Nazism because its conception of the good life required genocide and conquest to bring about "racial" dominance. MacIntyre's argument seems to imply an extreme form of ethical permissiveness. While moderate patriotism applies the constraints of morality to the pursuit of a community's well-being, MacIntyre's view exempts community practices from moral judgment.

What would moderate patriots do in this case, then? They would see that raiding as an exercise of community virtues is not legitimate. One's community may feel that the personal valor shown in such raids or the martial skills exhibited are the highest achievements, but these goods must not be purchased at the cost of innocent lives. For this reason, moderate patriots would favor ending the raids. This need not show indifference to their community, however. Unlike outsiders, moderate patriots might have a sympathetic understanding and appreciation of the value of the martial skills and virtues, and they would regret the loss of the goods associated with that way of life. Unlike outsiders, they might work to foster the development of other practices that preserve some of the community's traditional values.[6] They would not be indifferent to the community's losses, even though they think it necessary that the community pay this price. Unlike outsiders, they will also have a special desire for the community that they identify with to have a form of life that is worthy of support. The territorial raiders do not have such a form of life.

Finally, it is important to see that in reaching this conclusion, the moderate patriot is not simply choosing to side with the empire. Morality permits many goals but does not permit goals that require violating moral constraints against killing, injury, etc. Hence, the raiders' way of life is morally defective in a way that the empire's life is not. The empire (at least as here described) is not attempting to harm the raiders. Rather, it is responding to violations of moral constraints with the force necessary to prevent these violations.

## SUMMING UP

In this chapter, I have considered two serious objections against moderate patriotism. While MacIntyre correctly assumes that moderate patriots will not give unconditional support when their communities are involved in conflicts, he is mistaken in thinking that they are uncommitted to their communities. When conflict is legitimate or unavoidable as a means of defending the survival of the community, then moderate patriots will support their community. But this support will not be automatic or unconditional. That, however, is no criticism of moderate patriotism because automatic support of policies that lead to war and destruction is no virtue. Reasonable patriots should not offer that as part of their commitment to their country.

## NOTES

1. "Is Patriotism a Virtue?" 6.
2. For a similar argument, see Paul Gomberg, "Patriotism is Like Racism," *Ethics* 101 (1990), 145–46.
3. "Is Patriotism a Virtue?" 6.
4. For a discussion of this point, see Lawrence Alexander, "Self-Defense and the Killing of Noncombatants: A Reply to Fullinwider," in Charles Beitz et al., eds., *International Ethics* (Princeton: Princeton University Press, 1985), 98–105.
5. "Is Patriotism a Virtue?" 7.
6. William James makes a similar suggestion in his classic essay, "The Moral Equivalent of War," in *Pragmatism and Other Essays* (New York: Washington Square Press, 1983).

# 8

# Can We Judge
# Our Country?

A crucial aspect of moderate patriotism is its emphasis on critical judgment. For moderate patriots, it is essential, first, that people can attain sufficient detachment from their country's cause to judge its position in a conflict; second, that people can evaluate their country's way of life to see whether its core values are compatible with morality; and, third, that critically evaluating their society's policies and values is consistent with a patriotic attitude.

Many people, however, seem to think that this sort of critical judgment is either impossible or inconsistent with patriotic commitment. In order to be sure that critical evaluation of one's own country is both possible and compatible with patriotism, we need to understand both why the opposite view appears plausible and why it is mistaken. I will consider three arguments against the possibility of a critical form of patriotism: the "love is blind" thesis, the idea that individual values simply mirror social values, and the view that all moral values are "relative" to particular societies so that societies themselves cannot be judged.

## LOVE IS BLIND

One argument against patriots taking the role of critics arises from combining two ideas: the definition of patriotism as "love of one's country" and a romantic conception of love. I have no quarrel with the idea that patriotism is love of one's country. My own definition stresses that patriotism involves special affection and concern for one's country, an identification with it, and a willingness to act on its behalf. I take this account to be an analysis of what *love* of one's country amounts to. Anyone who loves her country must possess all of these features.

Suppose that a person expresses great affection for her country, speaks with genuine warmth and emotion about it, but does not think about its overall well-being and would be unwilling to act on its behalf. This would be a form of infatuation rather than love, and, as in personal relations, we would regard the emotion as shallow and unreliable. I suspect that there are people who are infatuated by their country. They respond to its victories and celebrations with genuine emotion, but they lack the commitment to its well-being that differentiates infatuation from genuine love. My analysis of "love of country" helps us to differentiate true patriotic love from mere infatuation with one's country or its successes.

Love is often said to be "blind." People who are in love are supposed to be unable to see any faults in the person they love. Along with this partial blindness goes an acute sensitivity to the positive features of the person loved. Love, on this view, is a partial obstacle to knowledge because it blocks one's perception of certain sorts of facts. It is also seen as an obstacle to critical reasoning because love is a strong emotion, a passion that interferes with our ability to deliberate and make critical evaluations.[1]

If this is what love is, then, one might argue, loving one's country makes one unable to evaluate it and its values in a critical, deliberate manner. A person who can engage in this sort of evaluation reveals herself as someone who does not love the country. For this reason, a critical stance towards one's own country is incompatible with a genuine patriotic attitude.

This argument fails because it relies on an exaggerated, highly romanticized account of love. There is no doubt that loving someone may blind us to his or her faults. Likewise, a person gripped by passionate emotion may be less able to engage in clear or critical thinking, especially about the person he or she loves. Nonetheless, to think that this condition of blind passion is typical of love is to caricature love and to overlook its complexity. It is, in fact, generally false that loving someone incapacitates us in this way. For this reason, the ability to engage in a critical evaluation of someone or something we love does not reveal an absence of genuine love.

The theory that love and critical perception are incompatible is part of a dualistic conception of human nature that has a long history. Ironically, both rationalists and romantics often hold this view in common.

Rationalists view the passions with distrust because they fear that strong emotions will incapacitate our power of reason. Romantics, on the other hand, see reason as having a chilling effect on our emotions and urge us to surrender our rational selves to the power of the passions.

Common to both views is the acceptance of an either/or perspective. Either one is rational or one is passionate. The two cannot coexist. This idea, however, is a grievous distortion. One can love one's parents, friends, or children without sacrificing one's power to think about them. Indeed, to the extent that love involves a concern for someone's good, we must think about them and become aware of actions, traits or practices of theirs (or ours) that are detrimental to their well-being.

Admittedly, it may be painful to become aware of negative facts about those we love. We do not simply observe and register these facts in a cold, detached manner. Rather, we are saddened or distraught or disappointed. Nonetheless, we are capable of seeing what the problems are, and our love is revealed in what we do with this knowledge, not in our inability to face up to it.

If these facts are true in our closest personal relations, it is hard to see why they would or should be different in our relationship to the larger political, cultural, and social communities to which we belong. If love of our family and friends need not be blind, then love of our country need not be so. If love of our friends and family may sometimes lead us to face unpleasant facts about them and voice criticisms to them, then love of our country ought to permit these as well.

## THE IMMERSION THESIS

Opponents of moderate patriotism might grant that a critical attitude is compatible with many loving relationships but deny that it is possible with our country or the larger society to which we belong. The problem, they might argue, does not rest on the incompatibility of reason and emotion. We can be critical in our loving relations with individuals, but this personal criticism occurs within a framework of values that each of us acquires from our community. As members of a community, we may criticize one another by using the standards of the society itself, but we cannot criticize the society and its values because we have nothing outside of it to appeal to.

One version of this view is what I call the "immersion thesis." According to this view, all of us are immersed in the values and practices of our community. Our development as persons consists in our internalizing the values of the community to which we belong. When we evaluate actions and policies, we do so by reference to these values. If someone were to suggest that we criticize these values, we would not know how to do so because we have no other values to use as standards of appraisal.

In my discussion of moderate patriotism, I have assumed that individuals can distinguish between patriotism and morality and can subject patriotism to moral constraints. MacIntyre, however, rejects this view and denies that morality and patriotism can be distinguished in this way. According to him, "What we have here are two rival and incompatible moralities, each of which is viewed from within by its adherents as morality-as-such. . . ."[2] MacIntyre denies both that there is a distinction between patriotism and morality as such and that we can detach ourselves from our particular community and evaluate its practices. He believes that our understanding of morality is itself so deeply entwined with our relationship to a particular community that no such detachment can be achieved.

MacIntyre does not claim to prove this view, but he presents it sympathetically. He develops a version of the immersion thesis that rules out the kind of criticism that is central to moderate patriotism. He writes:

> *If* . . . I can only apprehend the rules of morality in the version in which they are incarnated in some specific community; and *if* . . . the justification of morality must be in terms of particular goods enjoyed within the life of particular communities; and *if* . . . I am characteristically brought into being and maintained as a moral agent only through the . . . moral sustenance afforded by my community, *then* it is clear that . . . my allegiance to the community and what it requires of me . . . could not meaningfully be contrasted with . . . what morality required of me. . . . (10–11)

What MacIntyre is trying to show here is that the nature of moral development makes it almost impossible to carry out a moral evaluation of the morality of one's own community. Given the nature of moral development, a person's morality just *is* the morality of his community. It is not some separate system that he can use to judge the community. If this argument is correct, then the kind of moral reflection moderate patriots appeal to is either totally impossible or exists only as an atypical and aberrant version of normal moral reflection.

Michael Sandel has defended a similar view, referring to people as "encumbered selves" in an attempt to capture the extent to which we evaluate from the perspective of beings whose very nature is permeated by our social inheritance and special ties. For Sandel, the critical ideal I have developed involves a mistaken notion of the self as "unencumbered" and totally free of its location in time and place. Sandel, MacIntyre and other communitarians reject this conception as unrealistic and overly individualistic.[3]

## HOW CRITICAL CAN WE BE?

The issue here is whether we can get sufficient critical distance from the value conceptions of our own society to evaluate them. The communitarian account of the person and of moral development makes it difficult to see how that could occur, and in fact, there is no guarantee that it must occur.

It is possible to imagine people and societies that might conform to MacIntyre's description. For example, we can imagine people of limited intellect for whom morality is no more than the set of rules they are taught. Perhaps young children are in fact in this position, although it is worth noting how readily they find the rules and actions of adults unfair. Or imagine small communities of people who have strong traditions about what behavior is correct and who lack contact with any other societies. Lacking anything with which to compare their society's rules, they might simply accept them as natural rules of behavior. In these sorts of circumstances, MacIntyre's description might be correct. Finally, we can imagine totalitarian societies of the types depicted in novels like George Orwell's *1984* and Aldous Huxley's *Brave New World*. In these societies, social conditions, communications, and individuals are controlled in ways that make criticism difficult or impossible. In all these cases, something like the immersion thesis may provide an accurate description.

It is clear, however, that this is not our situation. Nor is it a typical condition in the modern world. We grow up in complex societies that contain many sets of competing moral authorities and teachers. Likewise, we are not a monolithic society so that we are exposed to varying sets of moral standards. In this situation, we are unlikely to emerge as individuals with socially fixed moral conceptions who lack any ability to subject our society itself to criticism.[4]

MacIntyre acknowledges as much himself, condemning mindless loyalty and explaining how loyal Germans could appeal to the principles of German society itself to criticize Nazism (14–15). The reason they could do this is that complex societies do not have a single, coherent moral code. Even if moral development consists of no more than internalizing the values of the society, this will not prevent criticism of social values since the society itself contains competing conceptions of what is good and right.

Typically, the morality of a community is not simply a collection of particular judgments. Rather, in addition to specific judgments, it contains an open-ended set of general values, rules, principles, ideals, and paradigms of proper behavior. The morality a person acquires from her community will, therefore, contain large areas of vagueness and indeterminacy. There is no rigid set of judgments that simply *is* the community morality. Hence, different notions of morality and of the requirements of loyalty may grow out of the same social soil and may make possible the sort of flexibility in moral thinking that permits individuals to contrast their community's acts and policies with the requirements of morality.

Even in small societies, the community's morality is likely to contain inconsistent, competing elements that generate conflict. Virtually every community, for example, encourages loyalty to the group as a whole. Yet, loyalty to one's own family is also likely to be encouraged, as is loyalty to one's friends. In most circumstances, people do not find it difficult to be loyal to all these groups, but sometimes the claims of one group conflict with those of others. The community morality may not provide any way of resolving such conflicts.

It may be that the idea of "morality as such" or "objective" morality emerges from just such conflict situations in which individuals feel the pull of competing claims but are unable to identify any one of them with what the community's morality requires. The more abstract notion of morality as such could be generated by the inability of the community morality to issue a verdict, combined with the individual's sense that there is a right answer to her moral quandary. The idea of objective morality could emerge as a distinct conception, even if it is an idealized version of the community morality. Once this degree of independence and abstraction is reached, there is nothing to prevent the sort of critical reflection that MacIntyre calls into question.

This leads me to a second point about MacIntyre's argument. Even if his communitarian conception of morality is correct and the process of moral development insures that some form of uncritical group loyalty would emerge as a central virtue, no conclusion follows about the importance of patriotism. The group to which our primary loyalty would be owed would be the group from which we obtain our moral understanding. This need not be the nation as a whole or any political unit, however. It could be one's family, one's village, one's religion. The nation need not be the source of morality or the primary benefi- ciary of our loyalty. It may be criticized and evaluated from the point of view of these other groups.

Even if some version of the immersion thesis is correct, then, it would not prevent us from engaging in the kind of moral reflection that moderate patriots recommend. Our capacities of moral reflection permit us to criticize our own societies, even if those societies are the ultimate sources of the moral standards we apply to them.[5]

## ISN'T MORALITY RELATIVE?

In answering the second argument against critical judgments of our country, I have not contested the idea that a person's morality just is the morality of his society. Rather, I have argued that social morality is enough of a hodgepodge to permit various interpretations of it and to leave room for substantial disagreement and self-criticism.

It is not clear that this social theory of morality leaves enough space, however, for the kinds of criticisms that moderate patriots want to make. Because moderate patriotism requires that societies themselves must be judged to see if they are worthy of loyalty, moderate patriots cannot rule out the possibility that they will come to see the basic values of their own society as unworthy of support. They need a con- ception of morality that permits this sweeping, radical kind of criti- cism. I have not yet questioned the immersion thesis itself or its equa- tion of one's society's morality with morality itself. Ultimately, however, the immersion thesis must be rejected if we are to make sense of the possibility that a person's society is not worthy of loy- alty.

We can imagine many cases in which the "hodgepodge" image of social morality will not come to the rescue of people who want to defend the possibility of deep moral criticism. Such criticism will be impossible in those cases where fundamental social values are at stake and there is a powerful consensus about what the morality of society requires. In these cases, it can be argued, there is no room for criti- cism of the sort moderate patriotism is committed to. For this sort of criticism to be possible, people must be able to appeal to moral stan- dards that are different from those of their society.

With this in mind, some might argue that moderate patriotism is defective because it presupposes a traditional conception of an abso- lute, transcendent morality. It assumes that there are moral truths that

are independent of particular societies. Suppose that this assumption
is false, however. Suppose that there are simply various social moralities and that moral beliefs are only true or false *relative to* some
particular social moral code. In that case, it will make no sense for
the moderate patriot to argue that her society's core values are mistaken. This makes no sense because there is no absolute standard of
morality to which moderate patriots can appeal in judging their society. The highest level of appeal is to the values of the society itself.

This kind of argument is suggested by MacIntyre's immersion thesis and by his discussion of the territorial raiders. In the latter case,
he argues that if a practice is central to a society's conception of the
good life, then that practice may not be criticized. Central values are
exempt from criticism in a way that peripheral ones are not.

Michael Walzer develops a historical and anthropological account
of justice that makes criticism impossible when there is an overwhelm-
ing social consensus in favor of a practice or a set of values. He writes,

> Justice is relative to social meanings. . . . There are an infinite number
> of possible . . . cultures, religions, political arrangements, geographi-
> cal conditions, and so on. A given society is just if its substantive life
> is lived . . . in a way [that is] faithful to the shared understandings of
> the members.[6]

He goes on to say:

> There are no external or universal principles. . . . Every substantive
> account of distributive justice is a local account. . . . Justice is rooted
> in the distinct understandings of places, honors, jobs, things of all sorts,
> that constitute a shared way of life.[7]

If this conception is true, then the ultimate standard of value is the
shared understanding, the moral consensus that exists in a community. Criticism is possible where no such consensus exists, but where
it is in place, criticism is necessarily mistaken because it appeals to
standards that are inapplicable to the society. Or, worse yet, it appeals to standards that do not really exist, since "there are no external
or universal" standards.[8]

Both the immersion thesis and the social consensus theory of morality appear to support the general thesis of ethical relativism. Both
deny the possibility of appealing to moral standards that are external
to a society and its values. If ethical relativism is true and if moderate patriotism presupposes a form of absolute morality, then moderate
patriotism is false. Hence, ethical relativism poses a serious threat to
the moderate patriotic view.

Although ethical relativism raises many large issues that I cannot discuss, I cannot ignore the relativist thesis because it threatens an important presupposition of moderate patriotism. Since many people profess to be skeptical about the possibility of absolute moral principles, this issue needs to be addressed. I believe that much of relativism's appeal rests on misunderstandings and that when these are cleared up, radical relativism does not look either plausible or appealing.

## WHAT IS ETHICAL RELATIVISM?

In order to describe ethical relativism, we need to understand ethical absolutism, since relativism is identified primarily by its opposition to ethical absolutism. In fact, there are several distinct views that people seem to have in mind when they talk about ethical absolutism. I will describe three versions of "ethical absolutism" and will consider the form of relativist counter-thesis that each provokes.

*The Absolute Principle View*: According to this view, a central part of morality consists of principles that are absolute in form. The model here is the Ten Commandments. Most of these commandments identify a type of action and instruct us never to perform actions of that type. In effect, this form of absolutism asserts that there are *exceptionless* moral principles that apply to rather simply defined types of action, such as killing, stealing, etc. While philosophers do not usually have this view in mind when they talk about absolutism, other people often appear to think of themselves as relativists because they do not believe that there are any exceptionless principles of morality.[9]

I believe that people are right to reject the existence of simple, exceptionless moral principles. There are justifiable exceptions to many commonly cited moral principles. Granting this does not commit one to relativism, however. People who believe, for example, that the principle "do not kill human beings" can be justifiably violated by killing in self-defense ought not to be thought of as relativists. Why not? Because they believe that killing in self-defense is *absolutely* right and hence that it would be wrong to condemn the act of a person who had killed in self-defense. So, one can believe in the absolute rightness and wrongness of certain actions while rejecting the idea that morality consists of simple, exceptionless principles.

When I talk about relativism, then, I will not mean the view that there are no simple, exceptionless moral principles, for this view is compatible with a belief in objective, universally applicable moral judgments and principles.

*The Single Moral Code View*: According to a second type of absolutism, there is a single set of fairly specific moral standards that applies to all human beings. According to this view, variations in culture or historical period make no difference to morality. From this perspective, if monogamy is a morally correct form of marriage relationship, then it is morally right for all people, and anyone who practices polygamy or polyandry is acting immorally. (Jacob, for example, ought not to have married both Rachel and Leah.) Likewise, if helping the needy is best carried out by public taxation in one society, then this is the appropriate form of public assistance for all societies. Any society that relies on private charity would be acting immorally.

This form of absolutism is implausible. It appears to be rooted in a rigid, unimaginative mindset that overlooks the fact that moral codes may differ on specifics while giving support to and expressing the same fundamental values.[10] Let me illustrate the problem I have in mind. Suppose that a person believes that we should show respect toward other people and that the way to do this is to bow whenever we meet someone. If this person holds the "single moral code" view, she would condemn as immoral a society in which people did not bow but instead showed respect by tipping their hats or smiling. The rigidity and lack of imagination inherent in the single moral code view emerges from the inability of its proponents to recognize that tipping hats and smiling may be capable of expressing respect just as well as bowing. They would mistake a trivial difference for a fundamental one. For this reason, it is worth rejecting the "single moral code" view. It fails to distinguish fundamental moral differences from different ways of implementing the same values.

While relativists are correct to reject the "single moral code" view, one can reject it without being a full-fledged relativist. One can reject this view without accepting the idea that there are *no* absolute values or *no* universally applicable moral principles. Rather, one could hold that some values (like the value of bowing) are "relative to" particular societies or persons, while others (like the value of treating people respectfully) are objective, universally applicable, and thus absolute. This view could be described either as moderate relativism or moderate absolutism. It is a form of relativism to the extent that it allows for some variation in moral practices, but it is equally a form of absolutism because it acknowledges the existence of some universal values or principles.[11]

*Some universal values view*: According to the view that I have just called "moderate absolutism," there are at least some moral values, principles, or judgments that are universally valid, true, or correct. While some values or principles may have only limited validity, others are absolute. Anyone who affirms values or principles that contradict the valid ones is mistaken.[12]

The form of relativism that denies this view asserts that there are no absolute values and that ethical validity is always relative to some framework or context. Two contradictory values or principles may be equally valid because each is embedded in a different context or framework. Value A is valid in framework A but invalid in framework B, while the opposite holds for value B. It is valid in B but invalid in A. Each is equally valid in the sense that it is valid within its appropriate context.

What is meant by a framework here? Generally a framework consists of a set of beliefs or practices that are adhered to either by a group or an individual. Thus there are social and individualistic forms of relativism, depending on how theorists describe the framework. This radical view is the form of relativism that I am most interested in. It is the form that MacIntyre and Walzer appear to support. Moreover, while it is the most extreme version of relativism, it is also the one most commonly asserted by people who think of themselves as relativists. What they say is that there are *no* absolute values, that *all* values are relative.

## EXTREME RELATIVISM

In explaining how the same act can be morally right in one place and morally wrong in another, relativists might draw an analogy with the law. In the United States, for example, the law requires us to drive cars on the right side of the road, while in Great Britain, the law requires drivers to stay on the left. We cannot say that driving on the left is legal or illegal and leave it at that. We must say "legal in Britain" and "illegal in the United States." Legality and illegality are relative to whatever system of law applies.

Relativists claim that just as the validity of laws is relative to countries, so the validity of morality is similarly relative. Indeed, given the existence of these laws and the dangers caused by violating them, we could all agree that it would be morally wrong to drive on the right side in Britain and morally right (in the sense of "obligatory") to drive on the right in the United States. So here is an example that makes it both intelligible and plausible to claim that an action can be morally right in one context and morally wrong in another.

The problem for the relativist emerges when we ask why it seems so obvious that we ought (morally) to drive on one side of the road in Britain and another in the United States. The obvious answer is that driving on the right is safe in the United States and dangerous in Britain, while driving on the left is safe in Britain and dangerous in the United States. Drivers are morally obligated to avoid dangerous practices because those practices are likely to injure and kill. The differences in appropriate driving behavior arise from the fact that the "same" act (driving on the right) is dangerous in one place and safe in another. Drivers in both countries are bound by the moral principle requiring that they avoid killing and injury. In spite of the local variation in appropriate driving behavior, a single absolute value underlies both practices.

One could only take this example of the traffic laws as an argument for extreme relativism by confusing it with moderate relativism. Moderate relativists and moderate absolutists agree that there can be ethical variation among societies, but they insist that the variation has to occur within the limits set by certain absolute principles. By appealing to this sort of argument, relativism gains in plausibility but loses in sting.

While the traffic law example may continue to serve as an illustration of relativity, its plausibility is not an argument for extreme relativism. If we accept extreme relativism, we need to be prepared to accept the following kind of case as well. Suppose that a particular society approves of killing human beings for fun, while other societies condemn this sort of act. We could say that in society A, it is morally permissible to kill people for fun, while in B, it is morally wrong. We would have divergent, conflicting practices, both of which are consistent with the basic principle that it is right to do what one's society approves.

In my previous examples, absolutists could accept local variability in forms of etiquette and traffic laws because the variations all were in accord with a moral value they accept—the protection of humans from death and injury. In this case, the absolutist will not readily accept the relativist view that killing for fun is morally right in the society that approves it.

Extreme relativists must be prepared to accept this unattractive conclusion. Ironically, however, their acceptance of this moral practice appears to commit them to an absolute value—the value of social conformity. If relativists did not give such importance to social conformity, they would not think it so important to do in Rome as the Romans do. Nor would they find themselves affirming the rightness of killing humans for fun.

Is this "social relativism" view relativist or absolutist? It contains elements of both doctrines, thus leading to confusion about how to classify it. It is relativist because the variations in behavior that it sanctions are quite extreme and require rejecting some moral evaluations that many would take to be absolutely valid. It is absolutist because it affirms the value and importance of social conformity. It makes one value (social conformity) absolute, while granting only relative validity to other important values, such as decent treatment of human beings.

In the end, there is little reason why absolutists should alter their view about the immorality of killing people for fun. They cannot be forced to do this by the claim that all absolutes have been shown to be baseless, since relativists themselves are committed to their own absolute—the value of social conformity. Nor can they be forced to reject the absolute wrongness of killing for fun on the grounds that social conformity is a higher value than sparing innocent human life. Faced with the necessity of choosing, they may say that social conformity is a lesser value and that any society that allows killing humans for fun shows itself to be in conflict with the moral commitment to protect people from death and injury. A society that sanctions killing for fun is simply mistaken or corrupt in its morality.

What relativists need is a way to argue for their case that has two features. First, it must avoid any commitment to substantive moral values of an absolute sort. Second, it must provide an argument strong enough to give absolutists reason to believe that moral principles that protect human life have only limited validity. What kind of argument might do this?

Relativists might argue that when we are faced with choices between divergent principles or frameworks, we have no way of telling which one is correct. Hence, relativism is more reasonable than absolutism.

This is a flawed argument, however. Our inability to make a rational choice might be an argument for *skepticism*, but it is not an argument for relativism. If, as the argument says, we are unable to determine which of two competing principles is correct, then perhaps we should agree with the skeptic that we cannot know *which* is correct. But it is odd to follow the relativist, who argues from our inability to judge which of competing principles is correct to the claim that *both* are correct, but only within the proper framework. This is an odd argument. There is no reason to believe that our inability to establish that *one* ethical principle is valid provides a sound basis for the view that *more than one* is valid.

## RESPECT FOR OTHER CULTURES

Relativists often fall into defending absolute values, even though these values are inconsistent with their overall theory. Walzer, in a passage I quoted earlier, denies that there are any "external or universal principles" of justice. He tells us that "Justice is rooted in the distinct understandings . . . that constitute a shared way of life." From these premises, he draws the moral conclusion that "To override those understandings is (always) to act unjustly."[13]

This final plea for tolerance raises two serious problems. First, if the practices involved are terrible enough, then a tolerant attitude might not be appropriate. We should be cautious, of course, in judging the practices of alien cultures. Our unfamiliarity with them and our own cultural limitations may lead us to error. (We do not want to repeat the errors of the "single moral code" theorist.) Moreover, even if a system is unjust, it may nonetheless be wrong for outsiders to intervene in order to change it. Doing so might cause more harm than good, and destroying a flawed way of life may be easier than rebuilding a good one. Nonetheless, with these cautionary ideas in mind, we might still view the practices of a society as so terrible that we judge it to be unjust, even if the society's practices conform to its own "shared understandings."

This brings me to the second problem. If Walzer rejects this criticism on the grounds that it is incompatible with respect for others as "culture producing" beings, then he is clearly appealing to a universal and absolute value himself. This is the familiar inconsistency found among many relativists, who first deny the existence of moral universals and then affirm toleration as a moral universal. That this inconsistency is well known and yet commonly occurs testifies to the power of two normative values: respect for individual autonomy (which leads to individualistic forms of relativism) and respect for community autonomy (which leads to social relativism). Individual conscientiousness and social conformity are recognized as values and are thought to require ethical relativism. That this view is so attractive explains its hardiness, but it does nothing to mitigate the genuine inconsistency that arises when one's commitment to these values expresses itself in the view that there are no absolute values.

Being a thoroughgoing relativist (and not just a moderate relativist) turns out to be more difficult than one might have thought. Once the difficulties of relativists are recognized, then the obstacles to embracing a moderate form of absolutism may not appear so daunting. Moderate absolutism recognizes a range of morally permissible variation among societies but sets limits to these variations. Some forms of action are wrong, even if they are consistent with basic, widely shared values of a society.

As outsiders, we can look at other societies and make these judgments. As insiders who share membership in a particular society, we can do the same. We are in a position to follow the moderate patriotic ideal that makes patriotic loyalty depend in part on whether our country is a worthy object of loyalty. We can ask whether it deserves the support that it calls for from its citizens.

## SUMMING UP

In this chapter, I have dealt with three arguments that are meant to show that moderate patriots are in no position to criticize their own societies. Against the "love is blind" argument, I claimed that love in fact permits and requires a critical attitude. Against the immersion thesis, I claimed that social inconsistencies leave plenty of room for a critical perspective, even if individual moral conceptions are absorbed from the society in which one grows up. Finally, I tried to show that doubts about absolute morality that arise from the appeal of ethical relativism are less serious than many suppose. While all ethical and philosophical positions have their difficulties, ethical relativism owes its plausibility to various confusions and seems especially liable to fall into inconsistencies.

In particular, if a relativist argues that we ought to honor our country uncritically because there are no absolute values by which to judge it, then the relativist is simply giving an absolute moral status to uncritical support of the country. Like other relativisms, this one is simply turning social conformity into an absolute. Anyone who does this is no longer a complete relativist.

## NOTES

1. For an affirmation of this view of love, see Freud's comments on idealization in *Group Psychology and the Analysis of the Ego* (New York: W. W. Norton, 1989), 56.

2. "Is Patriotism a Virtue?" 11. Subsequent page references are in the text.

3. Sandel develops his view in *Liberalism and the Limits of Justice* (Cambridge: Cambridge University Press, 1982). For criticisms of both Sandel and MacIntyre, see Amy Gutman, "Communitarian Critics of Liberalism," *Philosophy and Public Affairs*, 14 (1985), 308–22.

4. MacIntyre is certainly aware of this. In *After Virtue* (Notre Dame: Notre Dame University Press, 1981), he analyzes and laments the moral pluralism of modern society at some length.

5. For an attempt to show how serious criticism is compatible with the view that all values are community-based, see Michael Walzer, *Interpretation and Social Criticism* (Cambridge, Mass.: Harvard University Press, 1987), and *The Company of Critics: Social Criticism and Political Commitment in the Twentieth Century* (New York: Basic Books, 1988).

6. *Spheres of Justice* (Basic Books, 1983), 312–13.

7. *Spheres of Justice*, 314.

8. A similar social model of morality underlies Patrick Devlin's views in his famous essay "Morals and the Criminal Law." See Devlin, *The Enforcement of Morals* (London: Oxford University Press, 1965).

9. My impression is confirmed by some of the interviews in James Fishkin, *Beyond Subjective Morality* (New Haven: Yale University Press, 1985). See especially 52–56.

10. On this point, see Richard Brandt, *Value and Obligation* (New York: Harcourt, Brace & World, 1961), 435–36.

11. For examples of this type of view, see Philippa Foot, "Moral Relativism," in J. Meiland and M. Krause, eds., *Relativism: Cognitive and Moral* (Notre Dame: University of Notre Dame Press), 152–66; originally given as the 1978 Lindley Lecture at the University of Kansas; and John Ladd, "The Issue of Relativism," *Monist*, 47 (1963), 585–609.

12. In a widely reprinted discussion, W. T. Stace takes absolutism to be the view that "there is a single moral standard which is equally applicable to all men at all times. . . ." This formulation is ambiguous and could be taken as a statement of either the "single moral code" view or the "some universal values" view.

13. *Spheres of Justice*, 314.

# *9*

# The Dimensions of Loyalty

I have been defending the legitimacy of moderate patriotism against critics who do not find it to be patriotic enough. They see moderate patriotism as a tepid, grudging, and weak form of loyalty. In contrast, they see true patriots as people who will provide reliable, automatic support for their country. They reject the kind of critical, conditional support I have described, saying that it is not a form of genuine loyalty.

In completing this aspect of my defense of moderate patriotism, it will be helpful to examine the nature of loyalty. Once we understand loyalty better, the claim that moderate patriotism is not a true form of loyalty will be seen to be totally groundless.

## DEGREES OF LOYALTY

The first thing to note about loyalty is that it comes in degrees. We are not faced with a simple dichotomy between loyalty and disloyalty. Rather, there is a continuum, reaching from those who are fiercely loyal to those who are quite loyal to those who have no loyalty at all. Even people who are not actively loyal need not be disloyal, for their non-loyalty may arise from indifference rather than hostility. Lack of loyalty is not the same as active enmity and need not involve any desire to do harm. Nor need it imply loyalty to some competing group.[1] I am not, for example, loyal to France, but my lack of loyalty involves no negative feelings about France, no desire to see it harmed, and no commitment to its enemies.

The same points apply to patriotic loyalty. It, too, comes in degrees. Recall that patriotism includes a special affection for one's country, a sense of personal identification with it, a special concern for its well-being, and a willingness to make sacrifices in order to promote its good. Each of these traits may vary in intensity.

A patriot's affection for his country may be a passionate love or a milder but genuine affection. If it becomes too weak, then a person would no longer be a patriot, but there is a range of emotional strength within which different but genuinely patriotic feelings fall.

Likewise, a person's sense of identification with her country may vary considerably. One person might think of being an American as her primary identity, while for others, it is one way out of many in which they see themselves. Seeing themselves as parents, friends, members of a profession, members of a religion, residents of a region, they count their membership in the national community as just one part of who they are. Nonetheless, it may remain an important part. Considerable variations in degree are possible.

A person's degree of concern for the country may vary in similar ways, from passionate and constant concern to a genuine but less intense focus on the country and its needs. Again, the key point is that the concern can be genuine, even if it is less than the most extreme form.

Finally, people may vary considerably in the degree of sacrifice they are willing to make in order to promote their country's well-being. At one extreme is a person like Nathan Hale, who regretted that he had only one life to sacrifice for his country. Some patriots might be willing to devote a lifetime of energy and commitment to their country. Others may be happy to provide what they take to be their fair share of the burden of supporting the country while being reluctant to sacrifice their personal goals.

Once we see that patriotism consists of a set of different attitudes and that each of these attitudes is itself capable of appearing in different degrees of strength, that may help us escape the either/or perspective that often seems to underlie people's thinking about patriotism. It may help to get us beyond the crude assignment of all people into the categories of "with us" and "against us."

## LOYALTY AND ITS DIMENSIONS

Patriotism and loyalty are often equated. While they are related to one another in important ways, they are not the same, however. It is true that genuine patriots will exhibit loyalty, but not every loyal person need be a patriot. A mercenary soldier, for example, might be quite loyal to the country that pays him. He might be motivated by a sense of professionalism or a belief in the sanctity of contracts, while patriots are motivated by affection, concern, identification, and willingness to sacrifice.

Loyalty to one's country, however, is a central feature of patriotic people. I see this loyalty as a result of the other attitudes that make up patriotism (affection, concern, etc.). The word "loyalty" in this context draws our attention to a certain constancy in these attitudes. It conveys a sense of ongoing commitment to a person or group, a kind of reliability. We know that we can count on someone who is loyal, and because it is important that we be able to rely on people, we tend to regard loyalty as a virtue.

Nonetheless, loyalty is not always a virtue. One can be loyal to persons or causes that are unworthy. Likewise, loyalty can lead one to support actions and policies that are immoral and inhumane. In arguing for moderate patriotism, I have charged that the loyalty of extreme patriots is not a virtue at all. It is, instead, a vice, a form of excessive commitment to a nation that goes beyond the limits of what is morally desirable.[2]

In order to make clearer the ways in which extreme patriotism goes wrong and to strengthen my claim that moderate patriotism is a genuine and desirable form of loyalty, I want to distinguish several dimensions of loyalty. Having an analysis of these dimensions of loyalty will make it clearer how loyalty can be a vice. It will also render us less susceptible to the claim that attempts to moderate our loyalties will inevitably undermine them.

1. People's loyalties may differ with respect to the *number* of objects to which they are directed. At one extreme, a person may be loyal to a single person or group—one's child, friend, spouse, nation, or religious group. In other cases, a person may have ties of loyalty to many things. Loyalties, then, may be *exclusive* or *non-exclusive*, *single* or *multiple*. In most cases, people have multiple, non-exclusive loyalties. They have special ties to many persons and groups rather than being devoted solely to one.

Loyalties may sometimes conflict and compete with one another. It may sometime be impossible, for example, to be loyal to both of two friends. Nonetheless, we generally think that we can maintain multiple loyalties and do not think that loyalty to one person or group must threaten loyalty to others. Except in special cases, loyalty to one thing (e.g., one's family) is not a form of disloyalty to others (one's religion or profession).

2. Loyalties differ in their *basis*. Some loyalties are entirely rooted in brute facts over which we have no control. They are based on a sense of *personal connectedness* that we simply have with regard to some person or group. In contrast, a purely *criterion-based* loyalty derives from a judgment that something satisfies our criteria for being worthy of devotion. These loyalties depend entirely on an assessment of the value of their object.

There is a tendency to think of loyalties that derive from a brute fact sense of connectedness as being stronger than those that are criterion-based. As the saying "Blood is thicker than water" suggests, biological ties are seen as especially secure and binding. Socrates makes use of this idea in his political philosophy, arguing that his obligation to the state is a natural tie, analogous to his relationship to his parents.[3] The same idea is suggested by the root of the word "nation," which derives from the Latin word for birth, and by "patriotism" itself, which derives from "pater," the Latin for father.

Because of their invariability, natural ties may seem more reliable than criterion-based connections. A natural tie cannot be undone in the way that a conventional or criterion-based tie can. One cannot divorce one's parents or one's children. This should not lead us to think, however, that brute-fact loyalties are always more secure or dependable. People desert their children (to whom they are biologically related) just as they desert their spouses (to whom they are only connected by law). Likewise, naturalized citizens are often more enthusiastic patriots than those who are native to a country.

3. Loyalties may vary in the *scope* of the duties they involve. These duties may be *limited* or *unlimited*. Unlimited loyalties require us to do whatever is necessary to support the object of loyalty, while very limited loyalties call for some small and perhaps not too demanding set of actions. A particular job may require no more than punctuality and the performance of a few actions during the time one is working. The duties of a loyal family member are more extensive, lacking clear boundaries as to when they are to be performed and suggesting the possibility of acts that may involve considerable sacrifice. Patriotic duties have often been portrayed as essentially unlimited in scope.

A second aspect of the scope of duties concerns whether they are constrained by other duties or principles. Unlimited loyalties recognize no constraints on what may be done on behalf of the object of loyalty. Limited loyalties recognize that some actions ought not to be done even if they would advance the cause of the object of loyalty. Recognition of such constraints is, I have argued, crucial to making our special duties consistent with morality.

4. Loyalty-based duties may vary in their *strength*. Some people see their duty to an object of loyalty as *supreme* and *overriding*. Whenever there are conflicts of duties, a supreme loyalty will always take precedence. All other obligations are subsidiary to it. On the other hand, loyalty-based duties may be merely *presumptive*, providing a presumption (either strong or weak) in favor of action but one that still must be weighed against others when deciding what to do.

Loyalties, then, may provide the only or the most important reason for doing something. Or, they may provide one kind of reason that may be outweighed by other loyalties or by constraints that are not loyalty-based.

5. In addition to features relating to our object of loyalty, people's loyalties may include different attitudes toward people and groups to which one is not loyal. At one extreme, people loyal to one group may see the objects of other people's loyalties as *illegitimate*. For them, only one suitable object of loyalty exists, their own. Other objects of loyalty are seen as simply lacking in value or as having negative value because they conflict with what the extremist regards as the only proper loyalty. A religious fanatic might hold this view, thinking that all others should convert to his religion. Likewise, xenophobic people might resent the national pride that citizens of other countries have in their own traditions.

Opposed to this is the attitude that all objects of loyalty are *legitimate*, that there are no limits on legitimacy. A middle view would regard some objects of loyalty as legitimate and others as not, depending on what the object of loyalty is and what features it possesses.

There are several different attitudes, then, toward other people's objects of loyalty. One may regard them as illegitimate competitors, or one may be indifferent to them. Or, one may even have some degree of positive regard for them, even though one has no ties of loyalty to them.

6. Loyalties may include a variety of attitudes toward persons whose objects of loyalty differ from one's own. The extreme view would be that persons with other loyalties are to be *hated* or *disdained*. One hates them because they are, in a sense, traitors, people who fail to have the right object of loyalty. More moderately, one might simply be *neutral* or *indifferent* to them. Finally, one might have some degree of *concern* or *positive feeling* toward them, even though their loyalties differ from one's own.

These six dimensions of loyalty that I have described are summarized on the chart on the following page. Since there are six dimensions and since each one includes a range of different forms, it should be clear that there are many different possible forms of loyalty. For simplicity, I focus on three types: the fanatical loyalty that characterizes the most extreme form of patriotism, the moderate loyalty that I have defended, and the diffused loyalty of extreme universalists. The fanatic and the universalist represent extremes on each continuum and are thus more specific than the moderate type. The word "moderate" here applies to a range of possible middle positions. Not every position between the extremes will count as moderate patriotism, since some may be too close to the fanaticism of extreme patriots and others may be too close to the overly diffuse loyalties of the extreme universalist. The universalist position occupies a point at the opposite extreme from the fanatic loyalist. The chart makes clear why pure universalism is not a form of loyalty at all. It is instead a rejection of loyalty.

|                      | FANATICAL      | MODERATE          | UNIVERSALIST       |
| -------------------- | -------------- | ----------------- | ------------------ |
| NUMBER OF OBJECTS    | Single         | Many              | Indefinitely large |
| BASIS                | Brute fact     | Mixed             | Criterion-based    |
| SCOPE                | Unlimited      | Limited           | Variable           |
| STRENGTH             | Supreme duty   | Presumptive duty  | None               |
| OTHER LOYALTIES      | Illegitimate   | Variable          | Illegitimate       |
| OTHER LOYALISTS      | Hatred         | Variable          | Positive concern   |

Looking at these various dimensions of loyalty, we see more clearly what distinguishes illegitimate forms from acceptable forms of loyalty. By combining the first member of each of these dimensions, we can see what would constitute the most extreme form of *fanatical* loyalty and why this form of loyalty is morally unacceptable. Fanatical loyalty has a single object and recognizes no duties to any who fall outside of the circle of loyalty. The loyalty is entirely based on brute-fact connectedness, making the object of loyalty free of any evaluation or assessment. It involves a conception of unlimited and overriding duties, so that there are no limits on what may be done in pursuing the good of the object of loyalty. Moreover, other people's objects of loyalty are seen as illegitimate, and people with ties to the "wrong" objects of loyalty are viewed with hatred, contempt, and disdain.[4]

The chart also makes clear why extreme forms of universalism make genuine loyalty impossible. If one's loyalties multiply without limit to include all human beings, then one has no special loyalty to any. Likewise, if loyalties are entirely criterion-based, then they lack the essential element of personal connectedness that loyalists feel. They lack any special emotional tie to particular persons or groups. Or, if loyalty-based duties exist but are so limited in strength or scope that they are always overridden by other duties, then loyalty won't amount to much in determining how we ought to act. Extreme universalists reject all particular loyalties as illegitimate. Nonetheless, while they might lament the fact that people have special loyalties and might try to weaken their strength, universalists need not regard persons with these "mistaken" loyalties in a negative fashion.

Between fanatical loyalty and the universalist's non-loyal stance, there lie many different positions. It is within this space that we find moderate patriotism. Moderate patriots count their country as one of a relatively limited set of objects of loyalty. Their country is important to them, but it is not the only thing to which they are loyal. Moderate patriots recognize that the facts of birth, history, and shared experience may create bonds of affection and responsibility. Nonetheless, they believe that we should subject our loyalties to moral reflection and that persons or groups to which we are loyal may cease to merit our commitment to them. Thus, moderate patriots recognize the legitimacy of evaluation without arguing that loyalties must actually derive from rational, evaluative processes. They do not deny the relevance of brute facts such as birth or emotional attachment to determining what our loyalties are or ought to be.

Moderate patriots take the duties of citizenship seriously. They have both scope and strength in that they may make serious demands on us and may override other duties in some cases. Nonetheless, they reject the idea of unlimited and unconstrained duties. The claims of the nation are subject to constraints in the same way that loyalties of family and friendship are.

Moderate patriots are disposed to be tolerant of other people's loyalties. Once we see that facts of birth and emotional ties provide a basis for loyalties, we must then acknowledge that other people have as legitimate a basis for their loyalties as we have for ours. If my being born *here* is a basis of loyalty to my country, then I must acknowledge that your being born *there* is a basis of loyalty to yours.

Nonetheless, while loyalties that differ from my own may be legitimate, other people's loyalties are subject to assessment in the same way that mine are. Hence, moderate patriots will no more give unconditional approval to other people's loyalties than they will to their own. Their assessments of other objects of loyalties and of people with different loyalties will be, as the chart indicates, variable. There is an initial presumption of legitimacy, but this can be outweighed if the other loyalties are themselves morally unworthy.

## IN DEFENSE OF MODERATE PATRIOTISM

The moderate patriotic position is that special duties toward one's own country are legitimate so long as they honor certain constraints. As we have seen, this calls forth the charge that moderate patriotism is not a genuine form of loyalty. I have tried to answer that charge in a number of different ways.

One way of answering it is by pointing out that we accept this form of constrained loyalty as proper in all of our other relationships. No one thinks that genuine loyalty to one's spouse, children, parents, or friends requires that one will unconditionally do whatever they ask or unconditionally support them in whatever they do. No one thinks that being a loyal spouse, parent, child, or friend requires or permits us to abuse or disregard the rights, needs, and interests of other human beings. If we can recognize these limitations on our personal loyalties without thereby undermining them, it is hard to see why we cannot apply these same limitations to our loyalty toward our country without undermining it.

A second way of answering the charge that moderate patriotism is not genuine loyalty is by referring to the chart and suggesting that critics may be confusing moderate patriotism with extreme universalism. That is understandable since moderate patriots accept many of the criticisms that extreme universalists have made of extreme patriotism. It is understandable too because moderate patriots share with universalists the idea that we have duties to people who are not citizens of our own country. Both believe that we may sometimes have to forgo benefits to our own country because pursuing them would violate the rights of people beyond our borders. Our compatriots are not the only ones who count.

In spite of these overlaps between moderate patriotism and extreme universalism, the two positions are quite distinct. The chart should make that clear and should prevent further confusion.

Finally, a third value of this analysis is that it shows that people who think moderate patriotism is not patriotic enough are committed to supporting fanaticism. Extreme patriotism is a fanatical form of loyalty. Its overcommitment arises from its exclusive focus on one object of loyalty, its inattention to the qualities of the object of loyalty, its elevating of loyalty to the nation to a supreme status, its failure to observe any constraints on what may be done on the nation's behalf, and its unwarranted hostility and disrespect toward people with different loyalties.

Putting all these features together provides us with a description of the most extreme form of fanatical patriotism. One can be an extreme patriot by having some of these traits even if one does not have all of them. In any case, these extreme forms of patriotism are morally objectionable and when we reject them, the form of patriotism we are left with is moderate patriotism.

Those who think that patriotism is a virtue must make a choice. If they opt for extreme patriotism, they must give up their claim that patriotism is a virtue. If they want patriotism to be a virtue, then they must embrace the moderate form. If moderate patriotism is not genuine, then there is no morally legitimate form of patriotism.

## NOTES

1. On the diversity of attitudes displayed by citizens, see Paul Sniderman, *A Question of Loyalty* (Berkeley: University of California Press, 1981).

2. For a discussion of fanaticism as a form of overcommitment, see Jay Newman, *Fanatics and Hypocrites* (Buffalo, N.Y.: Prometheus Books, 1986), ch. 2.

3. For a discussion of Socrates' use of this idea, see my *Should We Consent to be Governed?* (Belmont, Calif.: Wadsworth, 1991), ch. 2.

4. For a brief but useful description of fanaticism, see John Kekes, *Facing Evil* (Princeton: Princeton University Press, 1990), 77–79. Kekes aptly describes fanaticism as "the ruthless pursuit of some goal."

*Part III*

# From the Moderate Patriotic Perspective

# *10*

# On Deciding Whether a Nation Deserves Our Loyalty

We have seen that while some forms of patriotism are illegitimate, there is a form of patriotism that is consistent with morality. While many issues have needed discussion to establish this conclusion, the conclusion itself does not tell us what to do. What has been shown is that patriotism is morally possible. It does not follow that anyone should actually be a patriot or give loyal support to the acts and policies of their country.

Anti-patriots might see this as a victory for their view. They might concede that patriotism is legitimate in theory while denying that it is ever legitimate in practice. Why? Because, according to them, no actual governments are worthy of our loyalty. All governments are implicated in evils and injustices that disqualify them from being proper objects of loyalty. Thus, for them, moderate patriotism may be legitimate as a purely theoretical possibility, but no one should actually be patriotic.

Defenders of patriotism may object from the opposite direction. Knowing that all governments have flaws, they may feel that moderate patriotism is merely a disguised form of anti-patriotism. They may see the argument for moderate patriotism as a trap. First, they claim, patriotism is defended, but only on the condition that governments must be worthy of loyalty. Then, all governments are shown to be defective and thus unworthy of loyalty. Finally, the conclusion is drawn that no one ought to be patriotic. Fearing that the defense of moderate patriotism is really an indirect attack on patriotism, defenders of patriotism may wonder whether moderate patriots do in fact support patriotic commitment.

I agree with defenders of patriotism that the genuineness of moderate patriotism would be called into question if no country could possibly satisfy the moderate patriot's criteria of worthiness. If the requirements of loyalty are unreasonably stringent, demanding, for example, that a society must be completely just in all its institutions and policies in order to merit patriotic loyalty, then no actual nations could possibly be legitimate objects of loyalty. A theory of patriotism that set the criteria for justifiable loyalty so high that only utopian societies could satisfy them would be misleading. While claiming that patriotism can be a virtue, it would imply that actual nations are never proper objects of loyalty and thus that patriotism is never appropriate.

While this is a legitimate concern, anti-patriots are correct to insist that whether any actual nation merits its citizens' loyalty is a contingent matter. It is certainly possible that no existing governments deserve the loyalty of their citizens. Patriotism might be a possible virtue that has the misfortune of not having suitable objects in the real world.[1] In a similar way, trust might be an attractive attitude in itself but might make no sense in a world inhabited primarily by untrustworthy people.[2] We can't rule out these possibilities. Nonetheless, a less radical view would be more plausible on its face. We should at least begin with the presumption that patriotism is (or has been) appropriate for at least some citizens of some countries at some times.

Anti-patriots, then, need to be assured that moderate patriots take seriously the criteria of worthiness that nations must satisfy to merit our loyalty. At the same time, pro-patriots must be assured that these criteria are not absurdly and unreasonably demanding. We can do both by beginning with the expectation that nations do sometimes merit loyalty without committing ourselves to this as a firm conclusion.

The acceptance of moderate patriotism commits us to taking seriously the question of whether our own government is a worthy object of loyalty. This is not a problem for extreme patriots. Their answer to this question is expressed by the slogan "my country, right or wrong." Extreme patriots tells us that citizens have an obligation to their country that is unconstrained by moral rules or ideals. For them, all that is required for a nation to merit my loyalty and support is that it be *my* nation. As long as the country is mine, I ought to give it my unquestioning and unconditional support.

In contrast, moderate patriots do not believe either that they ought to give automatic support to their country's policies or that any act is right simply because it is motivated by national loyalty. For them, loyalty to one's country is appropriate only when it has qualities that make it worthy of its citizens' devotion. Moderate patriotism is both *limited* by moral constraints on what actions are permissible and *conditional* on the nation's meriting our support.

## EVALUATING NATIONS

How can we evaluate a nation or country? This is a difficult question, but we can approach it by considering some ideas in Henry David Thoreau's famous essay on civil disobedience. While Thoreau himself was not a patriot, he took very seriously the problem of evaluating countries and governments and wrestled with the issues that this task raises. His deliberations suggest two rather different approaches to the problem.

The first approach emerges early in his essay and grows out of Thoreau's hostility to some of the policies of the United States. Writing in the late 1840s, Thoreau was deeply disturbed by the twin evils of slavery and the U.S. war against Mexico. He believed that both were profound and intolerable evils. Moreover, he thought, these policies had clear implications for a person's attitude toward the government. With these evils in mind, he asked, "How does it become a man to behave toward this American government today?" and gave the unequivocal answer that "he cannot without disgrace be associated with it."[3]

Thoreau's point here is clear. Any government that sanctions and supports an institution as unjust as slavery is not a fit object of loyalty. Indeed, to be associated with it is a matter of disgrace. Hence, a conscientious person will attempt not to be associated with it, and Thoreau withheld his taxes as a way of expressing his wish to be dissociated. As he said, "I simply wish to refuse allegiance to the State, to withdraw and stand aloof from it effectually" (654). Having decided that being a member of American political society was a matter of personal disgrace, Thoreau withdrew his loyalty from it.[4]

Thoreau's attitude is a form of conditional anti-patriotism. He makes the kind of judgment that moderate patriots say must be made and finds that patriotic loyalty is inappropriate. While he does not rule out patriotism in principle, he does reject it with respect to the American government of his time.

Thoreau's attitude may seem extreme, but it is not unreasonable. If a nation engages in terrible acts or supports immoral institutions, then being loyal to it and giving it one's support makes one an accomplice to those evils. If an individual kept someone caged in his house and used him as a slave, it would be wrong to ignore that fact and carry on one's friendship in a normal way. Likewise, the crimes and disgraces of war and injustice are too significant to ignore, and they make loyalty to the government that is responsible for them inappropriate. Thoreau rejected the idea that one should love and support a country that uses its resources to support slavery and sends thousands to kill and be killed in an unjust war.

That is one side of Thoreau's view—the profoundly anti-patriotic aspect of it. Later in his essay, Thoreau suggests a different evaluative perspective, describing the United States in more tempered words:

> Seen from a lower point of view, the Constitution, with all its faults, is very good; the law and the courts are very respectable; even this State [Massachusetts] and this American government are, in many respects, very admirable and rare things, to be thankful for, such as a great many have described them; seen from a higher [point of view,] they are what I have described them; seen from a higher still, and the highest, who shall say what they are, or that they are worth looking at or thinking of at all? (656)

In contrast with Thoreau's earlier condemnation of "this American government today," this statement highlights the difficulties of passing such a judgment. It does this by noting features of that very same government that are quite admirable. Thoreau acknowledges that the negative features are not the only important ones the government possesses. In addition, the statement suggests that there are multiple points of view from which we can assess the value of a government. Some of these perspectives are more demanding in their requirements, while others are less so. Since they generate different evaluations and justify different attitudes, we need to know which perspective to adopt when asking whether a country merits our loyalty.

In these later remarks, Thoreau suggests that evaluating governments and societies is a difficult matter. By noting the complex set of qualities that characterize nations and the multiple criteria that may be applied to them, he strongly suggests that it is a mistake to infer from the presence of significant evils that a government is necessarily unworthy of loyalty. He suggests that a government may merit loyalty even if it fails to live up to important moral principles and standards. We need to look at how this could be.

## THE PROBLEM OF BALANCED JUDGMENT

The first problem Thoreau mentions arises because the country that supports an evil like slavery also has many good features. The Constitution, the law, the courts, many features of the governmental system are, he says, "good," "respectable," even "admirable." If a country possesses both very positive features and very negative ones, what sort of overall judgment should we make?[5]

In some cases, we can judge a country by seeing how serious the faults are and whether they are central or peripheral to the system. Thoreau asked whether the defects are "friction" within the machine of government or an essential part of its function. Are they imperfections of a good system or deep flaws that render the system essentially evil?

Liberal reformers often see social injustice as friction in a system that on the whole works well. They strive to improve the system so that it distributes the benefits and burdens of social life more justly. In contrast, some Marxists see the oppression of working people as essential to any political system. Oppression, in their view, is not a defect in a system designed to produce justice. Instead, oppression is the function of the political system. In their view, since oppression is an essential feature of the system, the only way to end oppression is to destroy the system.[6] Early in his essay, Thoreau expresses the revolutionary position, declaring, "[W]hen the friction comes to have its machine, and oppression and robbery are organized, I say, let us not have such a machine any longer" (639).

Slavery, however, was a complicated case. It is not true that the government was set up primarily to maintain slavery or that slavery was essential to its nature. The fact that the federal government eventually destroyed slavery shows it was not essential. Nonetheless, the Constitution recognized slavery, and the machinery of government was used to maintain it for many years. One of Thoreau's special targets of criticism was the Fugitive Slave Law, which required states to return runaway slaves to their legal owners. Moreover, even if slavery was not essential to the system, it was a momentous evil, not a trivial defect. Thoreau estimated that one sixth of the nation's population was enslaved. This is not the sort of fact that can simply be passed over in assessing the United States before the Civil War.

Slavery, then, was a great evil that the government supported and maintained. While maintaining slavery was not essential to the machinery of government, slavery was too important an institution to describe as mere "friction." To further complicate matters, slavery was not the country's only feature. It had, Thoreau says, an admirable Constitution and a rare legal system for which one should be thankful.

In view of these facts, what overall assessment should we make?

Should we say that the system was fundamentally good but flawed in important ways? Or should we describe it as fundamentally flawed and hence unworthy of loyalty, affection, or respect?

## THE PROBLEM OF PROPER CRITERIA

It is not clear how to answer these questions, partly because it is unclear what criteria we should use in our assessment. I will mention two problems about these criteria.

First, there is the problem of determining how to make an overall assessment. Should we simply sum up the balance of goods and evils that are part of a system? Is there some amount of goodness in a nation's institutions such that if a nation possesses this amount or more, it will outweigh the evil of slavery? And if so, what amount is this, and how do we measure it? Or, is this model of summing up inappropriate? Is slavery so vile that no matter how good a nation is in other respects, the evil of slavery can never be counterbalanced by other goods—not because the other goods are insignificant but rather because the notion of counter-balancing makes no sense here?

Similar questions arise in thinking about individuals. No one would say that a person who had lived his life very virtuously could justify or excuse murdering an innocent person because the moral credit he had previously amassed outweighs the moral blame acquired by committing the murder.[7] No one would say that on balance he was still a good person. In the same way, one might think that nothing a country could do—short of doing away with its evil traits—could compensate for or outweigh its significant evils. Yet, even in the case of murderers, we distinguish between those who seem essentially evil and those who appear to have redeeming qualities. Perhaps similar judgments are possible about nations. In any case, before we can arrive at an overall assessment, we must decide whether we are dealing with a situation in which goods can balance out evils or whether this makes no sense.[8]

A second problem about criteria arises from the idea of "reasonable expectations." Thoreau calls the valuable parts of the American system "admirable and rare." These words suggest an appreciation of the difficulty of building and maintaining just institutions. Perhaps by comparison with most societies, the American system was quite impressive. Perhaps, viewed comparatively, American institutions ranked quite high, even if they were blemished by slavery and even if, from a higher perspective, we could not approve them.

According to this view, when we judge a particular nation, we must consider how other nations have fared and keep in mind the common failings of human nature and society and the compromises that even good societies make. In the United States, such compromises had been made to maintain the Union, for if the abolition of slavery had been insisted upon, the nation could not have been formed or sustained.

Using this reasoning, one may conclude that a nation can deserve our loyalty even if it contains significant evils. It tells us that when we evaluate a nation, we must not demand perfection as a condition of loyalty. Our expectations of nations must be reasonable, and our judgment of what is reasonable must be based on knowledge of both the historical context in which decisions have been made and general facts about human nature and society.

This argument makes a great deal of sense. Nonetheless, we must be careful that it does not lead us to accept weak, overly permissive criteria. Imagine someone arguing that given the combination of the bitterness of the German defeat in World War I, the economic dislocation and trauma of the 1920s, and the long tradition of anti-Semitism, it is unreasonable to expect that Germany would have refrained from the genocidal policies of the Nazi era. Surely, this conclusion goes too far. Nonetheless, we can easily get there on a slippery slope that starts off with talk about historical context, human nature, and realistic expectations. The end point of this slope is the view that nothing other than what actually occurs could be reasonably expected of anyone.

Having noted this danger, we are still left with the problem of where to draw line between what can and cannot be reasonably expected of people or institutions. This compounds the difficulties of arriving at an overall judgment.

## THE PROBLEM OF IDEALS VS. ACTUALITIES

Keeping in mind the notion of reasonable expectations, one might argue that while we know that no country lives up to its ideals, what is important is that the country's ideals be good ones. Even if it fails to live up to its ideals, at least it is attempting to move in the right direction. Thus, one might argue that while genocide flowed from the ideals of Nazism, slavery violated the ideals of the United States. Had the United States been dedicated to the proposition that all people are *not* created equal, then the country might not have merited respect or devotion. But, given that it was committed in principle to the fundamental equality of human beings, slavery could be seen as an aberration from its true nature.

There is some force in this defense. It does make a difference what the ideals of a country are, and it is not reasonable to expect a country to measure up to its highest ideals. Nonetheless, as with the previous argument from reasonable expectations, it is too easy to use this argument as an excuse for virtually anything.

One problem is that it is hard to tell what a nation's ideals actually are. Do we determine them by looking at ceremonial remarks and proclamations? Or do we decide by looking at how it actually behaves? Perhaps ideals and actualities are more closely related than the argument suggests. Perhaps the real ideals are revealed in the actual behavior of individuals and officials. Looking at the United States prior to the Civil War, it might be most accurate to say that it was actually dedicated to maintaining the fundamental *in*equality of human beings. Isn't that the message of the Fugitive Slave Law and the Dred Scott decision?

One might go further and argue that while it is bad enough if nations engage in evil practices, it is worse if at the same time they express lofty ideals that are contrary to their own practices. This adds the sin of hypocrisy to the already admitted evil of the institutions themselves. While calling ourselves the "land of the free," we permitted the buying and selling of human beings.[9]

Granted, then, there is a point about evaluating a nation by its aspirations, but the aspirations must be genuine, and the judgment that they are genuine must be based to some degree on actual practice. Recognition of its own failings may raise a nation in our esteem, but if not connected to remedial efforts, it may simply be evidence of hypocrisy.

## THE PROBLEM OF GOVERNMENT VS. NATION

The difficulty of evaluating nations is further compounded by the fact that it is not clear exactly what we are evaluating. We often speak of nations as if they were individual agents. We say that the United States permitted slavery, that Germany broke the Versailles treaty, that the Soviet Union invaded Czechoslovakia. This may be a useful and necessary way of talking, but it also obscures important facts.

Thoreau's harsh judgment—that it is a disgrace to be associated with the American government—suggests that the government and the country are single agents that have acted in evil ways. We know this is untrue, however, and so did Thoreau. Many people in the United States opposed slavery or had doubts about it, even if they supported compromises with those who favored slavery. Slavery was a source of conflict over many years, and only a minority of people actually held slaves. It may be unfair to judge the whole nation by the actions of some of its citizens.

Or, consider another example. The strategic bombing of cities carried out by Great Britain and the United States during World War II was a brutal and immoral policy that involved the intentional killing of vast numbers of innocent civilians. While Britain and the United States saw themselves as combating barbarism and inhumanity, their pursuit of victory led them to engage in large scale, indiscriminate acts of killing and destruction.[10] Yet, if one condemns these nations for their actions, one must at least consider the fact that only a minuscule number of people was involved in sanctioning and carrying them out. Most citizens had no knowledge that such attacks were planned and played no role in deciding to launch them. To condemn the entire nation for them seems to ignore these facts. More generally, many of the significant evils that blot the histories of nations have been carried out by a small minority of citizens. We ought not to condemn a whole nation for the actions of a small number of its people.

This argument requires us to take seriously the distinction between a government and a nation. Typically, when we speak of patriotism and national loyalty, we have in mind support for the government and its policies, and we judge nations by the actions of their governments. This may be a mistake, however. Not only are government officials a small minority of a nation's population, but the government itself is only one aspect of the nation's identity. A nation or country, one could argue, is essentially a cultural entity, and the political and governmental institutions are only a part of its nature. For this reason, one might argue, national loyalty may be appropriate even when a government does inexcusable deeds. Why? Because the government is not the nation, and the nation may be a worthy object of loyalty while the government is not.

In fact, we can distinguish at least three different subjects of evaluation—the people who hold office at any given time, the system of government, and the nation. Plato highlights the first of these distinctions at the end of the *Crito*, when the voice of the Laws tells Socrates that he has been "the victim of a wrong done not by us, the laws, but by your fellow men."[11] But just as we can distinguish the laws from the law enforcers, so we can distinguish the system of laws and government from the nation itself. The fact that evil rulers hold power or that an unjust system of government is in place need not reflect negatively on the citizens of a country if the government's power rests on overpowering force or massive deception.

What this point shows is that a nation may be a suitable object of loyalty, even though its government's laws and policies are systematically unjust. The patriot who remains loyal to the nation in this situation might not support either the current holders of office or the overall political system.

## WHAT ARE WE LOYAL TO?

Once we distinguish between the government and the nation, the extreme patriot might use this distinction to argue that the nation always remains a suitable object of loyalty and is in some sense beyond criticism, even when evil deeds are done in its name. This argument fails for two important reasons.

First, while we can distinguish nations from governments, it does not follow that nations are never tainted by the acts of those in power. If government policies are widely supported and reflect the dominant values of the nation and its people, then the nation itself may be made unworthy by the government's actions.

Second, if extreme patriots use this distinction to argue that the nation remains worthy of loyalty in spite of the actions of the government and that therefore citizens should support the government in its efforts, this argument clearly fails. "My country, right or wrong" is typically evoked when support is sought for what the government is doing. But if the *nation* remains worthy of support only because it is distinct from the government and not tainted by its policies, then the worthiness of the nation does not carry over to the *government*, and the kind of support for the nation that is appropriate is not the support of the government's policies.

So, while extreme patriots might invoke these distinctions to support loyalty and obedience, what they actually show is that there is even less reason to accept the notion that patriotism is necessarily exhibited in acts of obedience to law or support of evil policies. If state and nation are distinct, then national loyalty need not involve loyalty to the state.

This is a point that Randolph Bourne makes forcefully in his essay "The State." Bourne, writing during World War I, distinguishes among the government, the country, and the state. He captures some of the ordinary cynicism of common sense in his description of government. Government, he says, is

composed of common and unsanctified men, and is thus a legitimate
object of criticism and even contempt. . . . In a Republic the Government is obeyed grudgingly, because it has no bedazzlements or sanctities
to gild it.[12]

Bourne uses the word "country" to refer to the

non-political aspects of a people, its ways of living, its personal traits,
its literature and art, its characteristic attitudes towards life. (67)

Finally, Bourne says, the State "is the country acting as a political
unit." From this, he draws the conclusion that

The history of America as a country is quite different from that of
America as a State. (68)

Essentially, then, Bourne distinguishes among political leaders, the
country, and the state.

Bourne uses these distinctions very effectively to make two points.
The first is negative and critical. Like Tolstoy, he sees the State as
essentially warlike and competitive. Writing in a bitter state of mind
that grew out of his opposition to U.S. participation in World War I,
Bourne claims that "war is the health of the state" (71). As an opponent of war, he has no allegiance to the State.

Nonetheless, he is able to retain a sense of connection with and
pride in many aspects of American life. This is the second function of
his distinctions among political leaders, country, and state. Though
disillusioned with the leaders and the state, Bourne could remain
committed to the country. "country," he writes,

is a concept of peace, of tolerance, of living and letting live. But State
is essentially a concept of power, of competition. It signifies a group
in its aggressive aspects. (68)

The problem, Bourne thought, is that we are born into both a state
and a country, and our feelings for them are mingled "into a hopeless
confusion" (68).

Bourne himself rejects the term "patriot," seeing it as essentially
connected to the State whose values he rejects. Nonetheless, his discussion provides us with a model of a person who is loyal to his country even though he rejects the values of its government. The country,
for him, is different from the State. The positive function of his distinctions is to separate these objects of loyalty from one another so

that he can acknowledge his sense of connectedness with his country while at the same time disavowing the state policies he rejects.[13]

Jean B. Elshtain makes a similar point, using the distinction between the state and the "political and moral community." She writes:

> Patriotism . . . is part of our repertoire of civic ideals and identities. While its excesses may be lamented, it cannot, and should not, be excised, for patriotism also taps love of country that yields civic concern *for* country. Attached more to the sense of a political and moral community than to a state, patriotism can be, and has been, evoked to bring out the best in us—even as, when it shades into nationalism, it can arouse the worst. . . .[14]

Like Bourne, Elshtain rejects the violence of the state but defends a form of community loyalty that she thinks can bring out what is best in people.

Once we begin to make such distinctions, we can even make sense of the idea that a person could be both a patriot and a traitor—true to his nation, while betraying his government. A contemporary example of such a person is Alexander Solzhenitsyn, who was both a foe of the Soviet system and its ideology and a Russian patriot, someone who wanted the Russian nation and its culture to flourish and believed that this could not happen under the Soviet governmental system.[15] Or think of the Germans whose patriotism motivated them to attempt to assassinate Hitler.[16] People who love their country need not love or support its government or its policies.

## THE TASK OF EVALUATION

The task of evaluating nations is far from simple. As we have seen, it is not clear how to balance good and bad features. It is not clear what criteria of evaluation are appropriate. Nor is it fully clear just what the object of evaluation is.

Given all of these unclear ideas, one might wonder what of value emerges from this discussion. I draw several conclusions. First, the complexity of the evaluative process should indicate that moderate patriotism does not commit one to a quick rejection of actual nations as objects of loyalty. It is not enough to note the failings of a nation and simply infer that it is unworthy of any degree of loyalty. While Thoreau makes this quick, negative inference early in "Civil Disobedience," his later remarks suggest that the problem is more difficult.

Second, I conclude that moderate patriots set themselves a difficult task when they commit themselves to evaluating the nation for its worthiness. I do not raise this as a defect in moderate patriotism. Nor do I think that it is impossible to judge nations. Rather, I want to suggest that it is more difficult than one might think. If moderate patriotism provides the most appropriate perspective for citizens, then we are all saddled with these evaluative problems.[17]

Someone might object, however, that even going through the process I have described is incompatible with patriotism. Patriots, they might claim, are people who love their country, and people who love their country do not engage in elaborate processes of assessing it, calculating its degree of virtue, and deliberating about the appropriateness of loyalty. To play by these rules, one might argue, is to forsake love and loyalty right at the start. Real patriots will not engage in these deliberations at all.

This objection recalls the "love is blind" argument that we looked at earlier. It assumes that emotional commitment is incompatible with rational deliberation and moral evaluation. It requires that genuine patriotism be a form of blind loyalty. There is no reason, however, to accept these assumptions. There is no reason why the spontaneous affection that people feel for one another, as well as for the groups, institutions, and symbols associated with nations, cannot be critically evaluated.[18]

If our affections and loyalties are genuine and deep, then the failings of those we love will not quickly lead to the weakening of our love. It may lead us to explain, to seek improvement, to make excuses, and these reactions are not only understandable but may be appropriate and good. Certainly the most important response is to seek improvement, to try to help one's country move in the direction of goodness and a life that brings it honor. That, rather than blindness to faults, is the best expression of loyalty.

There may come a point, however, both in personal relationships and in relations to nations, when the presumption in favor of love and loyalty is undermined by events. When this happens, we can grit our teeth and in the name of loyalty ignore the failings of those we love and support them in all of their endeavors. Or, we can respond in anger and disappointment and simply cut ourselves off from them entirely. Or, if attempts to bring about change fail, we may need to consider whether the actions or traits that have caused us to be disappointed or angry are sufficiently serious so that our loyalty is no longer appropriate. This consideration strikes me as the best response, the one that is both fair to the person or nation involved and compatible with moral values and ideals.

Indeed, careful consideration of the issues involved may itself show that one takes the relationship seriously. Contrary to the charge that it reflects alienation and detachment, thinking about these problems may itself be evidence of loyalty. Moreover, though the process is rational and deliberative, it need not be "coldly logical." Where genuine loyalty is at stake, the process of thought may be anguished and painful.

Within the political realm, discussions of the worth of nations and their institutions are extremely important. With all of the pressures on governments to act opportunistically, the demand by citizens that governments live up to high ideals and make themselves worthy of loyalty is one of the ultimate checks on the use of power. In times of stress, when many citizens begin to wonder whether loyalty remains appropriate, they are in effect reconsidering the social contract. They are trying to decide whether the limits of loyalty have been exceeded and the demands of citizenship have become illegitimate.

Extreme patriots, of course, reject the legitimacy of this process, claiming that critical reflection about loyalty is incompatible with loyalty itself. In doing so, however, they ignore the lessons of history and overlook the important role that the "consent of the governed" plays in enabling governments to do evil. In contrast, moderate patriots show an awareness of the dangers of loyalty as well as its value. By insisting that criticism and reflection are compatible with patriotic attitudes, they do what they can to support the application of moral principles to the behavior of citizens and their nations.

## NOTES

1. MacIntyre appears to support a form of this thesis when he writes that "the practice of patriotism as a virtue is in advanced societies no longer possible in the way that it once was." See *After Virtue* (Notre Dame: Notre Dame University Press, 1981), 236.

2. This is a possibility considered by Herman Melville in his rather bleak novel, *The Confidence Man*.

3. From "Civil Disobedience," in *Walden and Other Writings* (New York: Modern Library, 1937), 638. Subsequent page references are in the text.

4. For a discussion of the desire to dissociate as a motive for protest, see Thomas Hill, Jr., "Symbolic Protest and Calculated Silence," *Philosophy and Public Affairs* 9 (1979), 83–102.

5. Some abolitionists condemned the Constitution for its recognition of slavery while others denied that the Constitution actually recognized it as a legitimate institution. For a brief discussion, see Sanford Levinson,

*Constitutional Faith* (Princeton: Princeton University Press, 1988), 65–68, 74–80.

6. For a very clear statement of the Marxist view, see V. I. Lenin, *State and Revolution*, ch. 1

7. The point and the example are due to Joel Feinberg. See his "Supererogation and Rules," in *Doing and Deserving* (Princeton: Princeton University Press, 1970), 23.

8. R. M. Hare appears to defend the view that the evils of slavery could be counter-balanced by other goods in "What Is Wrong With Slavery," *Philosophy and Public Affairs* 8 (1979).

9. Reinhold Niebuhr says of hypocrisy that it may be "the most significant moral characteristic of a nation." For his discussion of national hypocrisy, see *Moral Man and Immoral Society* (New York: Charles Scribner's Sons, 1960), 95–112; originally published 1932. For discussions that stress the gaps between the rhetoric and the realities of United States policies, see Noam Chomsky, *'Human Rights' and American Foreign Policy* (Spokesman Books, 1978); and Howard Zinn, *Declarations of Independence: Cross-Examining American Ideology* (New York: HarperCollins, 1990).

10. This policy is condemned by John C. Ford in "The Morality of Obliteration Bombing," *Theological Studies* 5 (1944), 261–309; excerpted in Richard Wasserstrom, ed., *War and Morality* (Belmont, Calif.: Wadsworth, 1970). For more recent discussion of both moral and historical questions about the bombing policy, see Michael Walzer, *Just and Unjust Wars* (New York: Basic Books, 1977), 255–62; and Kenneth Brown, "'Supreme Emergency': A Critique of Michael Walzer's Moral Justification for Allied Obliteration Bombing in World War II," *Manchester College Bulletin of the Peace Studies Institute* 13 (1983), 6–15.

11. *Crito*, translated by Hugh Treddenick, 54c.

12. "The State," in *War and the Intellectuals: Collected Essays, 1915–1919*, edited by Carl Resak (New York: Harper and Row, 1964), 65–66.

13. For further expression of Bourne's commitment to American cultural ideals, see his essay "Trans-National America," in *War and the Intellectuals*, 107–23.

14. *Women and War* (New York: Basic Books, 1987), 252.

15. For an expression of Solzhenitsyn's views, see his *Letter to the Soviet Leaders* (New York: Harper and Row, 1974). Solzhenitsyn is quite explicit about his Russian patriotism and its inconsistency with the Soviet system. He writes, ". . . the whole of this letter that I am now putting before you is patriotism, *which means* rejection of Marxism" (45).

16. This case is discussed by Alasdair MacIntyre in "Is Patriotism A Virtue?" 14f. For a discussion by a German historian, see Friedrich Meinecke, *The German Catastrophe* (Boston: Beacon Press, 1963), ch. 14.

17. For a powerful attempt to assess America and the appropriateness of loyalty to it, see Martin Luther King, Jr., *Where Do We Go From Here—Chaos or Community?* (Boston: Beacon Press, 1968).

18. Cf. Jean B. Elshtain's description of what she calls the "chastened patriot." Such a person, she writes, "is committed *and* detached: enough apart so that she and he can be reflective about patriotic ties and loyalties, cherishing many loyalties rather than valorizing one alone" (*Women and War*, 253).

# 11

# Patriotism, Military Service, and Unjust Wars

Many opponents of patriotism are disturbed by its connection to warfare. They believe that patriotism feeds belligerence and dulls our sense of the importance of shunning unnecessary violence. In describing moderate patriotism, part of my aim has been to show that patriotism need not involve enthusiasm for war.

Nonetheless, our most vivid associations link war and patriotism. Patriotic emotions rise to their highest levels during wars, and national holidays are often occasions for expressing patriotic sentiments about past wars. This may suggest that patriotism and war are necessarily linked. It may also raise questions about the way that moderate patriots view military service. Will moderate patriots serve in the military if they are called to do so by their country? Will they have an unconditional commitment to do so? Or will they only serve at their own discretion, subject to their own decision that a particular war is justified?

In this chapter, I will address these questions. The answer I will defend is that while moderate patriots may be willing to serve in the military, they need not be willing to do so. In addition, I will argue patriotic citizens ought not to fight for their country if it is engaged in an unjust war.

## PATRIOTISM AND MILITARY SERVICE

In spite of the strong associations between patriotism and military service, there is no necessary connection between them. If there were, a pacifist could not possibly be a patriot. But that is false. Although pacifists oppose all wars and are therefore unwilling to fight for their country, they may still be patriots. The simplest way to prove this is to refer back to the definition of patriotism. Patriotism, I have argued, is characterized by four qualities: special affection for one's country, a special identification with it, special concern for its well-being, and a willingness to sacrifice to promote the country's good. If we consider these traits, we can see that a person could possess all of them while still believing that all war is immoral and that taking part in any war is wrong. Such a person's opposition to war in no way precludes special affection for his or her country. Nor does it rule out special identification with it, concern for its well-being, or a willingness to make sacrifices on its behalf.[1]

Pacifists do, of course, draw a line between actions they will undertake on their country's behalf and actions they will refuse to do. War is an activity they refuse to participate in. Nonetheless, this does not undermine their claim to be patriots. There are many other activities that require sacrifice and that they could engage in for the sake of their country. They might be pleased to follow William James's famous call for a "Moral Equivalent of War" and join in a battle against the natural and social forces that threaten their nation's well-being.[2] Nothing keeps pacifists from making this type of positive commitment.

Moreover, in setting a limit to what they will do for their country, pacifists are no different from most citizens. There are undoubtedly many actions that most people would refuse to do if our government demanded them. Few of us think that patriotic loyalty requires us to mutilate our children or betray our friends if these acts are demanded by our government. Even if we take patriotic duties seriously, we need not regard them as supreme. Nor must we regard the government's specification of these duties as authoritative. So, most of us agree with the pacifist in rejecting the idea that our duties of obedience are totally unlimited.

Pacifists believe that a country may legitimately promote its own well-being, and if they are patriotic, they will support that goal. Where pacifists differ from most people is in their interpretation of the moral constraints on the pursuit of national well-being. They accept a constraint on action that forbids the organized violence involved in warfare. Though they reject neither the goal of national well-being nor most means of achieving it, they deny that it may legitimately be pursued through warfare. Pacifists are not alone in insisting that any morally acceptable form of patriotism must recognize some constraints. They differ only in where they draw the line.

That pacifism is compatible with patriotism was recognized by those provisions of the selective service laws that allowed at least some pacifists not to serve in the military.[3] By legally recognizing conscientious objection to military service as a right of pacifists, the law granted the legitimacy of this option and its consistency with full standing as a citizen.

One might argue that we should not infer too much from this. The selective service law severely restricted its allocation of conscientious objector status, requiring that objectors be opposed to all war and that their opposition be based on religious belief. Only absolute, religiously based pacifism qualified a person for exemption from military service. Noting this, one might explain the recognition of conscientious objector status by citing two facts: the generally favorable attitude toward religion in American law and, perhaps more important, the government's confidence that few people would qualify for this exemption. Because it did not recognize selective objection to war or objection based on moral and political beliefs, the government could be confident that the supply of people available for military service would not be threatened.

From this point of view, the granting of conscientious objector status is the exception that proves the rule. While this exemption was offered to a small minority, it was granted against a background assumption that military service is the norm. Military service, on this view, remains a central duty of citizenship and a paradigm of patriotic devotion.[4]

## WILLINGNESS TO SERVE IN THE MILITARY

In reply to this argument, we need to face directly the question of whether there is an essential link between patriotism and military service.

It is certainly true that military service is one way that patriotic people can show concern for their nation and willingness to sacrifice on its behalf. Nonetheless, it is a mistake to think that military service establishes that someone is a patriot. Patriotism is not the only motive that leads people to military service. It is no accident that military conscription is backed up by legal penalties. Some may serve simply to avoid legal punishment, while others may fear the disapproval of family or friends. Under a volunteer system, some may serve to gain education or economic benefits, while others do so because they lack non-military opportunities. Patriotic feeling is only one of many motivations for military service.

Likewise, it is obvious that one need not actually serve in the military or fight in war to be a patriot. If actual service were required, then disabled persons could not be patriots, people who are subject to a draft but not called would not be patriots, and women (until recently) could not be patriots.[5] So actually serving in the military cannot be an absolute requirement for patriotism.

Nonetheless, one might argue that all patriots (except those exempted by law) must be *willing* to serve in the military. This is a central part of the patriot's willingness to make sacrifices to advance the country's good. Moreover, one might claim, patriots must have an unconditional willingness to fight for their country during wartime. They cannot insist on picking and choosing the occasions on which they will fight for their country.

This view is defended by Alasdair MacIntyre. He notes that most political communities need standing armies to defend themselves. If this need is to be met, he says, then large numbers of young men and women must be willing to "sacrifice their own lives for the sake of the community's security." Moreover,

> their willingness to do so . . . [must] not be contingent upon their own individual evaluation of the rightness or wrongness of their country's cause on some specific issue, measured by some standard that is neutral and impartial relative to the interests of their own community and the interests of other communities.[6]

Military service, for MacIntyre, must be available unconditionally. It cannot be contingent on the judgment by individuals that their country is in the right and fighting justly.

Moderate patriots reject this view. Central to the moderate patriotic perspective is the idea that allegiance to a country should depend on the worth of the country and support of its policies should depend on the worth of those policies. Moderate patriotism rejects both unconditional allegiance to countries and unconditional support of policies.

Moreover, while many people think that war is a special circumstance that calls for the suspension of individual judgment, moderate patriots believe that the nature of war makes it especially important to evaluate war policies and decisions. The reason is that the prohibition of unnecessary violence is one of (if not) the most fundamental and stringent moral constraints. Killing and injuring other human beings are morally forbidden under almost all circumstances. Warfare is a uniquely disturbing activity because in a war these paradigmatically immoral actions become commonplace. Indeed, they are essential features that define war as a practice. Given war's destructiveness and the terrible suffering it causes, individuals have a specially stringent duty to insure that they only take part in war when the strongest reasons require it.

MacIntyre seems to believe that the survival of political communities requires that many people be willing to fight for their country unconditionally. For this reason, he sees the kind of thinking that moderate patriots call for as a threat to the survival of a community.

MacIntyre is clearly correct in thinking that the survival of a community may require its citizens to defend it against external enemies. His argument, however, overlooks other kinds of equally real threats to the survival and well-being of the community. There is the possibility that a community's leaders will lead it into unnecessary wars. These unnecessary wars may cause serious harm to the national community, bringing death and injury to its citizens, disrupting the lives of families, depleting the country's resources, and even exposing it to conquest by others. Likewise, leaders may take their countries into wars that may be winnable but are still costly and immoral. For MacIntyre's argument to work, he must show that the danger of people refusing to defend the community when it is actually threatened is greater than the danger that its rulers will take it into unnecessary and immoral wars. In a world in which war is commonplace and in which nuclear war could yield unprecedented destruction, it is not clear that the greatest threats to survival grow out of an excess of independent, critical judgment by individual citizens.

What if we were sure that political leaders would be extremely careful about entering into war and would do so only when it was morally or practically necessary? One could argue that if we were sure that the decision to go to war would always be taken responsibly, then unconditional willingness to serve would make sense. There are two problems with this argument. First, there is no reason to believe that this degree of wisdom and morality is always present in the decisions by leaders to go to war. Second, if it were, one's willingness to serve would not truly be unconditional. Rather, it would be conditioned on the understanding that political leaders will always act as wisely and morally as possible in making decisions about war and peace. This argument, then, does not justify unconditional willingness to serve. It justifies willingness to serve only on the condition that political leaders are so wise and morally conscientious that one could not improve on their moral judgment. This is, to say the least, a difficult condition to meet.

## JUDGING WARS

I have argued that willingness to fight in a war must be conditional on a judgment that the war itself is morally justified. This judgment in turn requires that we have some sense of how to go about evaluating war from a moral point of view. MacIntyre doubts the appropriateness of appealing to standards that are "neutral and impartial relative to the interests of . . . [one's] own community and the interests of other communities."[7] Nonetheless, such standards exist and are widely recognized. While the moral evaluation of war is a large topic, I will offer a brief sketch of a plausible view about it.

There are four types of views about the morality of war. One view, sometimes called "realism" or "realpolitik" is the idea that war is an amoral activity, something that nations do but that is beyond the scope of moral evaluation. Wars happen just as earthquakes and tidal waves happen, but, like these natural disasters, war cannot be judged from a moral perspective. Despite its apparent callousness, this approach often strikes people as sophisticated and realistic. It makes the moral judgment of war appear to be naive and inappropriate.

Whatever its initial appeal, this is not a plausible view. First, it ignores the crucial element of human decision, which is central to war but absent from natural disasters. Second, it is not a view that national leaders could express publicly. They work hard to cloak their activities in moral terms. Even if this is done cynically, it is evidence of the force of moral reasons in generating public support for war. Moral reasons have political force. Third, "realpolitik" makes no sense for citizens who are called to risk their lives for their country. They must have reason to believe that what they are doing is morally worthy. Classifying war as amoral would, in effect, deprive it of the justifications it needs to mobilize people's support. The attempt of the "realist" to denigrate the role of moral evaluation in this area is itself naive and unrealistic. It overlooks the fact that if enough people think a war is not worthwhile, then leaders will have a difficult time actually engaging in war.[8]

Among views that actually evaluate war morally, there are three possible approaches. The extreme militarist view is that war is always morally good. The extreme pacifist view is that war is always immoral. Neither of these views is widely held. Most people believe that war is sometimes justified, but they see it as a regrettable activity that is only justified by some form of necessity. Since absolute pacifism and extreme militarism are very much minority opinions, I shall not deal with them here and will focus on what I take to be the dominant view about the morality of war.[9]

The dominant moral view is that war should be neither totally approved nor totally condemned. According to this view, while war is a terrible activity, it may be morally permissible and even morally obligatory under very restricted conditions. This view is elaborated in the so-called "just war theory," which is an attempt to articulate the criteria by which wars may be evaluated.

There are two parts of just war theory, the *jus ad bellum* and the *jus in bello*. The *jus ad bellum* criteria set the standards that must be met to justify entry into a war, while the *jus in bello* criteria set the standards that govern the actual means of fighting of a war. A fully just war is one that is entered into under the right conditions and fought in the right way.

The following summary oversimplifies these requirements, but it will be sufficient for this discussion. According to the *jus ad bellum* criteria, one may engage in war if, first, one has a just cause, a serious enough, morally acceptable reason for doing so. Wars of aggression do not satisfy this requirement, while wars of self-defense do. Second, the war must be declared by a legitimate authority. Third, one must have the right intentions; that is, one must actually be motivated by such things as the desire to defend oneself or resist aggression. One cannot merely use these reasons as a cover for actions that have other aims. Fourth, entry into war must be a last resort. If there are other, peaceful ways of resolving a conflict, they must be tried first. War is justifiable only if all other options have been exhausted. Fifth, one must have a good chance of success. Finally, war must be a proportionate response. It would not be appropriate to go to war if the evil that the war will cause will be much greater than the evil that is being resisted.

These are the conditions that must be met to justify entry into a war. They are not the only conditions that need to be met, however. A country that has good grounds to enter a war may nonetheless act wrongly if it conducts the war in immoral ways. Even if one's cause is just, one's fighting may be immoral if it violates *jus in bello* (justice *in* war) constraints. In particular, while fighting a war, one must be discriminate, seeking only to kill and injure enemy soldiers and avoiding the intentional killing of civilians who are uninvolved in the fighting. Likewise, disabled soldiers and those that surrender must be well treated. Finally, the damage that one does in individual battles must be proportionate to the military value of winning that particular battle.[10]

This is not the place to elaborate or defend these requirements, but it is worth noting that they are widely accepted and are grounded in both ethical and religious beliefs, in military codes and traditions, and in international law. Even when political and military leaders feel free to violate them, they nonetheless pay "lip service" to these criteria and actively misrepresent facts to make it appear that they are adhering to them.[11]

## JUST WAR AND INDIVIDUAL RESPONSIBILITY

The just war criteria appear to have the form of necessary and sufficient conditions for engaging in war morally. That is, in order to fight a just war, one must satisfy both the *ad bellum* conditions for justified entry into a war and the *in bello* conditions for justified means of fighting. Failure to meet either test renders the war unjust.

What does this view imply for individual citizens who might be called to fight for their country? The most natural application of just war theory to individuals implies that individuals may only fight in a just war, a war that satisfies both the *ad bellum* and the *in bello* criteria. If a person's country enters a war unjustly or if, in the course of the war, immoral forms of fighting will be required, then morality does not permit participation in that war. Moreover, given the seriousness of the moral violations involved in immoral killing and injuring, it would be a person's moral duty to refuse military service. From this perspective, unconditional willingness to fight on one's country's behalf violates the moral duty individuals have to refrain from morally unjustified acts of killing and injuring.

While I find this the most natural way to understand the implications of the just war tradition for individual citizens, my interpretation differs from that of Michael Walzer, whose book *Just and Unjust Wars* contains an influential contemporary statement of just war thinking. Walzer appears to hold that the morality of a person's participation in a war is independent of the morality of the war itself. Moreover, he bases this view on his own interpretation of the just war criteria. If he is correct, unconditional willingness to fight for one's country is morally permissible and is sanctioned by just war theory itself. His argument, then, represents a serious challenge to my view that such participation is wrong and that willingness to serve in war should be conditional on the war's being just.

Walzer's view is that individuals are responsible only for the morality of their own actions in a war and not for the overall morality of the war itself. He writes:

> We draw a line between the war itself, for which soldiers are not responsible, and the conduct of the war, for which they are responsible,

at least within their own sphere of activity. . . . [B]y and large we don't blame a soldier . . . who fights for his own government. . . . We allow him to say what an English soldier says in Shakespeare's *Henry V*: "We know enough if we know we are the king's men. Our obedience to the king wipes the crime out of us.". . . . Not that his obedience can never be criminal; for when he violates the rules of war [i.e., the *in bello* criteria], superior orders is no defense. The atrocities that he commits are his own; the war is not.[12]

In this and other passages, Walzer suggests that it is morally right for individual citizens to fight for their country even if it is engaged in an unjust war. In order to act morally, they need only avoid violations of the rules of war, the *in bello* criteria. They are not responsible for whether the war satisfies the *ad bellum* criteria.

I believe that this view is too permissive. By sanctioning participation in unjust wars, it frees individuals from the duty to consider the morality of a war before supporting it by acts of killing and injuring. It is, in fact, a version of the view expressed by the slogan "My country, right or wrong," since it implies that whether one's country's cause is just or unjust is irrelevant to whether one ought to fight for it.

To anyone familiar with Walzer's writings, it will seem odd to attribute any version of this hyper-patriotic slogan to him. It is especially odd because later in his book Walzer explicitly says that citizens "cannot avoid" the pressing questions "should we support this war? should we fight in it?" (64).[13] Nonetheless, in the passage I have quoted, Walzer emphasizes the distinction between the two sets of just war criteria and claims that individual soldiers are responsible only for their own compliance with *jus in bello* rules and not for the war as a whole. For him, the *ad bellum* and *in bello* criteria represent a moral division of labor. The responsibility for judging the war as a whole belongs to political leaders and ordinary citizens but not with actual and potential soldiers. They need only worry about their own personal acts of war.

Given the moral seriousness of killing and injuring and the immorality of unjust wars themselves, there is a strong presumption in favor of the view that people have no right to fight in unjust wars and are morally blameworthy for the harms they inflict in the course of such wars, even if these harms are limited to the killing and injuring of enemy soldiers. Why does Walzer reject this? Why does he insist that soldiers on both sides of a war have an equal right to kill one another, even when those on one side are fighting a war of aggression, while those on the other are defending against attack?

One of Walzer's main arguments comes in the form of a reply to those who claim (as I have) that people ought not to serve "if they know the war to be unjust." Walzer answers that this knowledge is "hard to come by." Modern states, he says, give reasons for their wars and it

> takes courage to doubt these reasons. . . . [M]ost men will be persuaded to fight. Their routine habits of law-abidingness, their fear, their patriotism, their moral investment in the state, all favor that course. Or, alternatively they are so terribly young . . . that they can hardly be said to make a moral decision at all. (39–40)

In other passages, Walzer stresses the lack of individual volition involved in modern wars, contrasting modern soldiers, who do not choose to go to war, with the knights of old who did. Of the thousands who died in the battles of World War I, Walzer says that they died

> simply because they were available, their lives nationalized, as it were, by the modern state. They didn't choose to throw themselves at barbed wire and machine guns in fits of patriotic enthusiasm. (35)

He refers several times to participation in war as a form of "servitude" and stresses the idea that individuals are usually unable to resist military service.

There is certainly some truth in the points Walzer makes. Nonetheless, they do not undermine the view that people ought not to serve in unjust wars. A person may believe that service in unjust wars is morally wrong and still agree with Walzer that people who serve are not morally blameworthy if they have no way of knowing the war is unjust, if they are so habituated to obeying the law that they cannot violate it, or if they are so young that they cannot make an independent moral judgment. Facts like these may provide *excuses* for people who have fought wrongly, but they do not provide a *justification* for having done so. They do not show that citizens ought to fight for their country in an unjust war.

Throughout his discussion, Walzer overlooks both the distinction between justifications and excuses and the distinction between rights and duties. As a result, he does not differentiate between three different views. These are:

1. The "duty to fight" thesis: Citizens have a *duty* to fight for their country, even if it is engaged in an unjust war; i.e., it is morally wrong *not* to fight.

2. The "right to fight" thesis: Citizens have a *right* to fight for their country, even if it is engaged in an unjust war; i.e., it is morally *permissible* for them to fight.

3. The "no blame" thesis: Citizens who fight for their country are *not* morally *blameworthy*, even if it is engaged in an unjust war.

Since many of Walzer's statements are ambiguous, it is often hard to tell which thesis he is defending. He might be defending a duty to fight, a right to fight, or an excuse for those who fight on the wrong side. Or, he could be defending all of these views.

Walzer appears to reject the "duty to fight" thesis in a footnote late in his book. Speaking of people who refuse to serve in an unjust war, he says,

> They act very well if they refuse to fight, and we should honor those . . . who have the self-certainty and courage to stand against their fellows. (299n)

If those who refuse to fight are to be honored, then Walzer must not think that their refusal violates a duty to fight.

The same note provides evidence that Walzer holds both views 2 and 3, the "right to fight" thesis and the "no blame" thesis. After writing that we should honor people who refuse to fight in unjust wars, he adds: "That doesn't mean . . . the others [i.e., those who do fight] can be called criminals." As thesis 3 says, those who fight are not to be blamed for doing so. Finally, speaking of people who oppose a war because it is unjust, he says, "we should expect opponents of the war to refuse to become officers or officials, even if they feel bound to share combat risks with their countrymen" (300n). This final comment suggests that a sense of solidarity might lead one to fight in a war one disapproves. Walzer's apparent approval of this choice indicates that he holds view 2, the thesis that people have a right to fight for their country, even if it is on the wrong side of a war.

While Walzer wants to defend a right to fight in an unjust war, his argument fails to establish this conclusion. At most, Walzer's argument supports the third and most limited of the three views, "Citizens are not morally blameworthy for fighting for their country, even if it is engaged in an unjust war." It does nothing to justify thesis 2, "Citizens have a right to fight for their country, even if it is fighting an unjust war."

In fact, the argument fails even as a defense of thesis 3, the "no blame" thesis, since it provides a blanket denial of blameworthiness.

Even if one accepts Walzer's view that people are not blameworthy for immoral actions if they have no way of knowing that the actions are immoral or cannot avoid them, one might still insist that people are blameworthy for participating in war if they can know that the war is immoral and have the capacity not to serve. Walzer's argument provides no excuse for people in this position and hence no basis even for thesis 3, the most limited of his claims.

One part of Walzer's argument is especially odd, for he treats the fact that it "takes courage" to doubt the government's reasons for the war as a valid excuse. Later in his book, Walzer argues that the *in bello* rules require soldiers to accept increased risks to their own lives in order to avoid killing noncombatants (see 151–156). Surely, satisfying this rule requires considerable courage.[14] It is odd for Walzer to expect people to have the courage to risk their lives to uphold *jus in bello* rules, while he thinks it is too much to expect them to risk social disapproval in order to uphold the *jus ad bellum* criteria.

At best, then, Walzer's argument establishes that certain factors may excuse some people for participating in unjust wars. It does not show that such participation is a duty or a right. Nor does it show that fighting is always excusable. In saying this, I do not mean that all who fight should be considered war criminals. That kind of legal blame is different from the moral blame that I am discussing. My key point is that Walzer's argument fails to provide either a justification for serving in an unjust war or a blanket excuse for doing so. It does nothing to justify unconditional willingness to serve or to relieve people of the duty to consider the nature of the war they are being called on to fight.

## THE MORAL EQUALITY OF SOLDIERS

Let me now turn to a final argument that Walzer uses to support his view that soldiers may fight for their country in unjust wars. Walzer claims that whether they are on the right or the wrong side, soldiers on both sides of a conflict are "moral equals." Their moral equality implies that they have a right to kill one another, whether or not their country is in the right. In addition, it implies that neither has a right to engage in wanton killing of noncombatants, surrendered soldiers, and others who are not legitimate targets. Soldiers on both sides of a war, then, have an equal right to fight and an equal duty to observe constraints on the means of warfare. Just as soldiers whose country has a just cause may not violate the *in bello* rules of warfare, so soldiers whose country lacks a just cause nonetheless retain a right to fight.

We can strengthen Walzer's moral equality argument in the following way. If one denies that soldiers on the wrong side of a war have a right to kill other soldiers, this seems to imply that a person who finds himself in an unjust war is morally bound to permit himself to be killed. Morality, on this view, would require people who serve on the wrong side not to resist enemy attacks. As a moral requirement or a form of moral advice, this injunction to suicidal behavior is highly implausible. At the least, it seems, soldiers have a right to kill other soldiers. If the view that soldiers ought not to fight in unjust wars implies that they may not defend themselves in battle, that appears to be an absurd view.

In considering Walzer's appeal to the moral equality of soldiers, it is important to recall that we do differentiate among soldiers and do not always regard them as moral equals. While we may not usually view ordinary soldiers as war criminals, we do not regard those who fight unjustly in the same way as those who have fought against aggression. The dedication of Walzer's book honors those who fought *against* the Nazis. Not surprisingly, it does not include those who fought for Germany in World War II. But if honor is distributed differentially on the basis of the justice of one's cause, then surely soldiers on both sides of a struggle are not moral equals. Even if we believe that it is wrong to blame those who fight on the wrong side of a war, we do not think that one can justifiably be proud of such service.[15] Further, even if we do not blame people for such service, we would not regard shame or guilt as inappropriate responses to it. In fact, it would be hard not to think negatively of a person who had no qualms about having served in a cause that he now sees as unjust.

What about the argument that my view requires suicidal behavior by people in wartime by depriving them of a right to kill enemy soldiers? This objection is based on a misunderstanding. I do not deny that soldiers on the wrong side of a war have a right to kill enemy soldiers. This right, however, can be justified without appeal to Walzer's "moral equality" doctrine and his view that soldiers need not be consider whether their country is fighting justly or unjustly.

I suggest that while people who fight in an unjust war have no right to kill either noncombatants or enemy soldiers per se, they do have a right to defend their own lives. They are morally permitted to do that amount of killing necessary to survive. This derives from their own right of self-defense. Since noncombatants do not threaten, they may not be killed. Enemy soldiers do pose a threat, even if they are "innocent threats" who fight either involuntarily or justifiably.[16] Walzer is right that a soldier may kill enemy soldiers, even if his country is in the wrong. But this is only because soldiers have a personal right to defend themselves. Any killing that they do on behalf of the war effort itself, however, is morally wrong.

## SUMMING UP

Many people believe that patriotism requires unconditional willingness to fight for one's country in its wars. I have tried to show that this view is false. A patriot may be a pacifist, rejecting war altogether. Likewise, patriots who care about their country and are willing to make sacrifices on its behalf may nonetheless draw the line at supporting it in an unjust war. Countries ought not to fight unjust wars, and individuals ought not to fight in them. Patriotic people have both a right and a duty to judge their country's cause before supporting it in a war.

## NOTES

1. For expressions of the pacifist position, see Robert Holmes, *War and Morality* (Princeton: Princeton University Press, 1989); Staughton Lynd, ed., *Nonviolence in America: A Documentary History* (Indianapolis: Bobbs-Merrill, 1966); and John Yoder, *Nevertheless: The Varieties and Shortcomings of Religious Pacifism* (Scottsdale, Pa.: Herald Press, 1976).
2. "The Moral Equivalent of War," in *Memories and Studies* (London: Longmans, Green, 1911).
3. These laws were passed prior to World War II. I write in the past tense because they are not currently (1992) in effect.
4. For further discussion of this issue, see Kenneth Jensen and Kimber Schraub, eds., *Pacifism and Citizenship: Can They Coexist?* (Washington, D.C.: U.S. Institute of Peace, 1991).
5. The significance of the traditional exclusion of women from military service is insightfully explored by Jean Bethke Elshtain in *Women and War* (New York: Basic Books, 1987).
6. "Is Patriotism a Virtue?" 17.
7. "Is Patriotism a Virtue?" 17.
8. For more sustained critiques of realism see Michael Walzer, *Just and Unjust Wars* (New York: Basic Books, 1977); Robert Holmes, *War and Morality* (Princeton: Princeton University Press, 1989), ch. 2; and Marshall Cohen, "Moral Skepticism and International Relations," in Charles Beitz et al., eds., *International Ethics* (Princeton: Princeton University Press, 1985).
9. For a survey of various views, see Martin Ceadel, *Thinking About Peace and War* (Oxford: Oxford University Press, 1987).

10. For fuller accounts of the just war criteria, see William O'Brien, "Just-War Theory," in J. Sterba, ed., *The Ethics of War and Nuclear Deterrence* (Belmont, Calif.: Wadsworth, 1985), 30–44; and James Childress, "Just-War Theories: The Bases, Interrelations, Priorities, and Functions of Their Criteria," in M. Wakin, ed., *War, Morality, and the Military Profession*, 2nd ed. (Boulder, Colo.: Westview, 1986), 256–76.

11. Cf. Walzer on hypocrisy, *Just and Unjust Wars*, xv, 19–20.

12. Michael Walzer, *Just and Unjust Wars*, 38–39. Subsequent page references are in the text.

13. Likewise, his earlier book *Obligations* (New York: Simon and Schuster, 1971) presents and defends the views of anti-war dissenters.

14. In Tim O'Brien's novel about the Vietnam war, *Going After Cacciato* (New York: Dell Publishing, 1980), the soldiers are deeply resentful of an officer who forces them to search tunnels for civilians before destroying the tunnels. The burdens of complying with the *in bello* criteria are substantial.

15. Recall the controversy ignited by President Ronald Reagan's visit to the Bitburg Cemetery, a burial place for Germans who fought in World War II.

16. For a discussion and defense of the killing of innocent threats in wartime, see Lawrence Alexander, "Self-Defense and the Killing of Non-combatants: A Reply to Fullinwider," in Charles Beitz et al., eds., *International Ethics* (Princeton: Princeton University Press, 1985), 98–105.

# *12*

## Should Criticism Stop
## When the Shooting Starts?

The basic moral questions about the justification of war will always remain the same, since intentional killing and destruction are at the heart of war's nature. Nonetheless, these are not the only moral issues about war, and different wars raise distinct questions. During the Vietnam War, there was intense debate about both refusal to serve in the military and civil disobedience. There were good reasons why this occurred. With military conscription in effect, many people who opposed the war were eligible to be drafted for military service. When some refused induction, people debated whether they had a right to refuse or whether the government had a right to draft them in spite of their views. Some people claimed that exemption from military service should be extended to "selective conscientious objectors," people who did not reject all war but thought the one they were being called to serve in was immoral.[1]

Likewise, questions of civil disobedience arose because the war persisted in spite of widespread protests, and the government seemed unresponsive to the increasing opposition to the war. The lack of an anti-war candidate in the 1968 presidential election was the most powerful sign of the political system's lack of response. In this situation, some felt that illegal forms of protest were justified, while others thought that the constraints of the law remained morally binding on all citizens.

Neither of these issues arose with the same force during the 1991 war in the Persian Gulf. Because there was no military draft, there was no large pool of people who were faced with conscription into a war they opposed. There were some in the military who refused to

serve or filed for conscientious objector status. Doubtless many re-
servists and others who entered the military for economic or educa-
tional reasons were unhappy about the prospect of combat duty, but
their voluntary entry into the military made it more difficult for them
to object.

Likewise, while there were acts of civil disobedience, the war ended
rather quickly, leaving little time for widespread dissatisfaction with
it to grow. Moreover, the Congressional debate before the war provided at least the appearance of a responsive government. Opponents
of the war could hear members of Congress debate the wisdom of the
war and could see that there had at least been an opportunity to vote.
Due process seemed not to have been ignored as it had been during
the Vietnam War, and so the legitimacy of law was not called into
question in the same way.

## CRITICISM VS. SUPPORT

A question that arose with special force during the Gulf War concerned the duties of ordinary citizens who were not called for military service. Many of these citizens had opposed the war before it
began. Opinion polls just before the war showed the United States
about evenly split between people who favored going to war against
Iraq and those who opposed it. Those who opposed going to war were
faced with the problem of what to do when the shooting started.

There seemed to be three options for such people. They could offer
visible support for the war. They could remain silent. Or, they could
publicly dissent from the war policy.

Not surprisingly, those who dissented and continued to criticize the
war policy even after the war had begun provoked hostile reactions
from some war supporters. There seemed at times to be some effort to
prevent the extreme polarization that occurred during the Vietnam War.
Nonetheless, the war aroused strong feelings, and many expressed
doubts about whether it was right to criticize a war once the decision
to engage in it had been made. Many thought that people had a patriotic duty to offer moral support to the troops and to the war that they
were fighting. Some attacked protesters for their lack of patriotism.

Though the war is over, the question of what citizens should or
should not do in wartime remains with us. We continue to face the
question whether public opposition to a war is consistent with a patriotic regard for one's country.

I would like to approach these questions by considering two views that I heard during the war. I heard the first view from a former student who knew that I opposed the war. The student, who I knew to be a thoughtful, independent-minded person, told me that he believed strongly in the constitutional right of free expression and would oppose any legal penalties for speaking out against the war. Nonetheless, he strongly believed that once the war started, it was no longer morally right to criticize or protest. Citizens, he thought, have a moral duty to support their country in wartime.

A few days after the war ended, a colleague of mine expressed great bitterness toward those people who had opposed going to war but who supported the war once it began. This person condemned people who switched sides as cowardly and hypocritical. In his view, if they really thought the war was wrong, they should have held to their position once it started rather than leaping onto the bandwagon of support that quickly developed.

My own view differed from both of these. While I felt confident that it was legitimate to oppose the war even after it had begun, I did not feel contempt for people who switched sides after the shooting started. While some people, perhaps many, may have switched sides because they lacked principles, I suspected that many were motivated by feelings of genuine loyalty.

Were these people correct about what loyalty required? Or, were the protesters right in sticking to their position? What do citizens owe their country during wartime? Are we morally free to criticize it if we believe our country is in the wrong? Does loyalty to our country require that we stifle our doubts and support a war that we do not believe is right?

## THE CASE AGAINST SWITCHING SIDES

In trying to answer these questions, it is useful to look first at the criticism of people who had opposed going to war but switched sides when the war began. If we assume that moral consistency and acting on principle are important, we may be tempted to see these people as cowardly and hypocritical. If they believed before the war started that there were cogent moral reasons against going to war, then simple consistency required them to continue to criticize it. If, for example, someone opposed the war because it would result in widespread death and destruction, that expectation was not altered by the beginning of the very destruction that had been feared and opposed. It would be altered if the feared consequences failed to occur, but that change would not take place immediately and so would not justify switching sides as soon as the war started.

Likewise, if people opposed the war because they believed that economic sanctions provided an alternative, less violent means of forcing Iraq out of Kuwait and that the war was not a last resort, then the failure to go to war only as a last resort remained a failure once the war began. From this point of view, changing sides made no moral sense. The reasons for opposition to the war remained in effect even after the war began. For this reason, critics of those who switched sides do not see how switching could be morally justified or morally motivated.

Personally, I think it is a mistake to take a cynical view of all those who switched sides when the fighting started. The cynical reaction either overlooks or oversimplifies important issues about the ethics of criticism and the nature of citizenship. Before making a judgment, we need to consider what arguments could be offered for ceasing to protest once the shooting starts.

## THE CASE FOR SWITCHING SIDES

While the criticism of those who switched sides relies heavily on the ideal of moral consistency, one might argue that this criticism is too simple-minded. It assumes that if it is legitimate to criticize something at one moment, then it is legitimate to criticize it at the next. In fact, however, criticism is itself an action that can be right or wrong. Even if the content of a criticism is correct, facts about the context may make it inappropriate to voice the criticism. A familiar adage tells us that there is "a time and a place for everything." By implication, there are times and places when otherwise acceptable actions are inappropriate.

For example, suppose that someone has often voiced criticisms of a political leader and that these criticisms are true and justified. Nonetheless, if this person found herself at the politician's funeral, it would not be appropriate to voice these criticisms to the family of the deceased. Likewise, if someone is very ill or emotionally distraught, it would be wrong to criticize that person in ways that would be appropriate in other circumstances. While the truth of the criticisms is unchanged, the new circumstances make expressing those truths inappropriate.

So, context does matter when we judge whether the voicing of criticism is appropriate. Consistency neither requires us to express the same views in all situations nor justifies our doing so. Those who switched sides may have believed that the beginning of a war marks a shift to circumstances in which otherwise appropriate forms of dissent become inappropriate. While criticism of a proposed war is legitimate, criticism after the war starts is not.

A second argument can be used to strengthen this one. In many cases, the decision to adopt a policy by itself constitutes an important change in circumstances. Consider a case in which someone opposes the passage of a law. He may have many reasons for thinking the law to be a bad policy choice. Yet, once the law is enacted, all citizens have a duty to obey it, including people who opposed it before its passage. Their desire to be consistent with their prior opposition would not free them from that duty. In this case, then, the shift from deliberation about a proposed law to its enactment makes a significant difference to how one ought to behave. Prior objections do not justify disobedience.

Consider another example. Suppose that during the primary to select a party's candidate, a person supports candidate A, thinking A to be far superior to B. If the party selects B as its candidate, however, loyal party members are obligated to support B. Even though all the reasons why one had favored candidate A and opposed candidate B remain cogent, party loyalty requires that one now support B. From one perspective, one might think that nothing has changed, but from another, everything has.

According to this argument, a decision to go to war is like the enactment of a law or the selection of a candidate. People may work for any proposal or candidate they want, but when a decision has been made, they are duty-bound to go along with it. Further criticism is out of place. Likewise, loyal citizens may oppose a war before it begins, but once their country enters the war, they must support its war effort.

A third argument for supporting one's country in wartime is that this is simply one of the duties of citizenship, an implication of one's loyalty to one's own country. There is, of course, no specific list of duties that we have as citizens, but people might agree that certain activities are basic. Voting, paying taxes, and serving in the military if called are widely regarded as basic duties of citizenship.

Ordinarily, of course, citizens have a right to criticize government policies. This is part of the democratic process, and legally, we retain that right during wartime. Nonetheless, war is an extraordinary situation, and many of the ordinary rules of law and morality do not apply during wartime. Most importantly, during a war, people are permitted to kill, injure, and destroy in ways that are ordinarily forbidden. Likewise, people are required to risk death and injury in ways that they need not do in ordinary circumstances.

If war is a special set of circumstances in which different rules apply, then perhaps the ordinary rules that make criticism of government policy permissible are suspended or overridden by other rules that call for support of the country's war efforts. This is simply the appropriate behavior for a citizen at a time when fellow citizens are risking their lives. Prior opposition to entering into a war does nothing to absolve one from this duty.

A fourth argument begins with the idea that loyal citizens are people who always want their own country's well-being. In a war, the country's well-being consists of attaining victory. Those who oppose a war publicly make the attainment of such victory less likely and thus act in ways that are harmful to their country. Even worse, it is argued, to oppose the attainment of victory appears to indicate a desire for the victory of one's country's enemies. This desire is inconsistent with the loyalty and concern for one's own country that can legitimately be expected of citizens. Even citizens who opposed entering into a war have a duty to do what they can to ensure their own country's victory. Since continued criticism is an obstacle to victory, citizens have a duty to cease criticizing when the war begins.

These four arguments provide a respectable defense of those who switched from opposition to support once the war started. Together they defend those who switched sides from charges of cowardice and hypocrisy. If these arguments succeed, however, then I appear to have created a serious problem for myself, since I believe that continued opposition was the right response to the initiation of the Gulf War.[2] If these arguments show that those who switched sides did the right thing, it appears to follow that it was wrong to criticize the war after it began.

This conclusion, however, is mistaken. In putting forward a defense of people who switched sides, I am not claiming that switching sides was the *right* thing to do. I only want to say that if people were moved by the sorts of considerations I have described, then their decision to switch sides does not show them to be cowards or hypocrites. If they acted for reasons like those I have described, then their actions were motivated by moral values that are sufficiently plausible to shield them from charges of hypocrisy and cowardice.

This, at any rate, is my conclusion. The four arguments I have given, however, go further. They purport to show not simply that switching sides is a morally respectable option but that all citizens are morally required to support their country's military efforts during wartime. This is a conclusion that I do not accept, and I want to show why it is not justified. This requires taking a second look at the arguments for switching sides. When we see why they fail, we will better understand why criticism during wartime is morally justified.

## THE CASE FOR CONTINUED OPPOSITION

The first argument for switching sides is based on two correct points: criticism is itself an action that is subject to moral evaluation, and the context in which criticism occurs is relevant to evaluating its propriety.

These are important points, but they establish only a general need to consider the circumstances in which criticism is voiced. They say nothing about specific contexts. They tell us that there is "a time and a place for everything" without telling us anything about what times and places are appropriate for criticism. By itself, this argument is too general. It gives us no reason to believe that wartime is an inappropriate context for criticizing the conduct of a war.

The second argument moves toward a specific conclusion by describing actual cases in which opposition is appropriate before a decision is made but not afterwards. (These are the cases of a proposed law which is then enacted and a contest for choosing a party candidate.) In both cases, once the appropriate process is complete and the issue has been resolved, we expect people who had previously opposed it to accept the verdict. The argument draws an analogy between these cases and the situation in wartime. If we should "switch sides" and cease criticism after laws are passed and candidates chosen, then similarly we should switch sides and cease criticism after the decision to go to war is made.

While this argument has some force as a reply to charges of inconsistency and hypocrisy, it does not establish a duty to support a war one had opposed. Let me explain why.

First, in the case of an enacted law, while it is true that enactment is an important event that changes our duties, it is false that enactment rules out further criticism. Even if we have a duty to obey a law once it has been passed, we do not have a duty to refrain from criticizing it or seeking its repeal. If deciding to go to war is analogous to enacting a law, then continued opposition is quite in order because it aims for reconsideration and a repeal of the decision to engage in war.

Second, while the enactment of a law is important, it establishes at most a strong presumption in favor of obedience. Although civil disobedience remains a controversial and much-debated topic, it is hard to believe that there is an absolute duty to obey laws no matter what their content. Consider some familiar examples. No one would criticize the mother of Moses for failing to obey the Pharaoh's laws requiring the slaying of first-born children. Nor do people now criticize supporters of the "underground railroad" who worked to liberate slaves. If a law or policy is vile enough, disobedience is at least permissible and may be a duty. Even in the case of less vile policies, disobedience is often thought to be legitimate. The American colonists who participated in the Boston Tea Party are regarded as legendary heroes rather than villains and criminals, in spite of the fact that the tea tax they protested had been passed by parliamentary action.[3]

The idea that opposition to immoral laws may legitimately continue even after enactment is clearly relevant in this context. Initiating a war is an especially momentous kind of decision, and the awfulness of war's predictable consequences makes acceptance especially difficult. We can foresee that many people (possibly including one's friends and loved ones) will be killed and injured and that much destruction will be done. If a war is justified, these events are regrettable but necessary evils. If a war is not justified, however, if the cause is not sufficiently compelling or if alternatives to war exist, then the results of war are even greater moral and human horrors. The gravity of taking part in a war and the terrible evil of war's most direct consequences suggest that this is precisely the kind of case in which people ought not to accept a bad decision, even if it results from a legally authoritative process.

In fact, when we reflect on the horror of war's predictable consequences, we can appreciate more fully the force of the initial criticism of people who switched sides. If those people actually believed that the prospective war would be so dreadful, we might well wonder why they thought that an official decision to go to war should override their own judgment. If a law that required parents to kill their first-born children would be rejected because of its grave immorality, then one might wonder why those who believe a war to be gravely immoral would think that they have a duty to support it once it starts.

At the very least, one would think that the horrors of war would make it understandable why some citizens would feel a duty to continue their protest after the shooting starts. If one believes a war to be wrong, continued opposition appears to be the most natural and appropriate moral response. It is switching sides that begins to look like the morally questionable response.

The same point emerges if we reconsider the case of supporting a candidate whom one had opposed in the primaries. Ordinarily, party loyalty and a sense of the "rules of the game" yield a duty to support such a candidate. Nonetheless, there are limits to this duty, and if a winning candidate is bad enough, the duty to support him or her will be overridden by other duties.

Moreover, one of the strongest arguments against supporting a candidate is that he or she is likely to involve the country in immoral wars. While we might tolerate candidates whose views on policies differ from our own in many areas, disagreement on this sort of issue would make support very difficult. Again, the reason has to do with the nature of warfare and the extremity of the evils associated with it. It is hard to believe that party loyalty has sufficient moral weight to require supporting a candidate who would involve one's country in unnecessary wars.

At best, then, the examples of laws and party candidates support a presumptive duty to support a decision one had previously opposed. The argument fails to show, however, that this duty cannot be overridden by the stronger duty to oppose immoral or disastrous choices of laws, policies, or candidates.

The third argument for switching sides rested on the claim that supporting one's country in time of war is a central duty of citizens. This duty, it is argued, along with duties to vote, pay taxes, and obey laws, defines what the citizen's role is. If anything is a citizen's duty, an advocate of this argument might say, supporting one's country during war is.

This assertion is not really an argument at all. It is simply an emphatic statement of the opposing side. There is a disagreement about whether citizens have a duty to support their country in a war that they themselves had opposed, and this argument simply asserts that there is such a duty and that it is central to being a citizen.

Moreover, the assertion itself is weakened both by the amount of honest disagreement that exists on this question and by the vagueness that surrounds our conception of the duties of citizenship. It is worth noting, too, that while other acts such as voting, paying taxes, and obeying laws are often held up as obvious duties, there is widespread toleration of failure to vote, avoidance of taxes, and casual violations of laws (such as traffic laws, laws about reporting income, etc.).

Another problem with this claim is that it implies that pacifists could not be good citizens since they refuse to take part in wars and, presumably, refuse to give wars their verbal or political support. As I argued in the last chapter, this implication is false. It gains no support from an analysis of the nature of patriotism and is further weakened by the existence of laws that exempt religious pacifists from military service. The legal recognition of conscientious objection shows that opposition to war is compatible with full citizenship status.

The fourth argument for switching sides is that citizens should always support their country's good and that in wartime, the country's good is victory. Not to do so is, in effect, to support the victory of the country's enemies. Thus, people who support their country have a duty to support its victory in war.

While I suspect that something like this argument has a great deal of force in many people's thinking, it suffers from several serious flaws. First, even if one agrees that victory is in one's country's interests, one may believe that victory is impossible or that the costs of victory (human, moral, economic, or political) to the country itself make an end to war preferable to its continued pursuit. In these cases, it is precisely a concern for the well-being of one's own country that provides the motivation for opposition to a war.

Second, one cannot simply equate the good of one's country's with victory in war. A citizen might well believe that victory in a particular war will not make the country better off. A cessation of the war prior to further loss of life may be preferable even to military success.

Third, even if victory is both possible and in the national interest, the conduct of the war may still be wrong. Virtually everyone recognizes that there are moral limits to what a country may do in pursuit of its own interest. Someone might oppose a war even if it promises victory and benefits to the nation if engaging in the war violates important moral principles. After all, wars of aggression may well benefit the aggressor nation, but they need not be supported by citizens. Loyal citizens may well want their country to live up to high ideals and may oppose a war because it violates those ideals.

Many who opposed the Persian Gulf war did so because they thought it violated the principle that nations should go to war only as a last resort. Likewise, many opposed the war because they predicted that large-scale destruction would occur and that much of this destruction would be perpetrated by their own nation. Whatever the merits of these claims, they have nothing to do with supporting one's country's enemies. They grow out of a desire to see one's own country honor important moral constraints on the pursuit of national goals. These are not trivial ideals or principles, and it is hard to believe that people have a moral duty to turn their back on them simply because the decision to go to war has already been taken.

For all these reasons, people who morally opposed going to war had a right (and perhaps even a duty) to stick by that judgment. They did not have a duty to change their position simply because our political leaders had judged otherwise. Nor did they have a duty to remain silent. There is no duty to stop criticizing when the shooting starts.

## WAR AS A SPECIAL CIRCUMSTANCE

I believe, then, that criticism of a war policy does not become inappropriate simply because a decision is made to conduct the war. Nonetheless, when the Gulf War began, conscientious people did end up on different sides of the issue. In spite of their differences, there may be a common thread that links the beliefs of those who support and those who oppose criticism during wartime. The common thread is the idea that war is a special circumstance, that the moral rules that govern our actions in ordinary times do not apply in wartime.

Where war supporters and war critics disagree is on the proper response to the specialness of wartime. Those who support a war in spite of their qualms see war as a special circumstance that requires citizens to stand together in a time of need. Whatever doubts they may have, they believe that once the shooting starts, citizens must support their side. While debate and criticism are the life blood of democracy in ordinary times, they must give way to solidarity when the nation is engaged in war. Ordinary rights to criticize are overridden during the state of emergency that war brings with it.

War critics agree that wartime calls for special responses, but they differ about the nature of these responses. For them, whereas compliance and obedience to laws are ordinarily required of citizens, in war, the nature and results of the government policy are so dreadful that the ordinary presumptions toward obedience and public support are overridden. This explains why many felt the need to use their legal rights of protest and dissent and why some felt the need to engage in acts of civil disobedience.

## PATRIOTISM AND PROTEST

One might grant that protesting against a war one regards as wrong is legitimate but still think that it is incompatible with genuine patriotism. This idea receives some support from some remarks by

Bertrand Russell about his opposition to World War I. In his autobiography, Russell, who was a prominent opponent of the war, describes the conflict that he felt between his opposition to the war and his sense of patriotism. He writes:

> In the midst of this, I was myself tortured by patriotism. . . . Love of England is very nearly the strongest emotion I possess, and in appearing to set it aside at such a moment, I was making a very difficult renunciation. Nevertheless, I never had a moment's doubt as to what I must do. I have at times been paralyzed by scepticism, at time I have been cynical, at other times indifferent, but when the War came I felt as if I heard the voice of God. I knew that it was my business to protest, however futile protest might be. My whole nature was involved. As a lover of truth, the national propaganda of all the belligerent nations sickened me. As a lover of civilization, the return to barbarism appalled me. As a man of thwarted parental feeling, the massacre of the young wrung my heart. I hardly supposed that much good would come of opposing the War, but I felt that for the honour of human nature those who were not swept off their feet should show that they stood firm.[4]

There are many interesting points that could be made about this powerful description of what motivated Russell's anti-war activity. The question I want to raise is whether Russell, through his opposition to the war, was renouncing his patriotism.

The passage provides strong evidence that Russell saw his opposition in this way. He tells us that he was "tortured by patriotism," suggesting that he believed he had a patriotic duty to support England during the war. Moreover, when he gives his reasons for opposing the war, all of them have to do with personal and universal ideals. His opposition, he tells us, arose out of his conception of himself as a lover of truth and civilization. It arose out of his grief over the "massacre of the young." Finally, his protest was an effort to defend the honor of "human nature." All of these suggest that his patriotic commitment and his universal ideals were at war with one another and that his universal ideals carried the day.

This may be a true description of Russell. Nonetheless, I think he overstates the conflict between patriotism and universal ideals. Notice, for example, that the love of England that he describes as "very nearly the strongest emotion I possess" does not cease. He continues to love England. Moreover, while his talk of "making a very difficult renunciation" suggests that he was turning his back on England, this is preceded by the comment that he was only "appearing to set aside" his love of England.

Finally, while Russell implicitly contrasts his patriotic feelings with his commitments to ideals of truth, civilization and humanity, there is nothing that requires him to contrast these values in this way. Surely, as a lover of England, he wanted England to be a supporter and not a betrayer of his ideals of truth, civilization, and humanity. As a patriotic person, the betrayal of these ideals by his own country must have been especially painful to him. If this is so, then his opposition to the war was motivated both by his patriotism and by his universal ideals. The conflict existed not so much between his patriotism and his universalism as between his moral ideals and the conventional expectation that patriotic people will support their country's efforts in wartime.[5]

I would not criticize Russell or others for opposing war on the basis of strictly universalist ideals. The ideals Russell cites are worthy ones, and I have no desire to disparage them. Likewise, a person might justifiably subordinate his or her patriotism to these ideals in the way Russell suggests he did.

What I have argued, however, is that it is possible for opposition to war to be compatible with and even to derive from a person's patriotic feelings and commitments. While it is often assumed that patriotism and citizenship matter less to people who oppose their country's policy during war than to those who support it, there is no basis for this belief. The arguments that I have presented for opposing an ongoing war all grow out of a conception of citizenship itself. They are based in part on a concern that one's country act well. They grow out of the strong identification that people have with their country, an identification that leads them to feel pride when their country acts well and shame when it acts badly. Opposition to one's own country's war policies is compatible with and may be motivated by a deeply felt sense of patriotism.

## SUMMING UP

In this chapter, I have considered the question of whether citizens have a duty to support decisions to go to war that they personally disapprove. Some contend that there is such a duty, while others condemn such support as unprincipled. I have defended those who switch sides against charges of hypocrisy or cowardice. Nonetheless, I have argued, those who maintain their dissent have powerful arguments on their side and can legitimately claim both to be acted rightly and to be acting patriotically.

**NOTES**

1. For discussions of this issue, see James Finn, ed., *A Conflict of Loyalties: The Case for Selective Conscientious Objection* (New York: Pegasus, 1968).

2. For a retrospective debate on whether the Gulf War was a just war, see the essays in David DeCosse, ed., *But Was It Just?* (New York: Doubleday, 1992).

3. For classic defenses of disobedience to immoral laws, see H. D. Thoreau, "Civil Disobedience," in *Walden and Other Writings* (New York: Modern Library, 1937) and Martin Luther King, Jr., "Letter from Birmingham City Jail," in S. Lynd, ed., *Nonviolence in America: A Documentary History* (Indianapolis: Bobbs-Merrill, 1966). I discuss these issues in my *Should We Consent to be Governed?—A Short Introduction to Political Philosophy* (Belmont, Calif.: Wadsworth, 1992).

4. *The Autobiography of Bertrand Russell, 1914–44* (New York: Bantam Books, 1968).

5. For a vivid description of the difficulties in failing to meet the conventional expectations that one support a war, see Jane Addams's account of her opposition to World War I in "Personal Reactions During War," Staughton Lynd, ed., *Nonviolence in America: A Documentary History* (Indianapolis: Bobbs-Merrill, 1966), 178–91.

*Part IV*

# Challenges to
# Moderate Patriotism

# 13

# Patriotism and Global Injustice

Communities can only flourish if their members care about them and are willing to support them. One reason to defend patriotism is that it may motivate actions that promote the good of the national community. Without it, many people will be concerned only about their personal lives and will be less willing to share the burdens of social life. Without some commitment to patriotism or to other ideals that extend people's concerns into the public realm, it is hard to see how political democracy can survive or how the cause of economic and social justice can advance.

This is not to say that patriotism is sufficient to inspire civic action. One problem with the familiar type of patriotism in the United States is that its strong identification with military activity means that patriotic motivation can be aroused on behalf of war but not on behalf of domestic goals. Writing during World War I, Randolph Bourne noted that

> War . . . seems to achieve for a nation almost all that the most inflamed political idealist could desire. Citizens are no longer indifferent to the Government, but each cell of the body politic is brimming with life and activity. . . . In a nation at war, every citizen identifies himself with the whole, and feels immensely strengthened in that identification.

Bourne lamented the fact that a similar spirit could not be generated for constructive ideals and projects.

> Not for any religious impulse could the American nation have been expected to show such devotion *en masse*, such sacrifice and labor.

Certainly not for any secular good, such as universal education or the
subjugation of nature, would it have poured forth its treasure and its
life. . . . But for the sake of a war . . . , it would reach the highest
level ever known of collective effort.[1]

It was this contrast in citizen response that led Bourne to identify
patriotism with war and the state and to despair of its being mobi-
lized on behalf of the country and the well-being of its people.

Bourne's pessimism bears out the point that patriotism is not sufficient to stimulate support for improvements in the nation's domestic
life. It should not lead us, however, to think that patriotism is concerned exclusively with winning wars. If patriotism involves a concern for the well-being of one's country, then it should involve a desire
for improvements in its domestic life. It would be very strange to
consider a person genuinely patriotic if he or she does not care whether
the country flourishes economically, politically, culturally, or socially.
If there are people who are indifferent to every facet of their country's
life *except* its military strength and its success in war, we might suspect that their patriotism is not genuine. Real patriots will not value
war and victory for their own sake. They will only value them to the
extent that they are linked to the defense of the community and its
well-being.

There ought, therefore, to be carryover effects from patriotism to
civic pride and a desire for healthy, effective, and just institutions.
That these connections are often weak does not show that they must
be. In any case, even if patriotism is not sufficient for generating
concern about the well-being of the national community, it might still
be conducive to such concern. Without it, people may lack the social
concern required for sustaining the institutions of political and social
life.

## THE NEEDS OF STRANGERS

Patriotism broadens the range of our concerns. People who are
unknown to us become relevant by virtue of their being fellow citizens of our towns, cities, states, and nation. We come to think of
ourselves as sharing a certain fate with them, as part of a common
endeavor, even though we lack direct, personal connections to them.
Shared citizenship expands the scope of our concerns.

At the same time, however, it also narrows and restricts them. While
patriotism leads us to care about other members of our society, it also
tends to restrict our concerns to these people, cutting us off from other

people who may need our assistance and support. Because there are many millions of people in great need who are not our compatriots, some critics argue that it is wrong to give any special status to our fellow citizens. While patriots worry about the well-being of their own country and its citizens, it might be better if people who are well off worried about people in need, regardless of which nation they inhabit. Even if patriotism is legitimate in principle, they argue, it is not legitimate to prefer our fellow citizens if our own country possesses vast resources while others have too little to sustain a decent life.

This argument challenges the idea that patriotism should be encouraged at all. However necessary it may be to the well-being of particular communities, it may be wrong to encourage it if other "foreign" communities are very badly off. Why, one might ask, shouldn't one simply try to relieve the suffering of those in need? What difference does it make whether they are citizens of one country rather than another? Doesn't moderate patriotism share with extreme patriotism too great a preoccupation with the well-being of a particular community? Don't the pressing needs of people outside of our country show that we ought to abandon patriotism and embrace a "global humanist" perspective?[2]

One of the most forceful advocates of this global perspective is the philosopher Peter Singer.[3] Singer believes that citizens of affluent nations have a strong obligation to assist victims of famines and others who live in dire poverty. He cites former World Bank President Robert McNamara's description of "absolute poverty," a condition of life at "the very margin of existence." Absolute poverty is characterized by high infant mortality rates, low life expectancy, substandard nutrition, and insufficient food for children to permit normal growth and development. In the late 1970s the World Bank estimated that 800 million people, 40 percent of the population of developing nations, lived at this level.[4] At the same time, some citizens of developed countries live in a state of "absolute affluence," possessing both enough resources to meet their needs as well as a significant surplus for luxuries. Singer argues that this is a morally intolerable situation and that members of affluent societies ought to provide substantial assistance to those who lack what is needed for a minimally decent life. Singer sees this as a duty and not as a morally optional form of charity.

Singer defends his view with a simple, powerful argument. He begins with the uncontroversial assumption that "suffering and death from lack of food, shelter, and medical care are bad."[5] Second, he assumes that if it is in our power to prevent something bad from happening, without thereby sacrificing anything of comparable moral importance, we ought, morally, to do it.[6]

Singer illustrates this principle with an example. A person who is walking by a shallow pond and sees a child drowning in the pond has a moral duty to save the child. In Singer's example, there is no danger or difficulty in saving the child. One might, he says, get one's clothes muddy, but that is a trivial sacrifice to make in order to save a life.

From these apparently minimal assumptions, Singer derives a number of powerful conclusions. First, he claims, members of wealthy societies have a duty to save members of very poor societies in the same way that an individual would have a duty to save the child drowning in the pond. Why? Because it would be bad for these people to die or suffer and because members of wealthy societies have the ability to save them from death and suffering without sacrificing anything of comparable value. Thus, for example, relatively small monetary sacrifices, if made by all affluent people, would result in many lives being saved. By giving up some unnecessary luxuries, affluent people could provide food, medical care, and the means for producing food to people living at the absolute poverty level.

Singer notes that the level of assistance provided by governments of wealthy nations is extraordinarily low. Very few countries meet the goal of 0.7 percent of GNP that the United Nations has recommended as a reasonable target for assistance from rich to poor nations. In the absence of serious government efforts, Singer believes that individual citizens of wealthy nations should donate significant sums to Oxfam and other groups that provide assistance. While he sets a goal of 10 percent of income as a politically acceptable target for individual giving, he actually believes we ought to give much more. In fact, he believes that one ought to give whatever one has to others until the point where doing so harms oneself more than it helps the recipient. The result of doing this would be to reduce oneself nearly to the level of the absolutely poor because the benefits to them from our own sacrifices are so great.

## IS MEMBERSHIP A RELEVANT CHARACTERISTIC?

There are many challenging features to Singer's argument. Not the least of these is the high level of moral demand that it supports. Certainly commonsense morality is much less stringent. It allows us what James Fishkin calls a large "zone of indifference," a broad area of life that is free of moral demands and in which we may dispense our energy and resources as we wish. Commonsense morality also limits its demands, Fishkin says, by including a "cutoff for heroism."[7] In general, acting morally is not supposed to be extremely demanding and does not require heroic behavior. Singer, however, rejects these assumptions and argues that morality actually demands much more than we ordinarily demand of ourselves.

In considering Singer's argument, we need to ask why we think it wrong to allow the child (whom we can save) to drown in the pond when we do not think it wrong to permit children in far-off places (whom we can also save) to die from malnutrition and disease. Why is it that we think a person heartless and immoral if he passes the child and allows it to drown when we do not think people heartless and immoral when they spend money on luxuries instead of donating it to help those living in absolute poverty?

One difference is psychological. The child is right before our eyes, while the very poor are far away. Yet, as Singer argues, mere distance from a person is not a morally relevant feature. If I know that I can save someone, it does not matter whether the person is ten yards away or ten thousand miles away. Perhaps, as Singer says, distance was a morally relevant difference when communication was limited to one's immediate environment. In our high technology "global village," however, we can both know about and affect the lives of people at great distances from us. Distance by itself no longer either justifies or excuses inactivity.[8]

One might think that while mere physical distance is not morally important, the existence (or non-existence) of various special ties and relationships is significant. Indeed, moderate patriots are committed to this view, since they believe that it is morally permissible to devote more attention to our fellow citizens than to members of other societies.

Singer rejects this view and raises a serious challenge to moderate patriotism. Considering objections to his own extreme universalist position, he summarizes what he calls the "taking care of our own" argument. This is

> the argument that we should look after those near us, our families and then the poor in our own country, before we think about poverty in distant places.

He replies:

No doubt we do instinctively prefer to help those who are close to us. Few could stand by and watch a child drown; many can ignore a famine in Africa. But the question is not what we usually do, but what we ought to do, and it is difficult to see any sound moral justification for the view that distance, or community membership, makes a crucial difference to our obligations.[9]

Singer explicitly rejects "citizenship or nationhood" as an appropriate basis for determining which people we should try to benefit. He treats membership in a particular community as a morally arbitrary feature. The preference that people give to their fellow citizens, he says, is no more justified that the preference that racists give to members of their own race.[10] We may feel a greater obligation to help citizens of our own nation, but we do not actually have such an obligation. What we are morally bound to do is to help those in greatest need, and we must be prepared to reduce our own level of personal well-being substantially if that is necessary to provide minimally decent living conditions for all.

## ASSESSING SINGER'S CHALLENGE

Singer makes a powerful case for his view and deserves credit for putting the issue of world poverty on the philosophical agenda. Nonetheless, there are problems with his position. By calling into question our ordinary belief in the importance of special relationships, he must struggle against the power of a deeply entrenched feature of common sense morality. In addition, as he himself recognizes, the stringency of the duties he describes may actually diminish the force of what he has to say.

Singer weakens his case by posing the choices we must make in an extremely stark manner. According to him, we have only two choices. First, we can accept the idea that we have strong obligations to assist all people in dire need, while at the same time giving up the idea that we have special duties to family, friends, and fellow citizens. Or, second, we can insist that we do have special duties to those nearest and dearest to us and reject the view that we have any obligation to assist suffering strangers in faraway lands.

There are two serious problems with posing the choice in this way. First, as a practical argument for assistance to distant people, the argument is likely to backfire. Since almost no one is willing to renounce special duties to those near and dear, this argument is likely to make people reject the idea that we have genuine duties to distant strangers. As we saw earlier, the uncompromising universalist position is simply implausible. Special ties make up too much of what is central to life's value for us to forsake them. Without special ties, there is no love, intimacy, friendship, or personal trust, no community spirit or sense of solidarity. By linking his defense of a duty to assist the absolutely poor to an extreme universalist position that rejects all such special ties, Singer actually weakens his case for the duty to provide assistance.[11]

The second problem with Singer's argument is that it runs together two different defenses of the duty to aid the absolutely poor. One defense derives from extreme universalism, while the other is based on common sense morality. Singer unwittingly draws on common sense morality to support his view, while at the same time condemning common sense morality for its recognition of special duties and preferences. I believe that we can derive the duty to provide assistance to those in dire need from common sense morality itself. If we can do this, then we can recognize a duty to strangers without rejecting special ties to our family, friends, and nation.

Returning to Singer's arguments, I want to separate those that are based on extreme universalism from those that derive from common sense morality. I hope to show that we can make a better case for assistance to the absolutely poor on the basis of common sense morality than we can on the basis of extreme universalism.

The extreme universalist component of Singer's argument begins with the idea that everyone's interests should receive equal consideration. Whenever people act, they should perform the action that will create the best consequences for all. In doing so, they must treat everyone's interests as having the same significance. To take an earlier example, if I am about to buy an ice cream cone, I must (according to Singer's view) consider whether there is some better use to which I can put my money, and even if it turns out that buying ice cream is the best use, I must decide who would benefit most from it. If I had begun by wanting to purchase it for myself, I must consider whether someone else would enjoy it more. Or, if I had set out to buy it for my child, I must consider whether some other child would it enjoy it more.

This same kind of choice faces us with every decision and with every expenditure of resources (time, money, energy) at our disposal. Because others are in dire need and lack the necessities for a decent life, I must always use my resources to meet their needs because if I am not similarly needy, then my resources will do more good for them than for me. Hence, if I am well off, I must reduce my level of well-being substantially. Spending resources on myself is only legitimate if more good will come of it than if I spend it on others, and this will only occur when my level of well-being approaches theirs.

There is a possible exception. If I need a vacation to restore my energies to the point where I can do more good for others than I could if I don't take a vacation, then taking the vacation becomes justifiable. Apart from this type of situation, however, it would be wrong for me to spend my money on a vacation because the good it would produce is not morally comparable to the good of improving the lives of people at the absolute poverty level. This is Singer's radical universalist argument for the duty to assist others in great need, even at great cost to ourselves.

This argument is not without its power. After all, I and my family and my fellow citizens have no more intrinsic worth than faraway strangers.[12] Nonetheless, the argument leads to such demanding conclusions that it undermines itself as a practical argument. One might think that if morality really requires what Singer says, then only saints can be genuinely moral. Morality becomes a remote ideal rather than a guide for living. Singer acknowledges this problem when he asks "Might it not be counterproductive to demand so much?" He grants that it might be and concedes that if "we were to set a more realistic standard, people might make a genuine effort to reach it."[13]

## THE COMMONSENSE CASE FOR
## AIDING THE VERY POOR

Recall that Singer begins his argument with a simple example, the case of a child drowning in a shallow pool. Singer assumes that we would agree that a passerby would have a duty to save the child, even if this meant getting mud on his pants. Singer takes this case to illustrate a general assumption that we have a duty "to prevent something bad from happening" if we can do so "without thereby sacrificing anything of comparable moral importance."[14] Later, he uses this general assumption to undermine the morality of buying any luxuries for ourselves or people we love. Is this assumption as uncontroversially true as it seems to be?

I suspect that when we read Singer's assumption, we accept it because we mistakenly identify it with a different assumption that is part of commonsense morality. The commonsense assumption is that we ought to prevent serious evils if we can do so at little risk or sacrifice to ourselves. In Singer's example, the pond is shallow, we can save the child without endangering ourselves, and muddying one's pants is a trivial harm to oneself. These features of the example encourage us to equate Singer's assumption with the commonsense principle that we have a duty to prevent serious harm to others when doing so will not seriously jeopardize our own well-being.

In fact, Singer's principle differs significantly from moral common sense. Singer's assumption generates unlimited obligations that far exceed what we normally think is required of us. The commonsense assumption, while including a demand that we assist others in need, limits the amount of sacrifice required of us. It does not threaten to overwhelm us as Singer's principle does.

Nonetheless, the commonsense principle is not trivial, and it can be extended in significant ways. Suppose that in saving the child, it is not my pants that will be muddied but my child's pants. In this case, the ill effects fall upon my child rather than myself. Even though I have special duties to my child, this slight harm should not stop me from saving the drowning child. We can generalize, then, and say that I ought to prevent serious harms to others even if I or people I have special ties to will suffer some trivial harm as a result.

From this, we can move to the conclusion that Singer wants to establish about a duty to assist people living in absolute poverty. If I am sufficiently well off that contributions to assist those in need will not seriously diminish my own well-being or that of people I have special ties to, then I am morally obligated to make such contributions. More generally, anyone in this position has a duty to assist people living in absolute poverty.

Here, then, is an alternative argument for the duty to aid the very poor. Unlike the first argument, however, it does not appeal to radical universalist premises and does not reject the legitimacy of special concern for oneself and others that one is specially attached to. Moreover, by not requiring total impartiality, it does not have the extreme implication that I must spend myself down into poverty. For this reason, it does not violate Fishkin's "cutoff for heroism." Nor does it undermine a "robust zone of indifference," since many areas of life remain my discretionary domain.

I suspect that many people are influenced by Singer's overall argument because of the way that commonsense assumptions are woven into it. They reject Singer's view, however, when it becomes clear that it departs radically from commonsense morality. Common sense reasserts itself when Singer lowers the sacrifice requirement down to 10 percent of one's income. This is more plausible than his demand for extreme sacrifices because it is consistent with the principle that we should aid others when doing so does not jeopardize our well-being seriously. Ten percent of income is not a trivial sacrifice, but, unlike Singer's more extreme view, it is at least limited. It still leaves the greater part of our resources at our discretion, allowing us to use them for ourselves and people we care about. Hence, it is a more plausible requirement.

Singer also unwittingly appeals to commonsense morality in answering the objection that his view requires parents to give away their last bit of food while their own children starve. Singer's answer is that

> we are not faced with that situation, but with one in which our own children are well-fed, well-clothed, well-educated, and would now like new bikes, a stereo set, or their own car. In these circumstances any special obligations we might have to our children have been fulfilled, and the needs of strangers make a stronger claim upon us.[15]

Notice that Singer's answer does not depend on rejecting special duties. The idea is not that our children should count no more to us than strangers but rather that our children are already well provided for. In this case, our special duties to our own children are already fulfilled. We can, therefore, assist others without violating or rejecting the special duties we have to our own children. Here again, Singer's case gains plausibility when he departs from extreme universalism and appeals to moral common sense.

Most important, from the point of view of my defense of moderate patriotism, we can grant Singer's plausible claim that there is a duty to assist people living in dire poverty without rejecting the claim that special preferences for our own community are legitimate. We do have a duty to help others when they are in dire conditions and when our own community is sufficiently well off that it will not be seriously harmed by the diversion of our resources to others. We can recognize an obligation to distant strangers without rejecting the special duties we have to people close to us and to groups of which we are members.

## THE STRUCTURE OF COMMONSENSE MORALITY

One of the lessons of Singer's essay is that the description of commonsense morality I gave in chapter 4 needs to be supplemented. I argued that commonsense morality has a certain structure. While permitting wide latitude in our choice of goals, it imposes constraints on what we may do in pursuing our goals. The constraints I mentioned earlier are all negative. They require that we *not* kill, *not* injure, and *not* harm people except in certain exceptional cases (e.g., killing or injuring in defense of our own or other people's lives). In ordinary circumstances, we may not advance our own good by harming others.

Among the personal goals most of us have are certain other-directed aims. We want to promote the good of specific individuals and groups to whom we are especially attached. Morality permits us to act on their behalf so long as we honor these constraints. In addition to other-directed personal goals, we may have special duties to tend to the well-being of particular individuals or groups. In such cases, morality recognizes genuine obligations to specific people.

What Singer's essay makes clear is that commonsense morality sometimes requires *positive* actions on behalf of people to whom we have no special ties. That the child drowning in the pool is a total stranger does not alter the duty one has to save it. In this case, its humanity is sufficient. But, how does this duty fit in with the structure of commonsense morality?

We can interpret it in a variety of ways, but I think it is helpful to assimilate it to the idea of constraints on the pursuit of our personal goals. Morality, as I have said, allows us to pursue our own goals, but in doing so, we must be mindful of the effects of our pursuit on others. We need to be aware of the context in which we live and act, and this means that we cannot ignore strangers entirely.

In Singer's example, the person passing the pond is on his way somewhere. He is pursuing the private goal of arriving at a destination. This is a legitimate goal. Moreover, it does not require him to violate moral rules against killing and injuring others. Nonetheless, he suddenly finds himself in a situation where continued pursuit of this goal would result in the death of a child.

In this context, he is required to depart from his goal in order to save the child. Morality places an additional constraint on his action by forbidding him to pursue his goal as if there were no child drowning nearby. It forbids him to ignore the child when he knows that doing so will result in a serious evil, even though the evil (the drowning) is not something he intentionally sought. Put simply, it is wrong to go about one's business in the usual way when a child whom one can easily save is drowning.[16]

Similarly, well-off people in affluent countries are morally permitted to go about their own business, pursuing their own goals and devoting their energies to individuals and groups that they care about. Nonetheless, as Singer rightly claims, it is wrong for such people to continue going about their business when they know that they can provide substantial assistance to people in absolute poverty at little sacrifice to themselves.

This claim is more controversial than the comparable claim about the child in the pool. Nonetheless, I believe Singer is right that the duty to assist extends beyond people in our immediate environment. This idea, however, may seem like a departure from common sense morality rather than an extension of it. This is, as Singer rightly suggests, because human beings have not until recently been in a position either to know about the plight of distant people or to assist them. Changes in communication, transportation, and organizational capacities now make it possible for us to assist others whom we could not have assisted in earlier eras. The scope of our experiential environment has altered and is no longer limited by the natural range of our powers of seeing and hearing. Likewise, our ability to affect events is no longer limited by the location of our bodies. We are now able to know about and assist people who are far away but who are the moral equivalent of children drowning in nearby pools. The expansion of our knowledge and our ability to affect distant people brings with it an expansion of our moral duties.

One might challenge this claim by appealing to libertarian arguments that morality requires only that we honor negative constraints that forbid harming others. According to this view, we have a duty not to harm others but no general duty to help them. Libertarians reject the idea that there is a duty to offer assistance to anyone, including our fellow citizens. Since they deny that we have a duty to provide assistance to the needy of our own society, they would certainly reject Singer's more sweeping claim that we have a duty to help people in other countries.

I cannot mount a full-scale argument against this view here.[17] It is worth noting, however, that Robert Nozick, one of libertarianism's most prominent defenders, appears to accept the view that constraints on action may be altered by the circumstances of others. I have argued that while morality allows us to pursue our own goals as long as we do not harm others, it nonetheless requires that we depart from pursuing our goals if we can do so at little sacrifice and our doing so is necessary to prevent severe harm to others. Nozick, though he insists that morality consists mainly of negative duties, appears to agree. Discussing what he calls the "Lockean Proviso," Nozick tells us that property rights are limited by the circumstances of others. In his view,

> a person may not appropriate the only water hole in a desert and charge what he will. Nor may he charge what he will if he possesses one, and

unfortunately it happens that all the water holes in the desert dry up, except for his. . . . Similarly, an owner's property right in the only island in an area does not allow him to order a castaway from a shipwreck off his island as a trespasser. . . .[18]

Nozick concedes that morality does not always permit us to go about our business as if what happens around us does not matter. The right to tend to our own business is limited by changes in the circumstances of others. Conceding this, however, requires a rejection of the libertarian view that there is no duty to assist others. Just as we may not use our water hole for ourselves alone when the water supply of others has dried up, so we may not devote all our resources to ourselves and those we care about when the pool of resources required for a decent life is unavailable to distant strangers and when our sharing these resources can be done with little sacrifice to ourselves.[19]

Sometimes, situations simply demand our attention, even though we had nothing to do with bringing them about. We can see this in the expression "fiddling while Rome burns." While there is nothing wrong with fiddling, if a person playing the violin learns that Rome is burning and can do something to stop the fire, he or she has a duty to put aside this personal pursuit and try to prevent Rome from burning. The assumption that this is required is a part of moral common sense, not a departure from it.

## THE DUTIES OF AFFLUENT NATIONS

Singer focuses his attention on the duties of individuals. While he favors assistance by governments, he stresses the duties of individuals in situations where governments fail provide the needed aid. While I do not want to absolve individuals of responsibility, I think it is important to focus on what government institutions should do both to provide emergency relief and to help people develop the resources to care for themselves.[20]

But, one might ask, what has this got to do with patriotism? Doesn't the motivation to provide such assistance arise from global humanist concerns and not from patriotism? Don't patriots (even moderate patriots) have a special concern for their own country? Don't they want their own country to be as well off as possible? Finally, shouldn't patriots give highest priority to citizens of their own countries rather than to distant people?

Let me begin with the last of these points. People often say that it is wrong to provide food to the hungry in other lands when our own citizens go hungry. I think this is a reasonable objection, even though (as Singer notes) the degree of misery among those in absolute poverty is generally much greater than the misery of the poor in affluent nations. The proper reply to this objection is first to grant that it is wrong for us to allow our own citizens to live without adequate food, shelter, medical care, etc., and then to insist that we strive to improve their lot. Too often, the "let's not help others until we have helped our own" objection is followed by inaction and passivity on the home front. It is an excuse for doing nothing rather than a plea for setting priorities in the aid we give. The result is that neither the distant poor nor those close by are helped. Instead, poverty and the misery it produces are simply accepted as part of the human condition, and serious efforts to help those in need are put off indefinitely.

People who advance this objection sincerely must be willing to back it up with action. They should be concerned enough to do away with the misery of "relative" poverty among our own citizens so that we can then move on to the deeper misery of absolute poverty in other places. Priority for our own is not a permanent excuse for doing nothing for others.

But why should patriots care about people in other countries? The basic reason is that all of us are human beings, capable of suffering and capable of leading meaningful lives. The fact that the world is organized into countries does not alter the basic fact of our common humanity. Even if we want our own country to flourish, we need not want it to flourish at the expense of others. Nor does patriotism require us to want our country to be, for example, the most wealthy nation possible. Patriots may want their country to be morally good as well as wealthy or powerful. If patriots identify with their countries and if this identification is to be a source of pride, then patriotism may provide a motivation for wanting the country to share its wealth with less fortunate nations. Patriots may even believe that the country is only worthy of affection if it devotes itself to things other than the pursuit of its own wealth and power.

Taking a personal example may illustrate this. Parents certainly do not want their children to be impoverished. They want them to have sufficient resources to live a good life. Once this level is reached, however, parents will not necessarily want their children to acquire more and more material wealth. Indeed, if children are wealthy and use all of their wealth for personal self-indulgence, parents may come to feel ashamed of them. If the children use their large financial holdings for additional luxuries and never contribute to those in need, a parent might even regret the extraordinary financial success of the child because of its morally corrupting influence.

In the same way, many patriotic people do not like to think of their country as self-indulgent and callous toward the needs of others. They want their country to be committed to valuable, humanitarian goals that show it to be good as well as wealthy, compassionate as well as powerful. They want a country that is worthy of their own love and devotion. The mere accumulation of greater wealth or power beyond a certain point does not contribute to the goodness of the country. For that reason, just as we want ourselves and our children both to prosper and to live morally decent lives, so patriots will want their countries to live morally decent lives. To do so, wealthy nations must be attentive to the needs of other nations and peoples.

A morally worthy nation will honor the constraints of morality both by avoiding unnecessary wars and also by assisting people in other countries when this can be done without great sacrifice to its own people. Both sorts of actions are required by the constraints that morality imposes on how we pursue our own goals.

## HOW MUCH SACRIFICE?

In talking about government-sponsored programs of assistance to people living in absolute poverty, it is important not to gloss over the fact that such assistance is paid for by taxes collected from individuals. The cumulative amount of taxes collected may indeed represent a burden to many individuals. While I have stressed the common sense moral principle that we are required to assist people in need when we can do so at little risk or sacrifice, one might think that any meaningful assistance to others will require a larger sacrifice than morality demands. According to this argument, whether we think of sacrifice either individually or collectively, helping the world's very poor is simply too burdensome. It is more than morality requires, and a nation need not engage in such activity in order to be worthy of its people's loyalty or affection.

This objection raises many large issues, both moral and factual. I can only deal with them briefly.

A first question is how much of a nation's resources should be used for assistance to people outside the country. The U.N. target for development assistance is 0.7 percent of the gross national product. In the period from 1962 to 1975, U.S. foreign aid ranged from a high of 0.59 percent of GNP in 1963 to a low of 0.23 percent of GNP in 1973. Because most of us are not economists, we have difficulty interpreting such numbers. Nonetheless, we can get an idea of whether this was excessively burdensome by comparing it with contributions by other countries. Australian aid during the same period was never lower than 0.43 percent and was as high as 0.61 percent. Portugal, a rather poor country, ranged from 0.54 per cent to a high of 1.91 percent.[21]

This appears to indicate that levels approaching the U.N. goal are achievable. The U.N. goal is not merely utopian. Nor is it as demanding as Singer's goal for individuals. By setting the goal at under 1 percent of GNP, it does not require countries to significantly lower their well-being in order to provide assistance.

A second question concerns the morality of assistance. I have argued from a minimal moral requirement, in contrast to Singer's much stronger demand. I have claimed that morality requires that we assist others when we can do so at little risk or sacrifice. Even doing this, I think, would lead to a considerable increase in our aid to the distant poor. Nonetheless, a moral case can be made for more substantial assistance.

Consider the case of the drowning child again. If the child had been drowning in a stormy ocean and the passerby were a poor swimmer, there would be no obligation to risk his life for the child. To do so would be heroic, and we do not require that of people. Nonetheless, there are many intermediate cases. What if one's suit were to be ruined rather than merely muddied? Surely the life of a child outweighs the value of the suit. Suppose that one had to risk breaking a finger in order to save the child. This too would be a reasonable sacrifice to expect of a person in order to save a child.

If this is correct, then morality may demand more than the ultra-minimal kind of sacrifice I have assumed for much of this discussion. I do not know where the cutoff point is and will not try to discover it. Nonetheless, I want to suggest that more than minimal sacrifices may be called for in order to prevent grave enough evils.[22]

While this may appear as a controversial claim when approached from a discussion of aid to the world's needy, notice that patriots commonly assume that we are morally obligated to make large sacrifices to achieve our nation's goals. Those who believe in a duty to fight for one's country in a war certainly accept a very burdensome moral obligation. One has a duty, according to this view, to sacrifice substantial amounts of time and energy that could have been devoted to personal pursuits, to endure long separation from persons one loves, to accept physical hardship, to engage in brutal and horrifying battles, and to risk pain, injury, permanent disability, and death. Moreover, these sacrifices are not limited to occasions when the country's well-being or security is immediately in danger. They are often required in the service of high ideals: making the world safe for democracy, ending war, etc. Or, they are required simply to carry out the country's policies, even when its security is not threatened, as was the case in Panama in 1990 or in the 1991 Persian Gulf War.

If we take military service as our model, we might conclude that if there is a worthy enough goal, citizens and nations may be obligated to make very great sacrifices to achieve it. The level of minimal sacrifice I have assumed actually underestimates the ordinary view of the sacrifices that may legitimately be expected of people.

It would be worth comparing the goal of abolishing absolute poverty with the goals for which wars are often fought. When wars occur, great sacrifices are made for sometimes questionable goals. The value of sparing human beings from preventable hunger and preventable disease is both greater and more evident than the questionable political goals for which nations frequently expend their resources and the lives of their citizens.

Finally, one could argue that we already do make substantial sacrifices, even apart from wartime. After all, citizens already pay substantial amounts of tax money to support government programs. This is correct, and it suggests that much more effective government-sponsored assistance is possible without substantial increase in levels of taxation. One of the key problems is that such a large portion of the financial sacrifices of citizens has been devoted to military spending. According to Ruth Sivard, if world military budgets were decreased by only 5 percent, that would free $50 billion per year, enough money to make substantial progress in supplying clean water to the one-third of the world's population that lacks it, in providing improved sanitation for the one half of the world's population that lacks it, in dispensing immunizations that would save the lives of millions of children each year, and in conducting many other programs that could help the world's people.[23]

By itself, the United States could do many things at a similar scale. Since 1983, $24 billion has been spent on the Star Wars program alone, a project that most knowledgeable scientists saw as doomed to failure from the start. Hundreds of billions of dollars have been spent to develop, deploy, and improve weapons that go well beyond the legitimate requirements of national defense. While these vast sums have required substantial sacrifices by citizens, few have objected to them or thought the demands too great.

One might think that there is a crucial distinction between sacrifices made for the defense of the nation and sacrifices made to help those in need. Usually, we classify one as a necessity and the other as

charity. Ostensibly, however, this money has been spent not simply to
protect the nation and its well-being but also because of our commitment to moral ideals of freedom, individual dignity, democracy, etc.
It is hard to believe that we could not advance these ideals better by
making a serious effort to assist the world's poor. That we do not do
so is not a function of lack of ability. It is a function of our narrow
vision and restricted understanding of our own needs, goals, and ideals. We have allowed our concern for our country and its ideals to be
dominated by conceptions of military security and military strength.
If we can free ourselves of these distortions, we can use the wealth of
our nation to improve the lives both of our own people and of needy
people in other lands.

Setting such goals for ourselves and moving toward them would
make many people proud of their country. Just as, in a small way, the
formation of the Peace Corps enabled people to think of our country
acting in a positive and constructive way in accord with our highest
values, so would a redirection of our priorities give patriotic people
something to be genuinely proud of.

## SUMMING UP

In this chapter, I have argued that morality requires individuals and
nations to assist people in dire need, whether they are our own citizens or inhabitants of other countries. Unlike Singer, I believe that
the duty to provide assistance to strangers can be defended without
rejecting special duties to our own families, friends, and country.
Special duties to some do not require indifference to others. The constraints of morality require that while we pursue our own good and
the good of people to whom we have special ties, we need to be aware
of the circumstances of strangers and willing to assist them if their
basic needs go unmet while many of us have access to luxuries.

While I stressed that we can do much good while making minimal
sacrifices, patriotism has often sanctioned the demand for substantial
sacrifices, not only to defend the nation but also to promote its ideals. If a nation has humanitarian ideals, it may be reasonable to require more than minimal sacrifices to assist citizens of other countries as well as our own. Moreover, much of this could be achieved
without additional burdens because we already make substantial sacrifices to support the development of needless and destructive weapons. A redirection of resources, rather than an adding to our burden,
would bring our nation's practices closer to the ideals it espouses and
make it an appropriate object of pride.

## NOTES

1. "The State," in *War and the Intellectuals*, 71–72.

2. For a defense of a global humanist foreign policy, see Robert Johansen, *The National Interest and the Human Interest* (Princeton: Princeton University Press, 1980).

3. For Singer's views, see his essay, "Famine, Affluence, and Morality," and his book *Practical Ethics* (Cambridge: Cambridge University Press, 1979), ch. 8. Singer's essay first appeared in *Philosophy and Public Affairs* 1 (1972), 229–43. Page references here are to the reprinted version in Charles Beitz et al., eds., *International Ethics* (Princeton: Princeton University Press, 1985).

4. Cited in Singer, *Practical Ethics*, 159. For more recent statistics, see Ruth Leger Sivard, *World Military and Social Expenditures 1989* (Washington, D.C.: World Priorities, 1989), 24–35.

5. "Famine," 249.

6. Ibid.

7. *The Limits of Obligation* (New Haven: Yale University Press, 1982), 14–24.

8. On distance, see Singer, "Famine," 249–50.

9. *Practical Ethics*, 171.

10. For a similar claim, see Paul Gomberg, "Patriotism is Like Racism," *Ethics* 99 (1989), 535–52. For a defense of the relevance of group membership, see Michael Walzer, *Spheres of Justice* (New York: Basic Books, 1983), chs. 3, 4.

11. For a different, more elaborate justification of special duties, see Frank Jackson, "Decision-theoretic Consequentialism and the Nearest and Dearest Objection," *Ethics* 101 (1991), 461–82.

12. This point is stressed by Thomas Nagel in *Equality and Partiality* (New York: Oxford University Press, 1991), 11. Nagel's book provides an excellent discussion of the ethical and political problems that arise from our being able to view the world from both an impersonal and a personal standpoint.

13. *Practical Ethics*, 180–81.

14. Ibid.

15. *Practical Ethics*, 172.

16. On the duty to help those in distress within one's immediate environment, see Bernard Gert, *Morality* (New York: Oxford University, 1988), 154–57. For an extended discussion and a defense of "good samaritan" duties, see Joel Feinberg, *Harm to Others* (New York: Oxford University Press, 1984), ch. 4.

17. I offer a brief critique of libertarianism in my *Should We Consent to be Governed?* (Belmont, Calif.: Wadsworth, 1991), ch. 7.

18. *Anarchy, State, and Utopia* (New York: Basic Books, 1973), 180.

19. Norman Care invokes a similar idea in his challenging essay "Career Choice," *Ethics* 94 (1984) and in his book *Sharing Fate* (Philadelphia: Temple University Press, 1987).

20. For an excellent discussion of the role of government policy in this area, see Henry Shue, *Basic Rights: Subsistence, Affluence, and U.S. Foreign Policy* (Princeton: Princeton University Press, 1980). Robert Johansen analyzes actual foreign aid practices and goals in *The National Interest and the Human Interest* (Princeton: Princeton University Press, 1980), ch. 3.

21. Johansen, *The National Interest and the Human Interest*, 170.

22. For insightful discussions of related issues, see Lawrence Blum, "Moral Exemplars: Reflections on Schindler, the Trocmes, and Others," *Midwest Studies in Philosophy* XIII, 1988; and "Community and Virtue," in Roger Crisp, ed., *How Should One Live?* (Oxford: Oxford University Press, forthcoming).

23. *World Military and Social Expenditures 1989.* (Washington, D.C.: World Priorities, 1989), 43.

# *14*

# Patriotism and Nationalism

Patriots, even moderate patriots, have a special regard for their own country. It stands out from the many nations of the world as the one to which they are most attached, the nation they identify with and whose well-being they have a special interest in pursuing. Because patriotism gives a special value to one's nation, it seems natural to equate patriotism and nationalism.

In spite of the apparent logic of this conclusion, people often seem to regard patriotism and nationalism as quite different. While most people view patriotism as a positive trait, nationalism is often regarded with fear and suspicion. While patriotism seems to involve a proper affection for one's country, nationalism seems aggressive and belligerent. This raises a problem for defenders of patriotism. If patriotism is the same as nationalism and if nationalism is a dangerous, unworthy ideal, then patriotism is likewise dangerous and unworthy. Whatever reasons one has for rejecting nationalism would carry over to patriotism as well.

One way to defend patriotism would be to concede that nationalism is undesirable but to refuse to equate the two. If they are different, then we can reject nationalism while retaining patriotism. A second possibility is to concede that patriotism and nationalism are the same and to argue that nationalism, in spite of its bad associations, is itself a legitimate ideal. If nationalism is legitimate, we can admit that patriotism is a form of nationalism without having to reject it for that reason.

I will adopt a third approach and will argue that just as there are different kinds of patriotism that we must differentiate and evaluate separately, so too, there are different forms of nationalism that must be differentiated and evaluated separately. Because the word "nationalism" has several distinct meanings, there is no single thing that is nationalism. Therefore, we need to look at some of the many things people mean by "nationalism." When we have done this, we can decide which elements of nationalism may be embraced by moderate patriots and which should be shunned.

## FALSE DISTINCTIONS

Ordinary use of the terms "patriotism" and "nationalism" seems to rest on two illegitimate contrasts. There is a tendency to regard the national feeling for one's own society as a good, healthy, and constructive attitude, while at the same time regarding the national feeling of other countries as threatening, unhealthy, and destructive. This way of thinking is based on two biases: a radical distinction between "us" and "them" and an unwarranted assumption that our national spirit is good while that of other groups is bad.

These assumptions may be biased and subjective, but they are understandable. If the nationalism of other people leads them to assert their rights and interests, we may feel threatened by it. Expressions of foreign nationalism strike us as aggressive and hostile. Assertions of our own national rights and interests, however, appear as nothing more than a legitimate form of sticking up for ourselves. It is no wonder that we feel reassured by our own nationalism, which we ennoble with the term "patriotism," while feeling fearful and distrustful of other people's patriotism, which we see as a different phenomenon and label "nationalism."[1]

While these reactions are understandable, it is a mistake to transform our emotional reactions into allegedly objective differences between ourselves and others. We must not automatically think that our assertiveness is healthy while theirs is aggressive. Nor should we think that patriotism and nationalism are two distinct concepts, one of which applies to our legitimate national feeling, while the other applies to the illegitimate national feeling of others.

Sometimes, when people come to see that there is no real difference between our national spirit and that of others, they extend their fear and distrust of nationalism to our own national spirit. These antipatriots reject patriotism because they equate it with nationalism and see all nationalistic feeling as negative and dangerous.

Many thoughtful people have rejected all forms of nationalism.

Albert Einstein, for example, dismissed nationalism as "an infantile disease," calling it "the measles of mankind."[2] Einstein's comment expresses a common attitude among people who are drawn to globalism and universalism. The analogy with measles conveys several ideas. If nationalism is like a disease, it is clearly undesirable, and if it is like a childhood disease, it is a sign of immaturity. Finally, just as children outgrow their childhood diseases, so perhaps humanity will outgrow nationalism. In an ideal world, there would be neither measles nor nationalism. And, if nationalism and patriotism are one, there would be no patriotism either.

Einstein's comment expresses a view that many have held. In a survey of nineteenth-century views of nationalism, Isaiah Berlin notes that many "observers of a liberal type" saw nationalism as

> a passing phase due to the exacerbation of national consciousness held down and forcibly repressed by despotic rulers. . . .

These liberal observers believed that as different groups succeeded in throwing off oppressive rule,

> nationalism, which was a pathological inflammation of wounded national consciousness would abate: it was caused by oppression and would vanish with it.[3]

Here again, the disease metaphor is dominant and suggests that nationalism is a passing phase. While globalists may take heart from this, Berlin's article shows that those who have predicted nationalism's demise have underestimated its power. Unlike typical childhood diseases, nationalism might prove to be incurable or even fatal.

## NATIONALISM AS SUPREME LOYALTY

Berlin draws a contrast between normal levels of national consciousness and inflamed, exacerbated states of national consciousness. He sees nationalism as more than a sense of belonging to a particular group. It is instead

> the elevation of the interests . . . of the nation to the status of the supreme value before which all other considerations must . . . yield at all times. . . .[4]

Hans Kohn gives a similar definition of nationalism as "a state of mind, in which the supreme loyalty of the individual is felt to be due the nation-state."[5] For both Kohn and Berlin, it is the supremacy of the interests of the nation that characterizes nationalism and differentiates it from other feelings of personal and social attachment.

The claim to supremacy is one that nations do make. In wartime, for example, people are conscripted for service to the state, even though this severs them from their families, friends, professions, and other groups to which they have ties of loyalty and special duties. Whatever obligation one has to care for one's family is thought to be overridden by the call of the state. If a person claims that he or she has a primary obligation to family or friends, this would not generally be recognized as having priority over the duty to serve the state.

In other contexts, however, claims to national supremacy are tempered. The person who spies on friends or reports the activities of family members to government agencies is viewed with contempt. Even the state exempts people from testifying against their spouses in criminal trials. E. M. Forster is often cited approvingly for saying that if forced to betray either his friend or his country, he hoped he would "have the guts to betray" his country.[6]

The claim to supreme loyalty raises two questions. First, since we have many loyalties, why should loyalty to the nation take priority over all others? Second, why should any loyalty be exempt from the normal constraints of morality? The extreme nationalism that Berlin and Kohn identify requires that national loyalty always come first, pre-empting both other loyalties and the normal moral constraints on what we may do on behalf of those to whom we have special duties.

One way to oppose this form of nationalism is to argue that something other than the nation should be our object of supreme loyalty. There are many possible candidates for this position: family, friends, religion, ethnic group, profession, truth, beauty, etc. Someone whose primary commitment is to one of these agrees with the nationalist that there is a supreme object of loyalty but rejects the view that it is the nation. This is an important objection. It puts pressure on nationalists to defend their choice of the nation as supreme object of loyalty. What is so special about nations that we should take loyalty to our nation more seriously than any other loyalty?

There are two types of answer to this question. The first derives from an organic conception of the relationship of persons to nations. If we see ourselves as parts of nations in the same sense that a bodily organ is part of the whole body, then our independent existence cannot have any meaning apart from its connection to the group. According to Berlin, nationalists believe that the lives of individuals and of groups such as families, clans, and provinces are only meaningful because they contribute to the well-being of the nation.[7] Loyalty to our nation takes priority over loyalty to all other things since they have value only within the context of a flourishing nation. Apart from the nation, they have no independent meaning or worth.

This claim is hard to accept. As important as it is to belong to a linguistic, cultural, and political community, many of the goods we experience appear to have meaning apart from their connection to the larger community. The love of children for parents, for example, appears to be good independently of its contribution or connection to the well-being of the state. The same is true of the goods of friendship, creativity, discovery, compassion, etc. Many things have value and contribute to meaningful lives independently of their connection to a nation. If this is so, then the priority of the nation cannot be established by appeal to the idea that the well-being of individuals and subgroups is merely derivative from national well-being.

There is a second argument for the priority of the nation that is more pragmatic and political. One could argue along Hobbesian lines that a nation provides a framework within which conflicts between individuals and between groups can be resolved. If everyone put family loyalty first, for example, and refused to defer to the decisions of the nation, then there could be no social peace. No family could live securely. In order to have a peaceful social order, everyone must be willing to defer to the judgment of the nation in cases of dispute. If people are unwilling to do this, always placing family, religious, or ethnic loyalties first, then no one could live securely. Granting supreme authority and loyalty to the nation is necessary to secure a peaceful existence for all other groups.

This pragmatic argument for national supremacy has some force. Unless groups within a nation are willing to accept some institution as the ultimate arbiter of disputes, society may turn into a group of warring families, clans, or tribes. Historically, we know that the acceptance of national rule by competing religions brought an end to wars of religion. One could see this as an instance of a shift in the priority of loyalties. Where once religion was dominant and wars ensued, the nation became dominant and enforced a truce between religious groups.

In spite of the force of this argument, it has two flaws as an argument for the supremacy of national loyalty. First, it detracts from the alleged supremacy of loyalty to the state by making it conditional on the ability of the nation to provide peace and security to its inhabitants. If the nation fails to do so, the basis of loyalty is undermined.

This is not a view that extreme nationalists can accept. They want to argue that the nation should be accepted as the object of supreme and unconditional loyalty. By making loyalty conditional on its ability to maintain peace, this argument subordinates national loyalty to concerns for one's own security and the well-being of people one cares about.

There is a second problem with this argument. If the supremacy of the nation depends on its ability to provide peace and security, then if a supernational authority is necessary to keep peace between nations, the supernational authority should be the object of supreme loyalty rather than the nation. This, of course, is the argument used by advocates of world government.[8] On its face, it is a reasonable argument, but it is not helpful to believers in national supremacy. They will not be happy if the logic of their argument for national supremacy leads to the conclusion that supernational institutions might take precedence over the nation itself.

Neither of these arguments succeeds, then, in establishing the nation as the proper object of supreme loyalty.

## IS THERE A SUPREME OBJECT OF LOYALTY?

If we approach morality from the perspective of loyalty and other relationships, we will need to rank our objects of loyalty, asking *which* object of loyalty is supreme, which is second highest, etc. To whom do I owe my strongest loyalty: my parents? children? spouse? friends? religion? nation? We might think of a morality structured in this way as a "who-based" morality. Questions about what we ought to do are answered by seeing who is the beneficiary of our action or who would be harmed by it. Forster's remark that he would rather betray his country than his friend makes his priorities (friend over nation) quite clear and suggests a more general ranking of friendship over patriotism.

Is this the right answer? One can see its appeal. After all, our connections with friends are personal and direct, while our connection with our nation is indirect, mediated, and abstract. The nation is an "imagined community."[9] Nonetheless, Forster's answer is wrong. The reason it is wrong is not that nations are more important than friends. Rather it is wrong because the "who-based" conception of morality that it presupposes is mistaken. Forster appears to believe that he can answer the question whether to betray his friend or his country without saying any more about the nature of the conflict between them.

Suppose, however, that his country is promoting justice, while his friend is spying for personal gain or assisting an unjust foreign power. In cases like these, friendship ought not to take priority over national loyalty.

What this shows is that we cannot make a blanket statement that loyalty to one person or group should always take precedence over loyalty to some other person or group. Any reasonable morality must be "what-based" rather than "who-based." It must look at *what* our loyalty requires of us and evaluate the actions we are being called upon to do. Facts about special ties to individuals or groups are often relevant to our decision, but they are never sufficient to determine what we ought actually to do.

It is a mistake, then, to think that any particular loyalty is supreme. One can never say in advance that conflicting loyalties ought always to be resolved in one particular way. Which loyalty takes precedence depends on the character of the action required by each. Moreover, even if I have a greater loyalty to my country than I do to others, that does not mean that I may do to others whatever is necessary to benefit my country. Our loyalties must be fulfilled within the limits that morality imposes on us. Doing what is right is not the same as doing what would benefit persons or groups to which we are loyal.

To believe in the supremacy of the nation, then, is doubly wrong. It is wrong to believe that the nation is the supreme object of loyalty and wrong to believe that any object of loyalty always takes precedence over anything else. No loyalty is exempt from the general, impersonal constraints of morality.

If we understand nationalism as the view that the nation is the supreme object of loyalty and that nothing should stand in the way of advancing its interests, then this is an immoral doctrine that needs to be rejected. It is one of the forms of fanatical loyalty I described in chapter 9. Any form of nationalism or patriotism that has these features deserves our rejection, whether the country whose interests are at stake is our own or is foreign to us.

## SELF-DETERMINATION OF NATIONS

While nationalism is frequently a source of worry, we do not always view it negatively. One form of nationalism that often evokes positive responses is the desire for national autonomy. If a nation exists and rules itself independently, we tend to think it a bad thing for other nations to invade it or otherwise to subvert its independence. Nationalists who speak or act in defense of their nation's freedom in such contexts are not seen as fanatics. Instead, we take them to be making a reasonable and morally legitimate claim.

Likewise, if recognizable national groups lack a country of their own and are ruled by others, we often sympathize with the idea that these groups should have their own national governments. Recognizing that political boundaries do not always coincide with national groupings and that particular groups may be dominated or oppressed by others, we often sympathize with the call for "self-determination of nations," thinking it to be a worthy and legitimate goal.

Cases like these reveal a tendency to believe that nations should be permitted to rule themselves and should not be ruled by others. In the spirit of this claim, we can define nationalism as a belief in the legitimacy of national self-rule and the desire that one's own nation enjoy the good of self-rule. If, as seems plausible, this is an acceptable ideal, then this form of nationalism is legitimate.

While this is a plausible, widely accepted view, it covers over some very difficult problems that begin to emerge when we look at the term "nation" more carefully. "Nation" has two distinct meanings. In the context of international politics, a nation is a political entity, a government or state that has political authority and the ability to govern a particular territory. The rules of the international law that forbid aggression and condemn violations of national boundaries are rules that protect states.

There is a second sense of "nation" that designates an ethnic or cultural group. Such groups may exist whether or not they have a state. Prior to World War I, there was a Polish nation, for example, but no Polish state. Prior to 1948, there was a Jewish nation but no Jewish state. Currently, there is a Kurdish nation but no Kurdish state.

Because there are two senses of "nation," the ideal of national self-determination likewise has two separate meanings. The first protects the autonomy and sovereignty of *states*, forbidding aggression from the outside and legitimating action by the state against internal groups that seek to disrupt it. Because states are thought to have legitimate jurisdiction within their borders, other states are not supposed to intervene in each other's "internal" affairs. So, for example, while Iraq's invasion of Kuwait and its brutality toward Kuwaiti citizens were widely accepted as legitimate grounds for war, prior abuses of Iraqi citizens (including imprisonment, torture, and killings) by the Iraqi government were widely regarded as internal affairs that were not the business of other nations. Within the United Nations, states may complain about their maltreatment by other states, but individuals may not complain about maltreatment by their own states. These practices reflect a commitment to the autonomy and sovereignty of states.[10]

The second form of self-determination applies to nations as ethnic or cultural groups. It is the idea that each ethnic or cultural group has a right to rule itself by having its own state. Thus, arguments for the independence of Poland and Israel were based on the idea that definable groups of people existed but lacked a state of their own and that these groups have a legitimate right to their own state. The fact that these groups were ruled by others was regarded as an evil that needed to be rectified. The failure to do so was seen after World War I as one of the causes of war, and this led to Woodrow Wilson's advocacy of the principle of self-determination of nations.

Both of these principles have considerable appeal, and neither is necessarily linked with fanatical nationalism. State sovereignty, though it sometimes requires inaction in the face of injustice, is widely seen as an important principle in restraining states and preventing wars between them. A world without state sovereignty would permit states to use internal problems as pretexts for invasion. Likewise, the desire of people with a common cultural and ethnic background to rule themselves in their own state is distinguishable from the desire to dominate others or the desire for superiority. Ethnic and cultural nationalists often want only what they see others possessing already, a state that reflects and is responsive to its population. They want the legitimacy and recognition that go with a state of one's own. They may also believe that survival without such a state is impossible.[11]

In spite of the plausibility and widespread acceptance of both these principles, each one raises very serious problems. The simplest way to bring out their problematic nature is to point out that the two types of national self-determination, state sovereignty and self-rule for ethnic/cultural groups, are incompatible with one another. The incompatibility emerges very clearly in conflicting policies of the United Nations. The U.N. Charter of 1945 states:

> All peoples have the right of self-determination. By virtue of that right they freely determine their political status and freely pursue their economic, social and cultural development.

But, as Bernard Nietschmann points out, while the charter gives this right to all peoples (i.e., nations in the sense of ethnic/cultural groups), a 1960 U.N. declaration on colonialism condemns "any attempt aimed at the partial or total disruption of the national unity and territorial integrity of a country."[12]

These two principles are incompatible, however, because the only way that some nations (ethnic/cultural groups) can achieve self-determination is by disrupting the "unity and territorial integrity" of the state that rules over them. The practical force of this contradiction emerges when we confront the fact that while there are 168 states in the United Nations, there are between 3,000 and 5,000 nations.[13] We are, therefore, faced with a painful choice. We can give up the ideal of state sovereignty by recognizing the right of national groups to disrupt existing states. This, however would lead to widespread instability and disruptions of the international order. Or, we can give up the principle of a state for every national group. This, however, means rejecting the claims of many ethnic/cultural groups who live under states that do not recognize them and that are hostile to their efforts to preserve their own cultures.

All this complicates our assessment of nationalism. If we understand nationalism as the desire to affirm the rights and legitimate interests either of *states* or of *national groups*, then we seem to be able to affirm the rights of one but not the rights of the other. A nationalism of states conflicts with a nationalism of ethnic/cultural groups. Moreover, as some have pointed out, as long as the conflict between these two nationalisms continues, there will be wars, instability, and repression. According to Nietschmann, almost three fourths of the wars since 1945 have been between states and national groups. He estimates that such wars have produced five million casualties.[14]

Despite the costliness of these conflicts, we cannot simply blame them on the inherent immorality of these two forms of nationalism. Both state sovereignty and self-determination of national groups are credible ideals, neither of which is necessarily linked with fanaticism or war. The clash between them, however, does lead to war and is a cause of great human suffering.[15]

## TOWARD A THEORETICAL SOLUTION

It is possible to describe a theoretical solution to these problems. Implementing such a solution, however, is extremely difficult. Hence my proposing it is not meant to suggest that the conflict is easily resolvable or that it can be resolved once and for all times. The solution involves a modification of both the sovereignty and the self-determination principles that give rise to the theoretical aspect of the problem.

As a first step, it is important to see that while state sovereignty is important, existing states and borders cannot be regarded as eternal or sacrosanct. They have changed in the past and will change in the future. In some cases, secession by a part of an existing state may be the best solution for handling a conflict between different national groups within the same state.[16] Likewise, the move from centralized to federal forms of government may provide some groups with sufficient local autonomy to render their place within a larger state acceptable to them.

In addition, the principle of state sovereignty needs to be limited. The world community should not regard all ways of treating people within nations as a purely internal matter. Just as violation of international borders is accepted as a reason for intervention by other nations, so should widespread abuse of individuals or groups within nations be seen as a matter of legitimate concern for the international community. This is not to say that other nations should go to war at the drop of a hat to protect groups within states. It is rather to affirm that widespread abuse of people within nations is not permissible and should be met by diplomatic pressure and other means of attempting to secure people's rights within states. State sovereignty is not an absolute bar to interference.

Just as national sovereignty must be weakened, however, so must the claim to self-determination for all ethnic/cultural groups. Self-determination for all groups is not a realizable goal. It might be if the world consisted of localities inhabited solely by distinct ethnic/cultural groups. This is not the case, however. Virtually all areas inhabited by such groups are also inhabited by others. To grant self-determination to the major group in any area would result in the creation of new minorities. A homogeneous population can only be achieved by expulsion or slaughter, neither of which is a morally legitimate policy. Even if we were willing to have a world of thousands of mini-states, then, we would not solve the problem because territory does not coincide with ethnic/cultural divisions. Short of adopting methods of slaughter, expulsion, and rigid controls on population movements, there is no way of organizing the world according to the self-determination of nations principle.

The solution to these problems is the multi-national state. But the multi-national state cannot be defined simply by the presence of many groups within it. Rather, the ideal of such a state must be a political order in which diverse groups can live together, each having the right to live according to its cultural values. This means that the state cannot be used by one cultural/ethnic group to dominate over others, preventing them from living according to their traditions or sharing equitably in the wealth and power of the country. Likewise, states that have relatively homogeneous populations must be prepared to recognize the rights of minority groups and of individuals.[17]

In short, the only legitimate way to deal with the problem of co-existence among diverse groups and individuals is to adopt some form of pluralism. Each distinct national group may assert its legitimate right to a life according to its traditions, but it may not achieve this right by violating the rights of others. Or, to put it in another way, the nationalism of diverse groups is a legitimate interest only when it is constrained by universal principles of morality that recognize the same rights for others. The model of constrained self-assertion and con-strained pursuit of personal goals provides the criterion by which we can evaluate the legitimacy and desirability of various forms of na-tionalism.

Within a state, national groups may assert their separate rights and interests within the constraints set by a respect for the legitimate rights and interests of other national groups. Similarly, within the world community, individual states may assert their rights and interests within the constraints set by a respect for the legitimate rights and interests of other states.

If the nationalism of diverse groups and states conformed to this model, there would be nothing wrong with it. If this is the type of nationalism that a patriot is committed to, then that person's patrio-tism is legitimate as well. No one could criticize a patriot for seeking a recognition of the legitimate rights and interests of his or her state or his or her ethnic/cultural group if this person recognized the same rights in others.

In offering this sketch, my intention is to describe a principled solution to the clash of national sovereignty and ethnic/cultural self-determination. I am not suggesting that there are magic solutions to actual conflicts. Nor do I overlook the immense difficulties of achiev-ing a genuine pluralism. Competing claims for the same territory and histories of hostility are among the many factors that make disputes among and within nations especially difficult to resolve peacefully. When particular groups are badly treated over long periods of time, it is not surprising that their moral horizons narrow, leading them to care only that their group get its due, no matter how this affects oth-ers.

It is important to see, however, that there is a form of nationalism that permits and encourages efforts to reconcile the national and cul-tural interests of diverse groups.[18] The ways to reconcile them will differ and will need to be created, invented, and negotiated to suit the particular peoples involved. Difficult as these processes are, it is significant that a form of constrained nationalism exists that is compatible with such efforts. Caring for one's own group does not require caring for it alone.

## SUMMING UP

There is no single nationalism and thus no single answer to questions about the value of nationalism.[19] For this reason, the connections between patriotism and nationalism are an embarrassment to patriots only if all forms of nationalism turn out to be unacceptable. What I have tried to show in this chapter is that some forms of nationalism are acceptable while others are not. In particular, the view that the nation is the supreme object of loyalty is a form of fanaticism that it is important to reject. Likewise, it is important to overcome the view that it is only other nations that are nationalistic.

Some forms of nationalism are acceptable. A limited principle of state sovereignty plays an important role in preventing wars of intervention. Likewise, a limited principle of ethnic/cultural autonomy provides a basis for claims to self-rule by groups that are both different from and badly treated by dominant groups in many states. These are both reasonable forms of nationalism. Understood in these ways, moderate patriots can be nationalists without sacrificing their commitment to respect other people and to avoid hostility and violence.

## NOTES

1. For an insightful discussion of how such biases operate, see Uri Bronfenbrenner, "The Mirror Image in Soviet-American Relations: A Social Psychologist's Report," *Journal of Social Issues* 16 (1961), 45–56.

2. Quoted in David Baker, ed., *Political Quotations* (Detroit: Gale Research, 1990), 144.

3. "Nationalism: Past Neglect and Present Power," *Partisan Review* XLVI (1979), 342–43.

4. Ibid., 342.

5. *Nationalism: Its Meaning and History* (Princeton: Van Nostrand, 1965), 9.

6. "What I Believe," in *Two Cheers for Democracy* (New York: Harcourt, Brace, 1951), 68.

7. Berlin, 346.

8. For a clear, recent statement of the case for world government, see Benjamin Ferencz, *Planethood* (Coos Bay, Oreg.: Vision Books, 1988).

9. For an interesting account of the formation of nations as objects of consciousness, see Benedict Anderson, *Imagined Communities* (London: Verso, 1983).

10. For an interesting debate about how seriously national borders and state authority should be taken, see the articles by Michael Walzer and David Luban in Charles Beitz et al., eds., *International Ethics* (Princeton: Princeton University Press, 1985), 165–243.

11. The Israeli novelist Amoz Oz calls nationalism "the curse of mankind" but defends the state of Israel as a necessity for Jewish survival. See his *In the Land of Israel* (New York: Random House, 1983), 130–31.

12. "The Third World War," *Cultural Survival Quarterly* 11 (1987), 5.

13. Ibid.

14. "The Third World War," 11.

15. For useful discussions of this clash, see Elie Kedourie, *Nationalism* (New York: Praeger, 1961) and Dov Ronen, *The Quest for Self-Determination* (New Haven: Yale University Press, 1979).

16. For a discussion of arguments to justify secession, see Allen Buchanan, "Toward a Theory of Secession," *Ethics* 101 (1991), 322–42; and his *Secession: The Morality of Political Divorce from Fort Sumter to Lithuania and Quebec* (Boulder, Colo.: Westview Press, 1991).

17. For an excellent discussion of related issues, see Will Kymlicka, *Liberalism, Community, and Culture* (New York: Oxford University Press, 1988).

18. Such a constrained nationalism is advocated by Martin Buber in *Land of Two Peoples: Martin Buber on Jews and Arabs*, Paul Mendes-Flohr, ed. (Oxford: Oxford University Press, 1983).

19. For a particularly helpful survey of thought about nationalism, see Anthony Smith, *Theories of Nationalism*, 2nd ed. (London: Duckworth, 1983).

# *15*

# Popular Patriotism

In the preceding chapters, I have explained and defended moderate patriotism as a legitimate moral ideal. In fact, moderate patriotism is the only morally legitimate form of patriotism because it alone combines concern for one's own nation with respect for people of other nations and recognition of moral constraints on what we may do for our country. Finally, I have tried to show that many attitudes generally associated with patriotism are not essential to it. In particular, I have argued that patriotic people need not be willing to provide automatic support for wars in which their country is engaged.

Because many of these ideas differ from commonly accepted views of patriotism, both patriots and anti-patriots may think that what I have described is not genuinely patriotic. While I have argued against this charge in earlier chapters, there is one additional source of this skepticism about moderate patriotism that I need to address, the clash between it and popular images and ideas associated with patriotism.

## CONCEPTS AND IMAGES

If moderate patriotism is genuine, why does it seem so different from patriotism as we ordinarily think of it? One reason emerges if we distinguish between the concept of patriotism and the popular image of patriotism. The concept of patriotism is broad and inclusive. In its most usual definition, patriotism is love of one's country. I have taken that definition as my starting point and have tried to make explicit what is involved in such love. Patriotism, I have claimed, involves

special affection and concern for one's country, a special identification with it, and a willingness to make sacrifices on its behalf. It is
hard to see how a person with all these traits could be said not to be
a patriot. The fact that moderate patriots possess all these character-
istics is the basis of my claim that they are genuine patriots. Central
to my arguments, then, is the concept of patriotism as love of country.

When we think about patriotism, however, we often begin with
concrete images and associations rather than the general concept of
love of country. In the United States, the most prominent patriotic
images involve the flag and military service. Many national holidays
and rituals are occasions for displaying the flag and for remembering
wars and those who served in them. Patriotism comes to be equated
with rituals like saluting the flag or singing "The Star Spangled Ban-
ner," with celebrations of historic wars, with images of "bombs burst-
ing in air" and praise for those who fought. These highly focused rituals and the specific military associations they call forth have come to
overwhelm the broader, more open-ended values suggested by the
phrase "love of country."

In many people's thinking, the concept of patriotism is overwhelmed
by images of ritual activities and military endeavors. Describing popular patriotism in World War I America, Randolph Bourne wrote:

> We reverence not our country but the flag. . . . It is the flag and the
> uniform that make men's hearts beat high and fill them with noble
> emotions, not the thought of and pious hope for America as a free and
> enlightened nation.

Beginning with this comment about flags and uniforms, Bourne goes
on to equate patriotism with militaristic attitudes. "The flag," he says,

> is primarily the banner of war; it is allied with patriotic anthem and
> holiday. It recalls old martial memories. A nation's patriotic history is
> solely the history of its wars. . . .[1]

Bourne correctly describes the powerful associations among patriotism and flags, uniforms, and warfare. He notes how these have become the central features of patriotism and have eclipsed the idea of
love of country. Though he himself is dedicated to the "pious hope
for America as a free and enlightened nation," he sees himself as an
opponent of patriotism. Having come to believe that patriotism and
war are inextricably related, Bourne believes that opponents of war
must be opponents of patriotism.

Bourne's description of popular patriotism certainly rings true, but his conclusion needs to be resisted. We need to insist on the centrality of "love of country" as the defining characteristic of patriotism and resist equating patriotism with rituals that overemphasize military values.

Bourne's belief that patriotism is essentially tied to militarism grew out of the disillusionment he suffered after the United States entered World War I. This was a trying time for Bourne and others who opposed American entry into the war. He and other progressives saw many of their hopes and ideals overwhelmed by war hysteria.[2] While Bourne came to equate patriotism and war during this dark time, his earlier essays reflect a desire for a new and better patriotism and express his own passionate commitment to his country. In his 1916 essay "Trans-National America," he wrote:

America is a unique sociological fabric, and it bespeaks poverty of imagination not to be thrilled at the incalculable potentialities of so novel a union of men. To seek no other goal than the weary old nationalism—belligerent, exclusive, inbreeding, the poison of which we are witnessing in Europe,—is to make patriotism a hollow sham, and to declare that, in spite of our boastings, America must ever be a follower and not a leader of nations.[3]

In this earlier essay, Bourne seeks to transcend the poisonous effects of the "weary old nationalism" and wants to avoid making patriotism "a hollow sham." His sense of American uniqueness, his desire that America lead the way in developing a genuine pluralism, and his evident passion are all testimony to his own patriotism. In contrast, in Bourne's later essay, his loss of hope leads him to surrender patriotic ideals to those whose politics and cultural values he opposed.

While Bourne's remarks about popular patriotism are perceptive and while his personal disillusionment is understandable, he was wrong to accept the militarized values of popular patriotism as patriotism's essence. Indeed, his later view makes it impossible to see the genuine patriotism that motivated his early writing. It makes it impossible to classify him as the patriot that he was.

## THE LIMITS OF RITUALIZED PATRIOTISM

Bourne's remarks about the flag as an object of reverence continue to ring true. The flag and reverence toward it are central to popular images of patriotic devotion. In spite of this tight association, it is evident that patriotism and flag-centered rituals are quite distinct phenomena. This is not to say that the flag may not play an important role for patriots, but concern for the flag and expressions of reverence for it are not the same as patriotism.

One might wonder why we need the flag at all and why there must be holidays and other ritualized occasions for the expression of patriotic feeling. This kind of anti-ritual challenge is not one that I would embrace. We need ways to express and affirm our public values. Rituals and holidays can serve to provide these occasions and to strengthen our sense of connectedness with people who share these values. Rituals can keep alive a sense of history and help us to rededicate ourselves to our ideals. Flags, monuments, and holidays can all play a role in expressing. sustaining, and transmitting worthwhile attitudes and ideals. Saluting the flag may help to instill a commitment to the values of "liberty and justice for all" and to assure them a central place in the country for which the flag stands.

Nonetheless, we know that rituals may become empty, mechanical, and meaningless. Because they are performed according to a schedule, they can become mere habits that are not so much expressions of attitudes as substitutes for them. They may come to lack the spontaneity that animates our most genuine expressions of feeling. In addition, because rituals can be performed apart from the feelings they are supposed to express, they can be performed insincerely. They are subject to hypocrisy and to manipulation. As the visible signs of attitudes, they can be mistaken for the attitudes themselves and can lead us to lose sight of the values they are meant to affirm.

All these problems arise in connection with ritualized patriotism. Flag salutes, parades, and overt expressions of dedication to the country may come to take the place of genuine love and commitment. The result is an explosion of public avowals of patriotism that may or may not reflect genuine concern about the well-being of the country and its inhabitants. The visible signs of patriotic commitment may replace actual commitment.

To make these points is not to devalue patriotic rituals. We need publicly shared ways of expressing our values. Nonetheless, we need to be wary of both fake and shallow expressions of patriotism. Fake expressions are used by hypocrites who "wrap themselves in the flag," portraying themselves as patriots in order to advance their personal goals and interests. Shallow expressions are genuinely felt but are not backed by a willingness to promote the country's well-being when doing so requires personal sacrifice.

If we follow Bourne and equate patriotism with its ritualized expressions, then we can no longer differentiate genuine patriotism from fake and shallow patriotism. That such a distinction exists is quite evident, however, and provides a basis for arguing that ritualized patriotism is insufficient as a mark of genuine commitment to one's country.

## THE LIMITS OF MILITARIZED PATRIOTISM

A second component of the popular image of patriotism is the identification with military values. Wars provide occasions for increased patriotic feeling, and those who fight are accorded the highest respect as exemplars of patriotic virtue.[4] Indeed, more than any other activity, military service serves as the popular image's paradigm of patriotism. For those who are not in the military, giving support to the military becomes the primary way to express their patriotism.

This militarization of patriotic values is unnecessary, misleading, and harmful. Every country requires many things in order to flourish. Military defense is only one of its needs. For this reason, it is ironic that neither voting nor payment of taxes is usually linked to patriotism, even though these are essential duties of citizens. The military paradigm essentially tells us that love of country can only be expressed in one way, through military service or by support of military policies.

If we move away from this paradigm and reflect on the idea of love of country, we see immediately that there are many ways in which such love could be expressed. This multiplicity arises both from the many needs that countries have and from the diversity of talents that people possess. Given these facts, it makes no sense to focus on only one need of the country, treating it as if it were the only valid expression of patriotic commitment. When we do this, we overlook many other ways in which people can express their love of their country and their commitment to it.

It is instructive to recall that during the Iran/Contra hearings, Oliver North was able to counter questions about his actions by putting himself forward as an American patriot. His uniform, his military service, and his expressions of patriotic concern all served to identify him as a patriot who would risk all for the sake of his country. Among all those who took part in the hearings, North stood out as the representative of patriotism.

In contrast, the senators, representatives, and lawyers conducting the investigation were not generally seen as patriots. Even though they were defending our constitutional system of government, virtually no one saw their investigation as an expression of patriotic values. What is most telling is that when members of Congress attempted to validate their own status as patriots, they did so by recalling their own military service. Only military service was sufficient to validate their patriotism.

The attitudes revealed in this situation show how harmful the popular image of patriotism is. It allows those who fit the image to promote their values, even when these values conflict with fundamental ideals of democratic rule. Likewise, it leads us to overlook other patriotically motivated activities and to undervalue people who express their patriotism in diverse ways. While North gained automatic respect for his military service, members of Congress gained no similar level of respect for their service in public office. Similarly, people who work in government agencies to implement policies and do so out of concern for the national well-being are brushed aside as mere bureaucrats. Such judgments are unfair and reflect an acceptance of unfounded stereotypes.

This is not to deny that there are members of Congress or people who work in government agencies who are self-serving and are not motivated by patriotism. The same, however, is surely true of people in the military. People enter particular careers for many reasons. While it would be foolish to claim that all people in civilian government service are motivated by patriotism, we need to recognize that patriotism could motivate such service. We need to reject the common assumption that military service is the only way in which patriotic values can be acted upon.

The popular image of patriotism leads us to be too admiring of people in the military and insufficiently appreciative of contributions that others make. This set of attitudes is both unfair to people whose patriotism leads them into civilian service and harmful to the country itself. Given the diversity of a country's needs and the diversity of people's talents, patriotic ideals ought to encourage people to find different ways of promoting the good of their country. By focusing on one way (military service), we fail to encourage people to act constructively for the social good.

We know, however, that people might become teachers, nurses, fire fighters, social workers, or artists in part because they see these activities as contributing to their country's well-being. Through his writing, for example, Bourne tried to help create an America that lived up to the ideals he thought were best for the country. Other artists have wanted their country to have a rich culture that they could look to with pride and have used their talents to try to help produce such a culture.

Whether people are proud of their country depends a great deal on their personal ideals. Given the diversity of ideals, it is to be expected that concern about one's country could take make forms. Hans Kohn, discussing an 1820 essay by an English critic, tells us that

> Nothing stung the American writers and artists of the time as much as the question. . . ." In the four quarters of the globe, who reads an American book? Or goes to an American play? Or looks at an American picture or statue?"[5]

Kohn adds that this question preoccupied educated Americans for decades. They were stung by it because they took the mark of a worthy country to be its production of art and literature. It was difficult for them to feel pride in a country that lacked a real culture.

What was their response to this failing of their own country? They hoped for and, in some cases, contributed to the development of a richer, more valuable indigenous American culture. Patriotic feeling led them to seek changes that would bring the country closer to their highest ideals. Our popular image of patriotism makes it hard to see the writing of poems and novels or the creating of paintings and sculptures as an expression of patriotism, but it is evident that they can be.

The general concept of patriotism as love of country is, from this perspective, more constructive and more pluralistic. It rejects the single military paradigm of patriotism and encourages people to act on their concern for their country in whatever ways are available to them and in accord with their diverse ideals and abilities. It is perfectly natural that people especially concerned with health care, for example, would take pride in their country if the level of health care for people is good, while they would feel shame or disappointment if the country fails in this area. The same is true for people who especially value education, good architecture, preserving the environment, or scientific achievement. People with different ideals are sensitive to different excellences that nations may exemplify and to different failings as well. Military power is simply one kind of value among many and need not occupy a preeminent place in the goals that patriots hope their country will pursue.

If what I have said is correct, then it is a mistake to equate patriotism with the popular images of patriotism. While patriotic rituals and military service may have positive value, they are not identical with patriotism and do not begin to reveal the varied aims and activities that may derive from love of country.

The popular image of patriotism is a distortion. The distortion has a great deal of social and cultural power, however, and there is a strong tendency to capitulate to it by conceding that the distorted popular image of patriotism is true patriotism. To concede this, however, is to overlook the tension that exists in ordinary thinking about patriotism. Ordinary thought is not limited to the popular image. It also includes the general concept of love of country, and this concept provides the basis for criticizing the narrowness of the popular image. The challenge to moderate patriots is to transform the popular image of patriotism so as to sever the strong ties between it and military values. Neither flags nor military exploits are central to patriotism. The essence of patriotism is love of one's country.

## MILITARISM

In attacking the militarized popular image of patriotism, I am not suggesting that all values associated with military service are bad. The defense of people's lives and of their communities' vital interests is a necessary and valuable activity, and the courage and commitment that people exhibit in defense of these values are worthy of appreciation.

In talking about militarism, I mean to criticize an excessive regard for military values and the extension of military values to contexts in which they are inappropriate. These tendencies are harmful in several ways. An excessive regard for military values can lead to a failure to appreciate the importance and value of traits that are necessary to avoid unnecessary war. The ability to negotiate, to understand the interests of others, and to be creative in accommodating the legitimate interests of all parties are essential qualities if people are to live in peace and handle conflict without bloodshed. When values are militarized, every conflict is seen as a war, those with whom we are in conflict are seen as enemies, and attempts at accommodation and peaceful resolution are seen as signs of weakness. In such situations, political leaders seek popularity through the use of military force and displays of (what is taken to be) toughness. Belligerence becomes valuable for domestic politics, even though its likely outcome is increased hostility, a more threatening international environment, and harm to the country itself.[6]

A second problem with militarism is its tendency to undermine democratic processes. In a democracy, we assume that citizens will disagree among themselves about which policies are best for the country. Debate and criticism are seen as valuable activities, and freedom of expression is prized as a central value. Each person has a right to an opinion on matters of policy and a right to advocate or criticize particular policies.

Military organizations are not democratic, however. They are hierarchical and authoritarian. People in decision-making positions issue orders and commands that are not generally subject to debate by those in subordinate ranks. During battle, the situation demands high degrees of coordination that make relatively automatic assent to orders a reasonable and necessary requirement. [7] It is not surprising that the familiar features of democratic debate are absent from such situations.

When values become militarized, the rigid, authoritarian practices that may be legitimate in military institutions are transported to nonmilitary contexts and serve as a model for politics. When this occurs, the practices of democratic debate and dissent are seen as inappropriate. Agreement, support, and obedience become the central values. Citizens cease to be seen as sources of opinions about the worthiness of policies. Instead, they are conscripted as unquestioning supporters of policy. Democratic debate is subverted by the drive for the kind of compliance and uniformity that occurs in military organizations and battle situations. Even if these are appropriate values in military settings, their extension to the general political realm is inimical to democratic values.

A third feature of a militarized political culture is that those who disagree are seen as enemies and traitors. In spite of the clear lesson of history that wars are often mistakes and blunders that do no good for a country's genuine interests, people who reject wars are charged with betrayal and equated with the enemies of the country. Patriotism becomes identified with unquestioning support and those who fail to give this support are seen as anti-patriots. Once we distinguish support for a war from support for a country's best interests, however, we can see that this charge is unwarranted. The popular image of patriotism may require automatic support for a war, but the concept of patriotism as love of country surely does not.

## FRIENDS AND FOES

Ordinarily, we recognize that people have different interests, attitudes, feelings, and concerns, and we grant the legitimacy of this diversity. In the militarized image of patriotism, however, people divide up neatly into two categories. They are either patriots or traitors, friends or foes. In place of a mixture of diverse people, we substitute an absolute division between those who care for the country and those who wish it ill. From this perspective, patriotism is a duty and those who fail to be patriotic are traitors. This absolute division promotes a false and dangerous image. It needs to be tempered by reminders about what people are really like and what is reasonable to expect of them.

What is it reasonable to expect of people? Is patriotism a duty? Is lack of patriotism the moral equivalent of treason?

If patriotism is love of country, then it is not clear that patriotism can be a moral duty. Why not? Because there is no duty to have feelings or attitudes. We may be morally required as citizens to do our fair share in supporting the country—by paying taxes, serving on juries, voting, etc.—but we cannot be required to love the country. Love of country cannot be commanded or required in this way and cannot be a duty.[8]

Moreover, it is quite understandable why some people might not feel love for their country. Two categories of such people are those who are oppressed and those who are alienated.[9] By oppressed people, I mean those in a country who are treated unjustly, whose rights are violated, or whose interests are not taken seriously. If people within a country are not treated fairly by it and feel oppressed or abused, it would be odd to expect them to love the country.

In fact, many people who fall into this category do continue to love their country. They see their maltreatment as the fault of the government rather than the nation. Or they see their maltreatment as a failure by the country to live up to its own lofty ideals. They remain patriotic in spite of their poor treatment.[10] There is nothing wrong with this, but it is not something one could legitimately demand of them.

A second category of non-patriots are people who are alienated citizens. Alienated citizens do not love their country because they find its practices to be inconsistent with their deepest values. I have argued that a pacifist could be a patriot. Nonetheless, given the prominence of military values in the popular image of patriotism, it would be understandable if pacifists felt alienated and unable to muster affection for their country. Or, to take some different examples, people committed to particular cultural, artistic, or religious values and ideals might be distressed by the failure of their country to conform to these ideals and might cease to have affection for it. It was, after all, Tolstoy's commitment to Christian universalism that led him to reject patriotism. He was alienated because his country did not begin to live up to his central religious ideals.

These forms of alienation are understandable and may make it impossible for some people to be patriots. Interestingly, it does not mean that they might not be good citizens. A member of an oppressed group might be motivated to use the political process to bring about improvement. Such a person might be active politically and might effectively promote the well-being of the country by working to make it a more just society. Likewise, alienated citizens may take their status as citizens seriously and may work hard to improve the country by bringing it more into line with their ideals. These actions might be motivated by their ideals rather than by a love of the country. Nonetheless, if their ideals are worthy ones, that would not make their activities less valuable. Nor would it detract from the worth of these people as citizens.

What is crucial to see about these cases is that while such people are not patriotic, they are nonetheless good citizens. Contrary to the crude view that everyone is either patriot or traitor, friend or foe, such people turn out to be non-patriots who are not foes and who may make a significant contribution to their country. They may in fact share many interests and concerns with citizens who see themselves as patriots. In most contexts, one could not differentiate them from people who are patriotic, and in some cases, their contribution to their country's well-being exceeds the contribution of those who see themselves as patriotic.

The distinction between patriots and non-patriots may turn out to be a blur rather than a sharp line. If patriotism is neither necessary nor sufficient to motivate valuable actions by individuals, then lack of patriotism in an individual is not necessarily a threat. Just as patriotism is a respectable and legitimate ideal, so the lack of patriotism may in many situations be equally legitimate and respectable.

What is important is that people share a commitment to doing their share to promote a more just and peaceful society. Patriotism may be valuable in providing one motivation toward pursuing that goal. It is not the only motivation, however, and there is no need to disparage people who promote these goals for other reasons.

## FINAL THOUGHTS

The moderate patriotism I have defended in this book may seem so different from the patriotism we ordinarily have in mind that one may feel lingering doubts about the genuineness of moderate patriotism. I have argued that these doubts arise because of a discrepancy between the concept of patriotism and the popular image of patriotism. While the basic concept of patriotism, love of country, is pluralistic and open-ended, the popular image is dominated by rituals and militaristic values. Moderate patriotism may differ from popular images of patriotism, but it is true to the idea that love of country is the essence of patriotism. It is the popular image that is a distortion and that needs alteration. If we could shake it off, we would have an enriched and healthier popular conception of patriotism.

In any case, it is hard to see how anyone could deny that love of country (as shown by affection, concern, identification, and willingness to sacrifice) is genuine patriotism. By meeting these criteria, moderate patriotism shows itself to be the real thing. Moreover, by accepting appropriate moral constraints on the actions that are motivated by love of country, moderate patriotism defines itself as a morally legitimate and acceptable ideal.

Since my defense of moderate patriotism began with criticisms of extreme patriotism and has concluded with criticisms of the popular image of patriotism, one might think that popular patriotism is the same as extreme patriotism. This would be a mistake. In spite of the similarities between popular patriotism and extreme patriotism, they are not the same. While extreme patriotism is a doctrine that is explicitly committed to such values as national superiority and indifference to other countries, popular patriotism is not a definite doctrine at all. It is a diffuse and often inconsistent set of attitudes.

The diffuse and undefined quality of popular patriotism has two effects, one good and one bad. The bad effect is that the power of popular images of patriotism pushes the popular understanding of patriotism in the direction of extreme patriotism. Popular patriotism, especially in time of war, can be manipulated to support values that extreme patriots promote. That is the negative effect of the undefined quality of patriotism. Its lack of definition makes it easier to get people to support views that they would not generally accept.

The positive side of the undefined nature of popular patriotism is that mixed in with the types of views that support extreme patriotism are other views and attitudes that provide a basis for a more moderate conception of patriotism. When presented with an explicit formulation of extreme patriotism, most people would, I think, react with horror. Because commonsense morality contains many elements that are universal in scope and humane in orientation, most people would disavow the ruthless chauvinism of extreme patriotism.

For the most part, of course, these diverse moral and political ideals remain diffuse in our thinking. Various elements, some good and some bad, stand together under the umbrella label "patriotism." The bad parts are accepted along with the good because we fail to distinguish them and fail to think through their implications. My hope in writing this book is that by raising these ideas to the level of explicit consciousness, we can better understand and evaluate the many values that are included in the concept of patriotism. By making these ideas explicit, we can fashion a form of patriotism that leaves behind the distortions of extremism and that can unite us in the pursuit of a more peaceful and just world for all people.

## NOTES

1. "The State," in *War and the Intellectuals*, 87.

2. For a moving account of the difficulties of this period, see Jane Addams, "Personal Reactions During War," in Staughton Lynd, ed., *Nonviolence in America: A Documentary History* (Indianapolis: Bobbs-Merrill, 1966), 178–91.

3. *War and the Intellectuals*, 114–15.

4. If they join the ranks of dissenters, however, they may be attacked with special vehemence. On this, see Ron Kovic's moving account in *Born on the Fourth of July* (New York: Pocket Books, 1977).

5. Hans Kohn, *American Nationalism* (New York: Collier Books, 1961), 61.

6. For insightful discussions of these phenomena, see Murray Edelman, *Constructing the Political Spectacle* (Chicago: University of Chicago Press, 1988), chs. 3 and 4.

7. This is not to say that every order need be obeyed. An order to commit a war crime is illegitimate and should not be accepted. For a discussion of the limits of obedience, see Anthony Hartle, *Moral Issues in Military Decision Making* (Lawrence: University of Kansas Press, 1989).

8. Cf. Robert Paul Wolff's comment on the impossibility of loyalty as personality or character trait in *The Poverty of Liberalism* (Boston: Beacon Press, 1968), 72–73.

9. For discussions of both categories of people, see Michael Walzer, *Obligations: Essays on Disobedience, War, and Citizenship* (New York: Simon and Schuster, 1971), chs. 3 and 5.

10. This attitude is expressed by Martin Luther King, Jr. in *Where Do We Go From Here: Chaos or Community?* (Boston: Beacon Press, 1968).

# Selected Bibliography

Addams, Jane. "Personal Reactions During War." In Staughton Lynd, ed. *Nonviolence in America: A Documentary History*. Indianapolis: Bobbs-Merrill, 1966, 178–91.

Anderson, Benedict. *Imagined Communities*. London: Verso, 1983.

Axinn, Sidney. "Honor, Patriotism, and Ultimate Loyalty." In A. Cohen and S. Lee, eds. *Nuclear Weapons and the Future of Humanity*. Totowa, N.J.: Rowman and Allanheld, 1986.

———. "Loyalty and the Limits of Patriotism." In K. Kipnis and D. Meyers, eds. *Political Realism and International Morality*. Boulder, Colo.: Westview Press, 1987.

Baier, Kurt. *The Moral Point of View*. Ithaca, N.Y.: Cornell University Press, 1958.

Baron, Marcia. *The Moral Status of Loyalty*. Dubuque, Ia.: Kendall/Hunt, 1984.

———."Patriotism and 'Liberal' Morality." In D. Weissbord, ed. *Mind, Value, and Culture: Essays in Honor of E. M. Adams*. Northridge, Calif.: Ridgeview Publishing Co., 1989.

Barnet, Richard. "The Twilight of the Nation–State." In R. P. Wolff, ed. *The Rule of Law*. New York: Simon and Schuster, 1971.

———. *Roots of War*. New York: Penguin Books, 1973.

Beatty, Jack. "The Patriotism of Values." *The New Republic* 185 (1981), 18–20.

Beitz, Charles. *Political Theory and International Relations.* Princeton: Princeton University Press, 1979.

Beitz, Charles, et al., eds. *International Ethics.* Princeton: Princeton University Press, 1985.

Bellah, Robert, et al. *Habits of the Heart.* New York: Harper & Row, 1986.

Bentham, Jeremy. *Introduction to the Principles of Morals and Legislation,* 1789.

Berlin, Isaiah. "Nationalism: Past Neglect and Present Power." *Partisan Review* XLVI (1979), 337–58.

Blum, Lawrence. *Friendship, Altruism, and Morality.* London: Routledge and Kegan Paul, 1980.

————. "Gilligan and Kohlberg: Implications for Moral Philosophy." *Ethics* 98 (1988), 472–91.

————. "Moral Exemplars: Reflections on Schindler, the Trocmes, and Others." *Midwest Studies in Philosophy* XIII, 1988.

————. "Vocation, Friendship, and Community." In O. Flanagan and A. Rorty, eds. *Identity, Character, and Morality.* Cambridge, Mass.: MIT Press, 1990.

————. "Community and Virtue." In Roger Crisp, ed. *How Should One Live?* Oxford: Oxford University Press, forthcoming.

Bourne, Randolph. *War and the Intellectuals: Collected Essays, 1915–1919.* New York: Harper & Row, 1964.

Brecht, Bertolt. *The Caucasian Chalk Circle.* Translated by Eric Bentley. New York: Grove Press, 1966.

Bronfenbrenner, Uri. "The Mirror Image in Soviet–American Relations: A Social Psychologist's Report." *Journal of Social Issues* 16 (1961), 45–56.

Brown, Kenneth. "'Supreme Emergency': A Critique of Michael Walzer's Moral Justification for Allied Obliteration Bombing in World War II." *Manchester College Bulletin of the Peace Studies Institute* 13 (1983), 6–15.

Brown, P., and H. Shue, eds. *Food Policy.* New York: Free Press, 1977.

Buber, Martin. *A Land of Two Peoples: Martin Buber on Jews and Arabs.* Edited by Paul Mendes–Flohr. Oxford: Oxford University Press, 1983.

Buchanan, Allen. "Assessing the Communitarian Critique of Liberalism." *Ethics* 99 (1989), 852–82.

———. "Toward a Theory of Secession." *Ethics* 101 (1991), 322–42.

———. *Secession: The Morality of Political Divorce from Fort Sumter to Lithuania and Quebec.* Boulder, Colo.: Westview Press, 1991.

Care, Norman. "Career Choice." *Ethics* 94 (1984), 283–302.

———. *On Sharing Fate.* Philadelphia: Temple University Press, 1987.

Ceadel, Martin. *Thinking About Peace and War.* Oxford: Oxford University Press, 1987.

Clay, Jason. "Epilogue: the ethnic future of nations." *Third World Quarterly* 11 (1989), 223–33.

Cohen, Marshall, et al., eds. *War and Moral Responsibility.* Princeton: Princeton University Press.

Cottingham, John. "Partiality, Favouritism, and Morality." *Philosophical Quarterly* 36 (1986), 357–73.

Dahl, Robert. *After the Revolution? Authority in a Good Society.* New Haven: Yale University Press, 1971.

DeBenedetti, Charles, ed. *Peace Heroes in Twentieth–Century America.* Bloomington: Indiana University Press, 1986.

DeCosse, David, ed. *But Was It Just?* New York: Doubleday, 1992.

Dietz, Mary G. "Patriotism." In T. Ball, J. Farr, and R. Hanson, eds. *Political Innovation and Conceptual Change.* Cambridge: Cambridge University Press, 1989.

Doob, Leonard. *Patriotism and Nationalism.* New Haven: Yale University Press, 1964.

Dworkin, Gerald, ed. "Symposium on Impartiality and Ethical Theory." *Ethics* 101 (1991).

Elshtain, Jean B. *Women and War.* New York: Basic Books, 1987.

Falk, Richard. *This Endangered Planet.* New York: Random House, 1971.

Feinberg, Joel. *Harm to Others*. New York: Oxford University Press, 1984.

Ferencz, Benjamin. *Planethood*. Coos Bay, Ore.: Vision Books, 1988.

Feshbach, Seymour. "Individual Aggression, National Attachment, and the Search for Peace." *Aggressive Behavior* 13 (1987), 315–25.

Finn, James, ed. *A Conflict of Loyalties: The Case for Selective Conscientious Objection*. New York: Pegasus, 1968.

Fisher, Roger. *International Conflict for Beginners*. New York: Harper & Row, 1969.

Fisher, Roger, and William Ury. *Getting to Yes*. New York: Penguin Books, 1983.

Fishkin, James. *The Limits of Obligation*. New Haven: Yale University Press, 1982.

Forster, E. M. "What I Believe" In *Two Cheers for Democracy*. New York: Harcourt, Brace, 1951.

Freud, Sigmund. *Group Psychology and the Analysis of the Ego*. New York: W. W. Norton, 1989.

Gert, Bernard. *Morality: A New Justification of the Moral Rules*. New York: Oxford University Press, 1988.

Gewirth, Alan. "Ethical Universalism and Particularism." *Journal of Philosophy* LXXXV (1988), 283–303.

Gilligan, Carol. *In A Different Voice*. Cambridge, Mass.: Harvard University Press, 1982.

Goffman, Erving. *The Presentation of Self in Everyday Life*. Garden City, N.Y.: Doubleday Anchor, 1959.

Gomberg, Paul. "Patriotism is Like Racism." *Ethics* 101 (1990), 144–50.

Goodin, Robert. *Protecting the Vulnerable*. Chicago: University of Chicago Press, 1985.

———. "What Is So Special About Our Fellow Countrymen?" *Ethics* 98 (1988), 663–86.

Graham, G., and H. LaFollette, eds. *Person to Person*. Philadelphia: Temple University Press, 1989.

Grodzins, Morton. *The Loyal and the Disloyal*. Chicago: University of Chicago Press, 1956.

Group for the Advancement of Psychiatry. *Us and Them: The Psychology of Ethnonationalism*. New York: Brunner/Mazel, 1987.

Gutmann, Amy. "Communitarian Critics of Liberalism." *Philosophy and Public Affairs* 14 (1985), 308–22.

Hardin, Russell, ed. "Symposium on Duties Beyond Borders." *Ethics* 98 (1988).

Hare, R. M. *Applications of Moral Philosophy*. Berkeley: University of California Press, 1972.

———. "What is Wrong With Slavery." *Philosophy and Public Affairs* 8 (1979).

Harman, Gilbert. *The Nature of Morality*. New York: Oxford University Press, 1977.

Hartle, Anthony. *Moral Issues in Military Decision Making*. Lawrence: University of Kansas Press, 1989.

Hayes, Carlton. *The Evolution of Modern Nationalism*. New York: Macmillan, 1931.

Hill, Thomas, Jr. "Symbolic Protest and Calculated Silence." *Philosophy and Public Affairs* 9 (1979), 83–102.

Hoffman, Stanley. *Duties Beyond Borders*. Syracuse, N.Y.: Syracuse University Press, 1981.

Holmes, Robert. *War and Morality*. Princeton: Princeton University Press, 1989.

Ignatieff, Michael. *The Needs of Strangers*. New York: Viking Penguin, 1985.

Isaacs, Harold. *Idols of the Tribe*. New York: Harper and Row, 1975.

James, William. "The Moral Equivalent of War." In *Pragmatism and Other Essays*. New York: Washington Square Press, 1983.

Janowitz, Morris. *The Reconstruction of Patriotism*. Chicago: University of Chicago Press, 1983.

Jensen, Kenneth, and Kimber Schraub, eds. *Pacifism and Citizenship: Can They Coexist?* Washington, D.C.: U.S. Institute of Peace, 1991.

Johansen, Robert. *The National Interest and the Human Interest: An Analysis of U.S. Foreign Policy.* Princeton: Princeton University Press, 1980.

Kant, Immanuel. *Grounding for the Metaphysic of Morals.* Translated by James Ellington. Indianapolis: Hackett Publishing, 1981.

Kavka, Gregory. *Moral Paradoxes of Nuclear Deterrence.* Cambridge: Cambridge University Press, 1987.

Kedourie, Elie. *Nationalism.* New York: Praeger, 1961.

King, Martin Luther, Jr. *Where Do We Go From Here—Chaos or Community?* Boston: Beacon Press, 1968.

Kovic, Ron. *Born on the Fourth of July.* New York: Pocket Books, 1977.

Kuflik, Arthur. "A Defense of Common Sense Morality." *Ethics* 96 (1986), 784–803.

Kymlicka, Will. *Liberalism, Community, and Culture.* New York: Oxford University Press, 1988.

Kohn, Hans. *American Nationalism.* New York: Collier Books, 1961.

———. "Nationalism." In Philip Wiener, ed. *Dictionary of the History of Ideas.* New York: Charles Scribner's Sons, 1974.

Larmore, Charles. *Patterns of Moral Complexity.* Cambridge: Cambridge University Press, 1987.

Lenin, V. I. *State and Revolution.*

Lessing, Doris. *Prisons We Choose to Live Inside.* New York: Harper and Row, 1987.

Levinson, Sanford. *Constitutional Faith.* Princeton: Princeton, University Press, 1988.

Lynd, Staughton, ed. *Nonviolence in America: A Documentary History.* Indianapolis: Bobbs–Merrill, 1966.

MacIntyre, Alasdair. *After Virtue.* Notre Dame, Ind.: University of Notre Dame Press, 1981.

———. "Is Patriotism a Virtue?" The Lindley Lecture. Lawrence: University of Kansas Press, 1984.

Mack, John. "Nationalism and the Self." *Psychohistory Review* 2 (1983), 47–69.

Nagel, Thomas. *Equality and Partiality.* New York: Oxford University Press, 1991.

Nathanson, Stephen. *The Ideal of Rationality.* Atlantic Highlands, N.J.: Humanities Press International, 1985.

————. *Should We Consent to be Governed?—A Short Introduction to Political Philosophy.* Belmont, Calif.: Wadsworth, 1991.

————. "In Defense of 'Moderate Patriotism'." *Ethics* 99 (1989), 535–52.

————. "On Deciding Whether A Nation Deserves Our Loyalty." *Public Affairs Quarterly* 4 (1990), 287–98.

————. "Patriotism and the Pursuit of Peace." In K. Klein and J. Kunkel, eds., *In the Interests of Peace.* Wakefield, N.H.: Longwood Academic, 1990.

————. "Kennedy and the Cuban Missile Crisis: On the Role of Moral Reasons in Explaining and Evaluating Political Decision-Making." *Journal of Social Philosophy* XXII (1991), 94–108.

Navasky, V., ed. "Patriotism," Special issue of *The Nation* 253 (July 15/22, 1991).

Newman, Jay. *Fanatics and Hypocrites.* Buffalo, N.Y.: Prometheus Books, 1986.

Niebuhr, Reinhold. *Moral Man and Immoral Society.* New York: Charles Scribner's Sons, 1960.

Nietschmann, Bernard. "The Third World War." *Cultural Survival Quarterly* 11 (1987), 5.

Nisbet, Robert. *The Quest for Community.* London: Oxford University Press, 1969.

Nozick, Robert. *Anarchy, State, and Utopia.* New York: Basic Books, 1973.

O'Brien, Tim. *Going After Cacciato.* New York: Dell Publishing, 1980.

Oldenquist, Andrew. "Loyalties." *Journal of Philosophy* LXXIX (1982), 173–93.

Oldfield, Adrian. *Citizenship and Community.* London: Routledge, 1990.

Okin, Susan. *Justice, Gender and the Family.* New York: Basic Books, 1989.

O'Neill, Onora. "The Moral Perplexities of Famine Relief." In Tom Regan, ed., *Matters of Life and Death*. New York: Random House, 1980.

Oz, Amos. *In the Land of Israel*. New York: Random House, 1984.

Petersen, William, et al. *Concepts of Ethnicity*. Cambridge, Mass.: Harvard University Press, 1982.

Rachels, James. *The Elements of Moral Philosophy*. New York: Random House, 1986.

Railton, Peter. "Alienation, Consequentialism, and the Demands of Morality." *Philosophy and Public Affairs* 13 (1984).

Reidenbach, Clarence. *A Critical Analysis of Patriotism As an Ethical Concept*. Ph.D. Thesis, Yale University, 1918.

Reynolds, Charles, and Ralph Norman. *Community in America: The Challenge of "Habits of the Heart"*. Berkeley: University of California Press, 1988.

Ronen, Dov. *The Quest for Self–Determination*. New Haven: Yale University Press, 1979.

Royce, Josiah. *The Philosophy of Loyalty*. New York: Macmillan, 1915.

Ruddick, Sara. *Maternal Thinking*. Boston: Beacon Press, 1989.

Russell, Bertrand. "The Ethics of War." *International Journal of Ethics* XXV (1915), 127–42.

———. *Common Sense and Nuclear Warfare*. New York: Simon and Schuster, 1959.

———. *The Autobiography of Bertrand Russell, 1914–44*. New York: Bantam Books, 1968.

Sandel, Michael. *Liberalism and the Limits of Justice*. New York: Cambridge University Press, 1982.

Schaar, John. "The Case for Patriotism." In *Legitimacy and the Modern State*. New Brunswick, N.J.: Transaction Publishers, 1981.

Scheffler, Samuel. *The Rejection of Consequentialism*. Oxford: Clarendon Press, 1982.

Shue, Henry. *Basic Rights: Subsistence, Affluence, and U.S. Foreign Policy*. Princeton: Princeton University Press, 1980.

———. "Mediating Duties." *Ethics* 98 (1988), 687–704.

Singer, Peter. "Famine, Affluence, and Morality." *Philosophy & Public Affairs* 1 (1972), 229–44.

———. *Practical Ethics.* Cambridge: Cambridge University Press, 1979.

Smith, Anthony. *Theories of Nationalism.* London: Duckworth, 1983.

Sniderman, Paul. *A Question of Loyalty.* Berkeley: University of California Press, 1981.

Taylor, Charles. "Cross–Purposes: The Liberal–Communitarian Debate." In Nancy Rosenblum, ed., *Liberalism and the Moral Life.* Cambridge, Mass.: Harvard University Press, 1989.

Thompson, Dennis. *The Democratic Citizen.* Cambridge: Cambridge University Press, 1970.

Thoreau, Henry David. *Walden and Other Writings.* New York: Modern Library, 1937.

Tolstoy, Leo. *Tolstoy's Writings on Civil Disobedience and Non-Violence.* New York: New American Library, 1968.

———. *A Confession and Other Religious Writings.* London: Penguin Books, 1987.

Walzer, Michael. *Obligations: Essays on Disobedience, War, and Citizenship.* New York: Simon and Schuster, 1971.

———. *Just and Unjust Wars.* New York: Basic Books, 1977.

———. *Radical Principles: Reflections of an Unreconstructed Democrat.* New York: Basic Books, 1980.

———. *Spheres of Justice.* New York: Basic Books, 1983.

———. *Interpretation and Social Criticism.* Cambridge, Mass.: Harvard University Press, 1987.

———. *The Company of Critics: Social Criticism and Political Commitment in the Twentieth Century.* New York: Basic Books, 1988.

———. "What Kind of State is a Jewish State?" *Tikkun* 4 (July/August 1989).

———. "The Communitarian Critique of Liberalism." *Political Theory* 18 (1990), 6–23.

———. "What Does It Mean to be an American?" *Social Research* 57 (1990), 591–614.

Westbrook, Robert. "'I Want A Girl, Just Like the Girl That Married Harry James': American Women and the Problem of Political Obligation in World War II." *American Quarterly* 42 (1990), 587–614.

Wilson, Edmund. *Patriotic Gore*. Boston: Northeastern University Press, 1964.

Wolff, R. P. *The Poverty of Liberalism*. Boston: Beacon Press, 1968.

———. *In Defense of Anarchism*. New York: Harper & Row, 1971.

———, ed. *The Rule of Law*. New York: Simon and Schuster, 1971.

Yoder, John. *Nevertheless: The Varieties and Shortcomings of Religious Pacifism*. Scottsdale, Pa.: Herald Press, 1976.

Zinn, Howard. *Declarations of Independence: Cross-Examining American Ideology*. New York: HarperCollins, 1990.

# Index

# About the Author

Stephen Nathanson is professor of philosophy at Northeastern University. He is the author of three previous books, *The Ideal of Rationality, An Eye for an Eye?—The Immorality of Punishing by Death*, and *Should We Consent to be Governed?—A Short Introduction to Political Philosophy*.